The
Cook's BOOK

of Useful Information

by

John C. Lawrence

Golden West Publishers

Cover design by The Art Studio/Bruce Robert Fischer

Library of Congress Cataloging in Publication Data

Lawrence, John C.
  The cook's book / by John C. Lawrence.
      p.   cm.
    1. Cookery—Dictionaries.   I. Title.
TX349.L36 1988   641.5'03'21—dc 19   88-20572
                                          CIP
 ISBN 0-914846-38-8

Printed in the United States of America

Information in this book is deemed to be authentic and accurate by author and publisher. However, they disclaim any liability incurred in connection with the use of information appearing in this book.

Golden West Publishers   (602) 265-4392
4113 N. Longview Ave.
Phoenix, AZ 85014, USA

Contents

Terms Used in
Preparing and Processing Foods

bake—To cook in an oven with dry heat from 250 to 450 degrees Fahrenheit. Baking is a process used for breads, cakes, fish, meats, pies, poultry, etc.

barbecue—To roast fish, meat or poultry on racks over an open fire or coals, or buried in a pit.

bard—To cover a piece of meat, poultry or game with thin slices of salt pork, bacon, fatty fresh pork or beef fat. The barding is tied on and generally removed before serving. On game, it is left on and served with the dish.

baste—To spoon liquid or liquified fat on meat or poultry to moisten during roasting to prevent excessive drying.

beat—To mix ingredients by stirring rapidly and vigorously in an upward movement, thus adding air to the mixture.

bind—To add eggs or other binding agent to a combination of ingredients so the mixture will hold together.

blanch—To remove skins from tomatoes, nuts, etc., by putting them first into boiling water, then into cold water. Fresh produce to be frozen should be blanched.

blend—To mix thoroughly two or more ingredients until they combine.

boil—To heat a liquid until it is 212 degrees Fahrenheit (100 degrees Celsius), and air bubbles are rising continually and actively from the bottom of the pan. Also, to cook food in boiling liquid.

bone—To remove bones from fish, meat or poultry.

braise—To brown foods quickly in a small amount of fat, then to add a little liquid, cover the pan and cook the food slowly.

bread—To coat a piece of food with bread crumbs, crushed cereals or cornmeal prior to cooking.

bring to a boil—To heat a liquid only until the air bubbles break at the surface.

broil—To cook foods on a grid over embers. Also refers to use of the broiler section of a kitchen stove so foods are cooked under the heat source..

brown—To allow a dish to cook until the outer surface takes on a brown color: biscuits, meringues, etc.

brush—To apply butter, oils, beaten eggs, sauces and water to foods before, during and after cooking with a basting brush.

burn—To apply heat (generally accidentally) to food so that it becomes black, charred and usually inedible.

can—To preserve food in metal or glass containers.

candy—To coat fruits with sugary liquid or cook fruits in syrup until fruit becomes translucent.

caramelize—To give foods a light coating of melted sugar, which has turned brown.

carve—to divide a whole fowl or roast into portions by slicing.

chill—To cool by placing food in a refrigerator or a bowl of cracked ice.

chop—To cut food into small pieces by using a knife in an up-and-down motion.

churn—To make butter by whipping or agitating cream.

clarify—To clear a liquid or fat by removing solid particles. Butter is clarified by being melted and strained, with the resultant oil used in cooking.

coat—To dip foods into batter before breading and frying.

coddle—To bake eggs (or cook in a pan immersed in water) until the whites have set.

cook—To prepare foods for eating by baking, frying, roasting, etc.

cool—To permit hot food to return to room temperature.

core—To remove the fibrous central part of such fruits as apples, grapefruits, pears, etc.

corn—To preserve cuts of beef in salt brine with spices.

cover—To place a lid on a pot, pan or dish.

cream—To work a solid, such as butter or shortening, into a soft and fluffy mass by beating it steadily. Butter and sugar are creamed until they are softened and blended.

crease—To make a long indentation into dough, such as creasing the top of a bread loaf before baking.

crimp—To pinch together two pieces of dough, as in tart or two-crust pie-making, to produce slight ridges along the outer sealed edge.

crisp—To place fresh vegetables (such as carrots, celery, etc.) in cold water so they will become firm.

crush—To break and reduce hard substances to small particles by using a rolling pin or mallet.

crystallize—To allow sugar crystals to form on food.

cube—To cut into dice-shaped pieces. Also to tenderize meat by pounding cuts into a pattern of squares.

curdle—To thicken or coagulate.

cure—To preserve meat by drying, pickling or smoking.

cut—To separate a piece from the whole with a knife. To slice. To make a slash mark with a knife.

cut in—To combine butter or shortening into flour (or other dry substance) with the aid of two knives or a pastry blender.

deep fry—To cook food very fast in a deep pan which contains a large amount of cooking fat. There must be enough fat for the food to be completely immersed.

defrost—To thaw frozen food according to directions on package or according to specific tables for defrosting.

deglaze—To pour liquid (broth, vinegar, water, wine, etc.) into a pan where food has been cooked to aid in dislodging of any solids that might adhere to the pan. These solids are flavorful and make a sauce or gavy more tasteful.

degrease—To remove excess fat from soups, stocks, pan juices or sauces.

dice—To chop food into small pieces.

dip—To immerse a piece of food in a liquid before breading or cooking.

dish/dish out—To serve individual portions of food from a container.

disjoint—To separate pieces of meat or poultry at the joints.

dissolve—To infuse a solid into a liquid, such as combining sugar and water. The sugar then has dissolved.

dot—To place small pieces of butter or margarine on food before cooking.

drain—To remove liquid from cooking pot by pouring food into a colander, allowing liquid to drain away.

draw—To remove entrails (internal organs) from fowl and animals. Same as eviscerate.

dredge—To coat a piece of food with flour, cornmeal or other breading substance before cooking.

dress—To add stuffing to meat and poultry.

dress—(before cooking) To prepare fish, game, birds, poultry, for cooking by scaling, skinning, removing entrails, etc.

drizzle—To pour a liquid in a thin stream, generally referring to the application of a syrup or icing to cakes and pastries.

drop—To fill a teaspoon with a mixture (generally cookie dough) and allow a spoonful to drop of its own accord onto pan, about four to five seconds.

dunk—To immerse a piece of food briefly in liquid. Generally only a portion of the food is immersed at a time. Doughnuts, cookies, other sweet baked goods and breads can be dunked.

dust—To cover foods very lightly with a dry ingredient such as flour or sugar.

eviscerate—To remove the entrails (internal organs) from fowl and animals. Same as "draw."

filet/fillet—To remove bones from fish or meat.

fix—To prepare.

flake—To determine if fish has been cooked long enough by testing a piece with a fork to see if it separates (flakes) easily.

flame—To sprinkle a dish with alcoholic spirits which are then set on fire.

flip—To turn something over very quickly, like a pancake.

flute—To create grooves in vegetables and fruits by using a special knife. Also to make grooved indentations for decorative purposes in the rim of pie crusts.

fold in—To introduce a delicate mixture into a heavier one by turning one over the other in a vertical movement until they are combined. This process is used in making souffles and other dishes where beaten egg whites or whipped cream are used.

freeze—To preserve food by subjecting it to the temperature where water solidifies into ice. Most fruits and vegetables are blanched before freezing.

french—To trim meat and fat from the end of a chop.

french fry—To deep fry until golden brown.

fricassee—To serve stewed poultry parts in a thick sauce.

frizzle—To fry food until the piece being fried is curled and brown.

frost—To apply icing to a cake or a confection.

fry—To cook foods in heated butter, fat or oil. Shallow fry uses minimal amount of fat, while deep frying uses enough fat to cover the food itself.

glaze—To coat with a gelatinous or heavy syrup. To give a glossy coating to a dish.

grate—To rub a solid food against a rough surface (a grater), to reduce it to small particles. Usually, food grated is transformed into very thin strips or to powder.

grease—To apply cooking fat to the surface of pans, pots and dishes.

grill—To cook foods over direct heat, such as a barbecue grill.

grind—To reduce solid foods to small particles by use of a blender, grinder or food processor.

homogenize—To process whole milk so the cream is distributed throughout and will not rise to the top.

hull—To remove stems from strawberries, tomatoes, etc.

husk—To remove the non-edible green leaves and corn silk which surrounds an ear of corn.

ice—To apply frosting to a cake, cookie or other confection.

incase—To enclose a food in a covering, such as a roast, in puff paste.

incise—To make shallow cuts with a sharp knife in the skin of a fish that is to be grilled or fried.

incrust—To enclose in pastry.

inflame—To sprinkle a dish with spirits which are then set on fire. Same as flame.

infuse—To steep herbs or other flavorings in a hot liquid until the flavors are absorbed by the liquid. Generally, the liquid is strained before use. Tea is steeped.

irradiate—To treat foods by adding Vitamin D. Also a method of treating fresh foods with radiation for storing.

jointing—To cut up meat and poultry into parts.

juice—To extract liquid from fruits and vegetables.

knead—To work bread dough with the hands by pressing, folding and stretching dough until the desired texture is reached.

lade, ladle—To scoop or lift off by means of a ladle.

lard—To insert strips of fat into meats with a larding needle.

leaven—To cause foods to rise by use of such leavening agents as baking powder, baking soda and yeast.

macerate—To soak food, especially fruits, in a flavored liquid until the flavor of the liquid is absorbed.

make—To prepare food

marinate—To tenderize by soaking foods in a mixture of lemon juice, oil, vinegar or wine with herbs and spices.

marry—To combine two or more ingredients so their tastes are allowed to combine and set during cooking or preparation.

mash—To reduce food to a paste or paste-like consistency by use of a mashes.

mask—To change the flavor and/or appearance of food by using sauces, seasonings or garnishes.

melt—To liquify a solid by use of heat.

microwave—To use a microwave appliance for cooking foods speedily.

mince—To chop very fine.

mix—To combine various ingredients to insure even distribution.

moisten—To add liquid during cooking process.

mold—To shape food by pouring mixtures into hollow containers.

mull—To heat cider or wine and add spices.

oil—To coat baking pans or molds with grease.

oven fry—To place crumb-coated chicken parts or chops (or other foods) on an oiled sheet or low-sided pan and cook in an oven, uncovered.

pan broil—To cook in an ungreased, uncovered skillet on top of the stove with heat source under the pan. Salt can be used to keep food from sticking to the pan.

pan fry—To cook in a greased (uncovered or covered) skillet on top of the stove.

parboil—To partially cook food in water or other liquid, then finish the cooking in another manner.

parch—To dry or brown with dry heat, such as corn or rice.

pare—To remove the skin from fruits and vegetables. Same as peeling.

pasteurize—To sterilize by heating liquids to the point where most harmful germs are destroyed.

peel—To remove the outer skin from fruits and vegetables.

pickle—To preserve fruits, vegetables and meats in salt, sugar or vinegar brine.

pipe—To decorate by spreading a creamy substance (such as cake icing or mashed potatoes) in a thin line onto another surface, like a border of icing around the edge of a cake or cookie.

pit—To remove the stone from fruits, such as cherries, peaches, etc.

pluck—To remove feathers from fowl by pulling them out from the skin.

plump—To soak fruits in a liquid until they are rounded out and full of liquid. Plumping can also be accomplished by steaming.

poach—To simmer in a small amount of liquid or water. Eggs are often cooked in this manner. (See Egg poacher)

plank—To use a piece of lumber cut thicker than a board on which to grill and serve meat or fish. This method of cooking imparts the flavor of the wood to the food.

pound—To strike repeatedly, such as striking a raw steak with a mallet until the steak is thin.

preheat—To heat an oven to a desired temperature before starting to cook.

preserve—To can, dry, pickle or freeze food to prevent spoilage.

prick—To puncture, such as inserting the tines of a fork into the top of a pie crust.

proof—To set yeast bread dough to rise away from drafts or changes in temperature.

proofing—To let yeast dough rise.

pulverize—To grind to a powder.

puree—To rub food through a fine sieve or process in a blender or food processor to produce a paste.

put up—To can or preserve foods for future use.

reduce—To intensify the flavor of a liquid by cooking it rapidly until it is decreased in volume.

reheat—To rewarm foods heated previously.

render—To heat meat fats to remove the oils. This process is used to produce lard.

rice—To force food (like boiled potatoes) through a ricer to produce minute particles for creaming.

ripen—To let something reach its peak of maturity.

roast—To cook meats by dry heat (in an oven) using an uncovered pan.

roll, roll out—To flatten pastry dough and spread it thin by means of a rolling pin.

rub—To work seasonings, fat, flour or other ingredients into the surfaces of foods to be cooked.

rub through—To force a substance through a sieve.

saute—To fry quickly in a small amount of fat.

scald—To pour boiling water over foods (generally vegetables) until the skins loosen. Also, to heat milk almost to the boiling point.

scallop—To bake in layers (as potatoes and onions) in a casserole dish, sometimes with a crumb topping.

score—To place shallow slits part way through the outer surface of food (usually meat or bread) for functional or decorative purposes. Scoring meat allows the fat to drain and tenderizes tough connective tissue.

scramble—To beat eggs lightly with water or milk, then pour into a hot, greased skillet, constantly stirred with a fork, and cooked just until set (not browned).

sear—To burn or scorch the surface. Roasts should be seared on all sides to help seal in meat juices.

season—To add spices, herbs or salt to enhance the flavor of a dish.

serve—To offer food or drink for consumption.

sharpen—To intensify the spiciness of foods by adding lemon juice or vinegar.

shell—To remove and discard the inedible outer covers of nuts, peas, etc.

shred—To tear or cut into strips.

shuck—To remove the husk from an ear of corn.

sift—To pass flour, cornmeal, sugars and other dry foodstuffs through a fine screen (sifter) to remove lumps.

simmer—To cook very gently below the boiling point, once the boiling point has been reached.

skewer—To thread small pieces of meat, vegetables and fruits on a slim metal rod before grilling.

skim—To remove the top part of a liquid (such as cream which rises to the top of non-homogenized milk, or scum from soups and stews).

slaughter—To butcher animals for meat.

soak—To immerse in a liquid and allow to remain awhile.

souse—To pickle.

spading—To work with a spatula the warm fondant or other candy mix in candymaking. The spatula turns the mixture over onto itself again and again.

spread—To set a table with food.

sprinkle—To drop minute particles of food (such as grated cheese) over the surface of a dish.

steam—To cook food in water vapor by surrounding it in a cloud of steam using special pots and pans for this process.

steep—To soak in a liquid to soften or extract flavor. Steeping tea leaves in hot water will produce tea.

stew—To simmer slowly.

stir—To mix ingredients by agitating them in a circular manner with a spoon, fork or spatula.

stir-fry—To use the sauteing technique for frying vegetables and meat.

stone—To remove the seed from such fruits as apricots, cherries, peaches and plums.

strain—To pass food through a sieve or strainer, removing lumps or liquid matter.

stuff—To fill cavities in poultry and vegetables, such as stuffing a turkey or a tomato.

taste—To eat a small quantity of food to perceive the flavor.

thaw—To permit frozen food to come to room temperature.

thicken—To make a liquid more dense by adding flour, tapioca, etc.

tint—To lightly color food by adding small amounts of food coloring.

toast—To brown or crisp lightly by direct heat.

toss—To mix lightly, as in a tossed salad, to permit salad dressing to cover ingredients.

truss—To sew or tie poultry or roasts with a trussing needle in order to retain their shape.

uncork—To remove a cork from a bottle; to open a bottle without disturbing the sediment.

wash—To brush the surface of a pastry before or after baking with egg, milk, water, etc.

whip—To beat vigorously with a fork, whisk or rotary beater and thus introduce air into the beaten mixture.

work—To manipulate ingredients (generally by hand) in order to combine them.

CHAPTER I

Dictionary
of
Cooking Terms

Key to Abbreviations Used

(Am) American	*(Kor) Korean*
(AmInd) Am. Indian	*(L) Latin*
(Arm) Armenian	*(Ma) Malaysian*
(Aus) Australian	*(Mex) Mexican*
(Bel) Belgian	*(mil) military*
(Ch) Chinese	*(Nor) Norwegian*
(col) colloquial	*(OE) Old English*
(Cr) Creole	*(Or) Oriental*
(Cz) Czechoslovakian	*(Per) Persian*
(Dan) Danish	*(Por) Portugese*
(Du) Dutch	*(PR) Puerto Rican*
(Eng) English	*(Rom) Romanian*
(ErAm) Early Am.	*(Rus) Russian*
(Fr) French	*(Sc) Scottish*
(Ger) German	*(sl) slang*
(Gr) Greek	*(SoPac) South Pacific*
(Heb) Hebrew	*(Sp) Spanish*
(Hin) Hindustani	*(Sw) Swedish*
(Hun) Hungarian	*(SW) Southwestern U.S.*
(Ind) Indian	*(Swis) Swiss*
(Ir) Irish	*(Tur) Turkish*
(It) Italian	*(Viet) Vietnamese*
(Ja) Japanese	*(Yid) Yiddish*

How to Use This Dictionary

All words and phrases are listed in alphabetical order. Only letters of the English alphabet are used. The Spanish letters 'ch', 'll', 'n', 'rr' and the German letter ' ß' are not recognized as separate letters. The German letter ' ß ' is roughly equivalent to the English letter 's' and is treated as such.

Translations, if any, appear after the word definition. These translations are also listed separately. Designation of parts of speech and genders are not given. For proper pronunciation and usage please consult the appropriate dictionary.

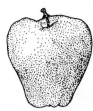

A, AA—Grades of fresh eggs. 'AA' is the highest quality. 'A' slightly less.

abalone—A sea mollusk whose meat is very delectable. Care should be taken in preparing and cooking the flesh. If not fixed properly the meat will be very tough. The shell is the source of mother-of-pearl.

abats de coucherie *(FR)*—*(See 'offal')*

abatte *(Fr)*—A fairly broad, thick, flat double-edged knife used for flattening meat.

abattis *(Fr)*—Giblets

abbachio *(It)*—Spring lamb

abricot *(Fr)*—Apricot

abricot-peche *(Fr)*—peach-apricot

abrotenite *(Fr)*—Herb-flavored wine.

absinthe—a liqueur originally flavored with wormwood and any of a variety of spices. The use of wormwood was outlawed in 1914 in France. Spain is reportedly the only country that permits the use of wormwood in the making of absinthe. May be served as a cocktail, aperitif or digestif. Is used in some mixed drinks.

Abziehen *(Ger)*—String bean

acacia—Another word for gum arabic.

aceite de oliva *(Sp)*—Olive oil

aceituna *(Sp)*—Olive

acetic acid—The acid that gives vinegar its tartness.

aceto *(It)*—Vinegar

aceto balsamico *(It)*—A vinegar made from Trebbiano grapes. Aged in a series of barrels of different woods. Found in specialty shops. Dark, sweet and pungent.

achiote *(Sp)*—Annatto seeds

acid—A substance that is tart or sour.

acidulate—Water that has had a small amount of an acid added. Usually lemon juice or vinegar. Used to keep cut vegetables and fruit fresh looking before cooking. This acidulated water is not used for cooking.

acorn—The nut of the oak tree.

acqua *(It)*—Water

acre *(Fr)*—Tart, acid.

ades—Literally any fruit-flavored drink. The best ades are made with fresh juices. Canned juices can be used. Flavoring is available in powdered or liquid concentrate form. Some are pre-sweetened. Usually mixed with water. Ades are served cold with ice.

aebleskiver *(Dan)*—A fried bread made of flour, sugar, eggs, butter, yeast and flavorings. May be deep fried or baked in special pans. Serve hot with powdered sugar, jam or applesauce.

agar-agar—A gelatin substance derived from seaweed. Used as a thickening agent.

agave—Variety of plants whose juices and pulp are fermented to make an alcoholic beverage.

aged—Foods and beverages such as cheese, meats, spirits, beers, cakes, cookies and wines that have been stored under controlled conditions for days, months or years. Besides maturing the flavor, aging often improves their color and texture.

aglio *(It)* Garlic

agneau *(Fr)*—Lamb

agneau de printemps *(Fr)*—Spring Lamb

agnello *(It)*—Lamb

agnolotti *(It)*—Macaroni stuffed with lamb.

agua *(Sp)*—Water

aguacates *(Sp)*—Avocados

aigre *(FR)*—Sour

aigre-doux *(Fr)*—Sour and sweet

aiguillette *(Fr)*—A thin slice of cooked meat

ail *(Fr)*—Garlic

aix oignons *(Fr)*—With onions

ajo *(Sp)*—Garlic

a la or ala *(Fr)*—In the mode of.

a la Anglaise *(Fr)*—*(see Anglaise)*

a la bordelaise *(Fr)*—Food cooked with or garnished with Bordeaux wine or mushrooms or mirepoix or artichokes and potatoes.

a la broche *(Fr)*—Cooked on a spit or skewer.

a la carte—Dishes on a menu offered and priced individually as opposed to table d'hote.

a la Creole *(Fr)*—Dishes that usually contain rice or are served with rice. This term can apply to both hot and sweet dishes.

a la diable *(Fr)*—Refers to dishes served with diable sauce.

a la Francaise *(Fr)*—In the French style or manner.

a la frascati *(Fr)*—Garnishes for meat dishes made of sliced foi gras, mushrooms, truffles and asparagus.

a la gauloise *(Fr)*—Garnish consisting of the cocks' comb and kidneys

a la grecque *(Fr)*—Vegetables prepared in the Greek style; seasoned with oil, vinegar, spices and served cold.

a la jardiniere *(Fr)*—Food plainly prepared with chopped parsley, butter sauce and lemon juice.

a la meuniere *(Fr)*—Sauteed in butter. Can also be dusted with flour then sauteed. Generally refers to fish fillets.

a la Milanaise *(Fr)*—Generally food that is dipped in egg and bread crumbs, mixed with grated parmesan cheese, and fried in butter. Also a macaroni dish with cheese.

a la mode *(Am)*—Slice of pie served with a scoop of ice cream.

a la mode *(Fr)*—Large cuts of braised beef.

a la monselat *(Fr)*—Dishes which contain truffles, artichokes and fried potatoes when appropriate.

a la montmorency *(Fr)*—Dishes, cakes and confections which have added to them cherries in one form or another.

a la Mornay *(Fr)*—Dishes that use Mornay sauce.

a la Newburg—Dishes (generally seafood) served in a sauce consisting of butter, cream, egg yolk and wine.

a la orientale *(Fr)*—Dishes cooked with tomatoes, garlic and sometimes saffron.

a l'Orly *(Fr)*—Fish that is filleted, skinned then dipped in a light batter and deep fried. Served with a tomato sauce.

a la parmesane *(Fr)*—Dishes that almost always contain grated parmesan cheese.

a la Parisienne *(Fr)*—Garnishes of various elements that must include potatotes.

a la paysanne *(Fr)*—Meats and poultry braised and served with a garnish of carrots, onions, turnips, celery cooked in butter, chopped fried bacon and potatoes. Vegetables should be cut into small uniform sized pieces.

a la Provencale *(Fr)*—Dishes cooked or prepared with garlic or onions.

a la Russe *(Fr)*—In the Russian style or manner.

a la serviette *(Fr)*—Food served in a napkin.

a la tartare *(Fr)*—*(see Beef Tartare)*

albacore—1) A species of tuna fish. A large fish that is also known as yellow fin tuna. 2) *(Por)* Swordfish

albahaca *(Sp)*—The herb basil.

albaricoque *(Sp)*—Apricot

albicocca *(It)*—Apricot

albondiga *(Sp)*—A meat ball of forcemeat or ground/chopped meat.

albumen—Egg white

alcachofa *(Sp)*—Artichoke

alcaravea *(Sp)*—Caraway seed

alcohol—1)A chemical compound present in beers, wines, whiskies, vodka, gin, liqueurs and other beverages. When consumed they have the effect of making one light headed. 2) When using alcoholic beverages the alcohol will evaporate when the dish is cooked. Of course this does not hold true uncooked dishes.

alcole *(It)*—Alcohol

alcool *(Fr)*—Alcohol

al dente—Foods that are cooked so that they are very firm or crisp.

ale—An alcoholic beverage that is similar to beer but usually more bitter. Made from malt and hops.

alecost *(Eng)*—Costmary *(See Spices section)*

alfoncigo *(Sp)*—Pistachio

al fresco—An informal meal served out of doors.

alinar *(Sp)*—Dressing for salad or other foods.

Alkohol *(Ger)*—Alcohol

alligator pear—Avocado

alloro *(It)*—Bay leaves

all purpose flour—A blend of hard and soft wheat flours. A flour for all uses.

allumettes *(Fr)*—Little cakes of puff pastry that may be filled or garnished. Generally are baked and served as an hor d'oeuvre.

almendra *(Sp)*—Almond

almond—A widely used nut in confections, as a snack and as a garnish for certain meat, fish and vegetable dishes. Also ground into a paste for use in various sweets. Skins are removed and they are toasted before use. As a snack the nut is often flavored with onion, garlic, salt or other spices.

almond powder—Almonds that have been finely-ground. Used in various confections.

alose *(Fr)*—Shad

aloyau *(Fr)*—Sirloin or ribs of beef.

Alpinia Cardamomum *(L)*—Cardamon

alum—A crystalline compound, containing aluminum, that is sometimes used to make pickles crisp. CAUTION—use only when a particular recipe calls for it.

amande *(Fr)*—Almond

amaretto *(It)*—Macaroon. Also an almond flavored liqueur.

amapola *(Sp)*—Poppy

amaranth—An annual plant whose seed is widely used in Central America. The seed is ground into a flour. The young leaves may be used as a potherb. The amaranth was once the sacred food of the Aztecs. Its history as a food goes back over 6,000 years. Can be found in some health food and organic food stores.

ambrosia—Generally a fresh fruit salad with coconut and nuts.

American process cheese—*(see Processed Cheese)*

American whiskey—Bourbon whiskey

ammonia (household)—A solution of ammonia and water used in the home for various cleaning chores. Has a very strong odor and should not be breathed directly. Is generally mixed with additional water for use. CAUTION—Should *never* be mixed or used with other cleaners.

anana *(Sp)*—Pineapple

ananas *(Fr, It)*—Pineapple

Ananas *(Ger)*—Pineapple

anchois *(Fr)*—Anchovy

anchois farcis *(Fr)*—Stuffed anchovies.

anchovy—A small sea fish. Used as a garnish in salads, on pizzas and other dishes. Usually available canned in oil. Has many bones. Quite salty in taste.

andouillette *(Fr)*—A forcemeat ball.

aneth *(Fr)*—Dill

aneto *(It)*—Dill

angel food cake—A cake made of egg whites, sugar, flour and flavorings. Generally baked in a tube pan. Two forks or a cake wire should be used for cutting. This is a very light cake.

anglaise *(Fr)*—A mixture of eggs, salt, pepper and oil. Pieces of meat, fruit or vegetable are dipped into the anglaise then into the appropriate coating. Food prepared in this manner is called l'Anglaise.

angostura bitters—A mixture of various spices, herbs, fruits, quinine and rum. Used to flavor certain alcoholic drinks. It is used sparingly.

anice *(It)*—anise

animelles *(Fr)*—Lamb's fry

anis *(Fr, Ger, Sp)*—Anise

anisette—A liqueur flavored with anise.

antipasto *(It)*—Hors d'oeuvre, appetizers. May be cold or hot. Generally served before the main course. Can be elaborate with many different foods or very simple with one or two.

anti-splash lid—A pan covering made of wire mesh. Generally has a handle. Placed over skillet when frying foods. Helps prevent grease splatter.

A-1 sauce—Brand name for a seasoned sauce that is used on steaks and on or in other dishes.

aperitif *(Fr)*—Appetizer. Generally refers to a before dinner liqueur, wine or cocktail.

aperitivo *(Sp)*—Appetizer

Apfel *(Ger)*—Apple

Apfelmost *(Ger)*—Apple cider

Apfelsine *(Ger)*—Orange

apio *(Sp)*—Celery

Apollinaris—A naturally carbonated water from Germany's Rhineland.

appareil *(Fr)*—Mixtures

appetite—A desire for food or drink.

appetitost—A semi-hard cheese made from sour buttermilk

appetizer—Anything eaten or drunk to increase one's appetite.

apple—A popular and versatile fruit. Can be eaten raw in-hand or in salads. Can be baked, fried, stewed, made into applesauce or applebutter. Is used in cakes, pies and various pastries. Dries well. There are many varieties.

apple butter—Cooking apples that have been simmered with sugar and oil of cinnamon to produce a thick dark sauce. Used as a bread spread and in various cakes and pastries.

apple cider—Juice of apples. Served as a breakfast or snack drink. Also in fruit punches. When allowed to ferment it becomes alcoholic and is called 'hard cider.' Vinegar is also made from apple juice.

apple dumplings—Pastry squares or rounds filled with apples, sealed then baked with a little water. Sugar and cinnamon are used as flavorings.

apple jack—A distilled alcoholic drink made from fermented apple cider.

apple peeler, patent—Device in which an apple is mounted. Turning a handle will rotate the apple against a sharp metal blade, removing the peel. Handy when peeling large quantities of fruit. An electrical model is available.

apple sauce—Sauce made by cooking apples until they are a mush. Sometimes flavored with sugar and spices. Served as an accompaniment to pork roast. Used in cakes, pastries and other confections.

apricot—A fleshy fruit related to the plum. Apricots are eaten fresh, canned, stewed, dried. Made into jams and preserves. Should not be peeled. The dried fruit makes excellent fried pies. The jams and preserves can be used for cake and tart filling. Used in other confections.

Aprikose *(Ger)*—Apricot

apry *(Fr)*—Apricot flavored liqueur

aquavit—A liqueur from Scandinavia. Often flavored with herbs and spices. Used in cooking, as an aperitif and digestif.

aragosta *(It)*—Lobster

arancia *(It)*—Orange

arbiter elegantiae *(L)*—A judge of excellence.

arborio rice—A short-grained rice imported from Italy.

arils—Raisin or grape seeds. Any small seed that has had a flesh coating.

Armenian cucumber—Chinese cucumber

aroma—A pleasing odor.

arrowroot—A thickening agent. Makes a clear sauce with no after taste. The word comes from the American Indian word 'araruta,' which means flour root. It is made from starchy extracts of the roots of various tropical plants.

arroz *(SP)*—Rice

arroz con pollo *(Sp)*—Chicken with rice.

artichaut *(Fr)*—Artichoke

artichoke—The unopened flower of a variety of thistle. It is boiled or steamed until the fleshy part on the bottom (button) is tender. The center cluster of leaves (choke) is removed before eating. Care should be taken to remove all of the small thistles. The leaves are pulled off and the flesh on the lower end is removed with the teeth. The leaves may be dipped in a sauce or melted butter. After eating the leaves the button is eaten. Leaves are eaten with the fingers, the buton with a fork. Can be used as a salad course or stuffed with various meat salads and served as a luncheon entree.

Artischocke *(Ger)*—Artichoke

asparago *(It)*—Asparagus

asparagus—The edible young stalks of a perennial herb. It is related to the lily. The stalks are steamed or gently simmered until they are al dente. Serve hot with butter, oil, lemon juice or various sauces. When served cold, a vinaigrette dressing is used. Are best fresh although they may be purchased frozen or canned.

asparagus bean—A variety of cowpea.

asparagus pan—Tall two-piece pan with lid. The asparagus spears stand upright in the pierced insert. Steamed until al dente.

aspartane—An artificial sweetener. It is low in calories and contains no sugar. It is used as a table sweetener. Not suitable for cooking.

asperge *(Fr)*—Asparagus

aspic—A gelatin dish which can contain, in addition to the flavored gelatin, fruits, vegetables, meats and juices. Can be a dessert or salad. Popular item for the buffet table. Generally a fancy mold is used.

assaisonnement *(Fr)*—Condiment, seasonings, to season

assiette *(Fr)*—A plate, dish

atole *(AmInd)*—A hot beverage made from blue corn meal, water and milk. Sugar, honey, ground red chilies or chocolate can be added for flavor.

atun *(Sp)*—Tunny, tuna

aubergine *(Eng, Fr)*—Eggplant

au berre *(Fr)*—With butter

au beurre fondu *(Fr)*—In melted butter; with butter sauce

au beurre roux *(Fr)*—With browned butter

au gratin—A dish covered with bread crumbs, butter and/or cheese then browned. Meat casseroles are often finished in this manner.

au jus *(Fr)*—The natural juices given off by meat as it cooks.

au lait *(Fr)*—With milk

au naturel *(Fr)*—Simply or plainly prepared.

Aurum *(It)*—An orange-flavored liqueur.

Auster *(Ger)*—Oyster

aux choux *(Fr)*—With cabbage

aux confitures *(Fr)*—With preserved fruit or preserves.

aux cressons *(Fr)*—With watercresses

aux morilles *(Fr)*—With morels

ave de corral *(Sp)*—Fowl

avena *(It, Sp)*—Oats

avocado—The soft edible fruit of a tropical tree. Generally eaten raw. May be seasoned with salt, pepper, lemon juice, mayonnaise or to one's taste. Can be mashed with seasonings to make a chip dip, soup or a sandwich filling. Is used as a garnish for some soups and stews. Excellent in tossed salads. Avocados are the basis for the Mexican dish guacamole. When cut, the fruit should be sprinkled with lemon juice or water to prevent the flesh from turning black. The fruit is picked green. To ripen let set in a warm place or place in a brown paper bag. They do not ripen well in the refrigerator.

avoine *(Fr)*—Oats

azafran *(Sp)*—Saffron

azi *(Fr)*—Rennet

azucar *(Sp)*—Sugar

azy *(Fr)*—Rennet

B—Grade of fresh eggs. This grade is lower than 'A.' Generally not found in stores. Used by bakeries and other users of large quantities of eggs.

B & B—A liqueur that is a combination of brandy and benedictine.

baba or baba au rhum *(FR)*—A rich cake soaked in syrup and rum. A rum cake.

babeurre *(FR)*—Buttermilk

baby corn—A special variety of corn. The ears are picked when about 2-4 inches long. The ears are generally pickled and used as an appetizer or garnish.

bagels—A doughnut shaped hard crusted roll. Sometimes sprinkled with poppy seed or sauteed onions. Traditional Jewish bread served with lox and cream cheese.

bail—The wire handle on a pot or bucket

bain-marie *(Fr)*—A pan of boiling water in which the container of food is set. It is then placed in the oven to cook.

baisure *(Fr)*—*(See Kissing Crust)*

Baked Alaska—An elegant dessert. A block of hard-frozen ice cream is wrapped in a fine pastry or meringue and baked very quickly to brown. It should be served as soon as it comes out of the oven. The contrast between the cold cream and the hot covering is delightful. It may be browned in the regular oven, the salamander oven or by a hand-held salamander.

baked blind—To bake tartlet shells, pie crusts and the like without a filling.

baker's dozen *(col)*—Thirteen. In days past when breads and pastries were purchased at the bakery, the baker would give an extra doughnut or cookie to show the customer his honesty and appreciation. Another way of saying thank you. Hence when a dozen of an item were purchased, one extra was put in the bag without charge.

baking beads—Dried beans, peas, rice, ceramic pellets or aluminum pellets that are placed inside the pastry shell when baking blind. Helps keep the shell from puffing up and becoming misshapen. All are reusable.

baking beans—*(See Baking Beads)*

baking pans—Any container used for baked goods—pies, cakes, breads, cookies, quiches roasts, fowl, etc. Can be of metal, glass or ceramic.

baking powder—A leavening agent. Generally available as the double acting type.

baking sheets—Flat metal sheets that are round, square or rectangular in shape. May have raised sides. Can be used for baking breads, cookies, tarts, flan cases or when oven toasting is needed. *(See Tins)*

baking soda—*(See Soda, Baking)*

baklava *(Gr)*—Confection of layered phyllo leaves, nuts, various spices, butter and sugar syrup.

baliki *(Rus)*—Salted and smoked sturgeon.

balmoral loaf tin—A rigid tin used for baking fruit cakes and breads where a decorative surface is desired. Shape and size similar to a bread loaf tin.

balsamic vinegar—*See Aceto Balsamico)*

bamboo shoots—The shoots are cut as they break the surface of the ground. They are then sliced and added to various dishes. Widely used in Oriental cookery. Can also be boiled, sliced and added to the relish tray.

banana—This tropical fruit grows in large clusters, is elongated in shape and generally yellow. It is used fresh in salads and eaten in hand or as an addition to dry breakfast cereal. May be lightly sauteed in butter and brown sugar as a side dish. Used in pies, breads and cakes. The fruit is ripe when the skin is yellow and flecked with brown spots. Should be allowed to ripen at room temperature. *(See Banana buds in the Spice Section)*

banana split—A confection of sliced bananas, scoops of ice cream and various syrups and preserved fruits. Sometimes whipped cream and chopped nuts are added. Served in a long flat dish shaped similar to a banana.

banane *(Fr)*—Banana

Banane *(Ger)*—Banana

banneton—A sloped sided bowl made of reeds. Used for the second rising of yeast bread. Gives an interesting design when the dough is turned out and baked.

bannocks *(Scot)*—Similar to scones. Made with cornmeal, oatmeal, buttermilk, leavening and seasonings. Baked in a large round. May also be cooked on a 'girdle' (griddle). To serve, cut into wedges.

banquet—A dinner attended by many people, generally in honor of a person, holiday or other event.

bantam—A variety of dwarf chicken. Sometimes eaten.

baobab—The edible fruit from an African tree.

bar *(Fr)*—Bass fish

barbabietola *(It)*—Beet

barbeque grill—Device on which foods are cooked over hot coals.

barbeque sauce—Generally a highly seasoned sauce used to baste the food being barbecued.

barbera *(IT)*—A red wine made in Piedmont

barley—A cereal grass. Cooked as a breakfast dish and used in soups and in various casseroles.

baron—Usually means a very large piece of beef that is cooked in one piece. Can weigh up to 100 pounds. When cooked and served as such it is called Baron of Beef.

baron d'agneau *(Fr)*—This cut of lamb comprises the two rear legs and saddle, all in one piece. Saddle of lamb.

barquettes *(Fr)*—Oval tartlet shells. Can be filled before baking or baked blind then filled

bartenders sugar—A very fine granulated sugar. Used in mixing various alcoholic drinks. Can also be used in making confections.

basilic *(Fr)*—Sweet basil

basilico *(It)*—Basil

Basilienkraut *(Ger)*—Basil

basin—A bowl with sloping sides.

basted (egg)—Method of cooking eggs in a fry pan on top of the stove. The hot cooking fat is gently spooned over the tops of the eggs until the whites are firm. A lid may be put on the pan so that steam will form and the eggs are basted in this manner. The eggs are not turned over.

basting brush—Small brush made of natural fibers, used to apply sauces to roasting meats.

bataclan *(Fr)*—Dessert pastry made with almonds, eggs, sugar, flour and other ingredients. Baked in fluted tins then given a vanilla icing.

batata *(Sp)*—Yam

batter—Mixture of flour and other ingredients that is thin enough to be poured (such as cake, cornbread or pancake batter).

batterie de cuisine *(Fr)*—Kitchen equipment

Bauernsuppe *(Ger)*—Peasant soup

Bavarian cream—A sweet pudding with whipped cream. Molded in a round, plain or decorative mold. It is a very light (fluffy) dessert. Various flavorings and fruits may be added. It is served cold. Can be made to be served as a cold drink. Similar to an egg-nog.

bean—Any of a variety of pod-producing plants. In some varieties the pod with the immature seed are cooked. Other varieties the dried seed is cooked. *(See individual listings of beans. Also see Dried Beans)*

bean curd—Custard-like squares made of soaked, mashed and strained soy beans. Found in Chinese and Japanese specialty stores. Should be eaten when fresh.

bean pot—Fat earthenware pot with a narrow opening and a tight-fitting lid. Very good for baked beans or stews. Very little moisture is lost in cooking. Cooking is generally done with low heat in the oven. Can be used on top of the stove.

bean sprouts—Various types of beans and legumes are forced to sprout. These sprouts are used in Oriental dishes, in salads and on sandwiches. High in vitamins. If cooked, they should be al dente.

bear claw—A type of filled breakfast roll.

Bearnaise sauce—Sauce made of shallots, tarragon, chervil, spices and herbs, egg yolks and butter, served warm with grilled meat and poultry.

beaujolais—A red wine which is best drunk within six months of bottling.

becasse *(Fr)*—Woodcock (game bird)

beccafico *(It)*—Italian table delicacy consisting of song birds that have been fed on figs and grapes.

becfigue *(Fr)*—*(See Beccafico)*

bechamel *(Fr)*—Rich cream sauce.

beche-de-mer *(Fr)*—Trepang or sea slug. A Chinese delicacy.

beechnut—Small nut of the beech tree. Can be used as a coffee substitute or eaten raw or roasted. In some areas it is used as food for swine.

beef—A bovine which is raised for its flesh. The male calf is castrated at a young age. It is then called a steer. There are several breeds raised for their meat. All ages and sexes of this animal are edible. It is the steer that produces the tenderest and most flavorful flesh.

beef, cuts of—Names for the same cut of meat can differ from area to area. Also in some areas there will be cuts not found in other parts of the country.

BRAINS may be braised, fried, creamed or served with scrambled eggs.

BRISKET can be cooked fresh or pickled in brine and spices for corned beef and pastrami.

GROUND, various grades are used. Chuck and round are generally the best cuts to use for loaves and patties. Rather lean.

HAMBURGER, scraps and the less tender cuts are usually ground for hamburger. Can be used in meat sauces and other highly-seasoned dishes. High fat content.

HEART is not as tender as veal or lamb heart. Must be cooked a long time. Moist cooking is a must.

HIDE *(See Skin below)*

KIDNEYS have a strong odor and a pronounced flavor. Generally take longer to cook than veal or lamb kidneys.

LIVER is dark reddish-brown in color. Less expensive than veal or calf. Can be fried, braised or sauteed.

ROASTS may be roasted dry or moist, braised and sometimes grilled over charcoal. Some cuts are: Center cut chuck, Chuck shoulder, Standing rump, bottom round, Top rib, Top sirloin, Eye of round, Rib (standing rib, prime rib), strip loin, pot and 7-bone).

SKIN is tanned to make leather.

STEAK may be pan fried, broiled, braised or grilled. Some cuts are: Round, T-bone, Filet mignon, Sirloin, New York and London broil (Flank).

STEW MEAT, scraps and the less tender cuts are often cut in small pieces for making stew.

TAIL, tough, takes long cooking. Used in stew and soups.

TONGUE may be boiled, chilled, sliced thin and treated with a vinegar sauce. Use as an appetizer.

TRIPE, little flavor. This is the stomach tissue of the animal. May be purchased fresh, corned, pickled or cooked. Used in various spicy stews like the Mexican dish 'menudo.'

beef, grades of

USDA PRIME, the highest quality of beef. The most expensive. Thick outer layer of fat and heavily marbled. The juiciest and tenderest of grades.

USDA CHOICE is the most popular grade of beef. Less fat and marbling than Prime.

USDA GOOD is not as widely used as Choice. Low fat content. Often used for hamburger meat.

USDA STANDARD is rarely found in stores. Low fat. Long moist cooking needed.

USDA COMMERCIAL is meat from older cattle. Used in luncheon meats, sausages, wieners, etc. Generally not found in stores.

beef jerky—Thin slices of beef that have been dried. Excellent snack and backpackers food.

beef stroganoff—Dish made of strips of beef, mushrooms, onions, sour cream and seasonings. Served on rice or egg noodles.

beef tartare—Raw beef steak that is finely-chopped or ground. Shaped in a mound with a depression in the top into which a raw egg is slipped. Generally served with salt and fresh ground pepper. Chopped onions can be served on the side.

beef wellington—Method of preparing a boneless roast, usually one of the tender cuts—sirloin, rib eye, tenderloin. The meat is wrapped in pie crust or puff paste. It is then baked until the crust is brown. Not recommended for meat that is cooked well done unless the meat is precooked. Meatloaf may be prepared in this manner.

beer—An alcoholic beverage brewed from malted grains. Usually served cold. Can be served at lunches and outdoor fetes. Some people drink it in place of cocktails and highballs. Is used to some extent in cooking. When cooking with beer, the container should be opened one to two hours before using. This will permit it to warm to room temperature and the carbonation to die somewhat.

Beer Nuts—A trade name for peanuts that have a brittle sweet coating. Sold in bars as a snack.

beet—A dark red root vegetable. It is boiled and served with butter or may be pickled. The young leaves are useable as a potherb. When cooking do not peel or cut the skin. After cooking, the skin will slip off by rubbing under running cold water. If the skin is cut or punctured before cooking the color will tend to cook out.

beetroot *(Eng)*—Beet

beignet *(Fr)*—A fritter. Doughnut

beignets de pommes *(Fr)*—Apple fritters

belcher water *(sl)*—A glass of soda (seltzer) water.

belegtes Brot *(Ger)*—Sandwich

bell pepper—Any of the sweet green peppers.

beluga—English spelling of Russian words "byeluga" and "byelukha" for white sturgeon which produces a fine roe for high quality caviar.

Benedictine *(Fr)*—A French liqueur invented by the Benedictine monks at the Abbey of Fecamp. Flavored with aromatic herbs.

berenjena *(Sp)*—Eggplant

- 25 -

berries—A small pulpy fruit. Can be eaten fresh, with sugar and cream, stewed, in pies and tarts. Also made into jelly and jam. Varieties include—blackberry, dewberry, loganberry, boysenberry and raspberry. Berries are a very delicate fruit. Handle gently. They do not ripen after picking. Don't wash unless absolutely necessary.

berro *(Sp)*—Watercress

besan *(Ind)*—Chick pea flour

betterave *(Fr)*—Beet

beurre *(Fr)*—Butter

beurre *(Fr)*—A soft pear. A butter pear.

beurre fondu *(Fr)*—Melted butter.

beurreter de Montpellier *(Fr)*—Butter that has been colored green. Although it is edible, the main function of this butter is decorative.

beurre manie *(Fr)*—Butter and flour that has been shaped into small balls. Used to thicken sauces. A supply may be made and stored in the refrigerator.

beurre noir *(Fr)*—Black butter (butter which is browned and has chopped parsley added.

beverage—Liquids taken by mouth such as coffee, tea, milk, carbonated drinks, punch, etc. Water is not a beverage.

bezugo *(Sp)*—Buffalo fish

bibleleaf *(ErAm)*—Costmary

bicarbonate of soda *(Eng)*—Baking soda

Bier *(Ger)*—Beer

Bierstube *(Ger)*—Taproom, beer bar.

biere *(Fr)*—Beer

bifteck *(Fr)*—Beefsteak

bifteck a l'americaine *(Fr)*—Beef tartare

hilli-hi—A cream of mussel soup with many variations. French-American in origin.

bin—A storage box used for storing fruits and vegetables that do not require refrigeration. Usually built into the kitchen cabinets or in the pantry.

birds nests—*(See Potato Baskets)*

Bird's nest soup *(Ch)*—The swallow (a bird) secretes a substance it uses in holding its nest together. The dried nest is used in making the soup. The soup has a distinct flavor.

Birne *(Ger)*—Pear

birra *(It)*—Beer

bisarge *(Mex)*—A spiny cactus that is sometimes sliced and candied.

biscuit *(Fr)*—Cooky, cracker, wafer

biscuits—A bread made with flour, milk (or water), baking powder, fats and seasonings. Usually are rolled and cut in rounds and baked. May also be dropped by spoon and baked or fried in fat. Cheese, onions, bacon, spices may also be added. Served hot with butter, jam, jelly or honey. Can be used as base for a meat or vegetable cream sauce. A dessert can be made by spooning on the cold biscuit fresh strawberries and whipped cream. A popular breakfast bread, especially with gravy. Some cooks add an egg to the dough.

biscuits *(Eng)*—Cookie or cracker.

bishop—Port wine flavored with roasted orange peel and cloves, then mulled before serving.

bishop's bread—A dessert bread with almonds, raisins, chocolate chips. After baking in a loaf pan, the bread is let set for 24 hours before slicing very thin.

bisques—1) Any of a variety of fish, meat or vegetable based soups thickened with milk or cream. 2) An ice cream with crushed nuts or cookies.

bitok *(Rus)*—Meat cakes made from various meats. Mixed with bread moistened with milk, onion and spices, it is formed into cakes and fried in butter. The cakes are then simmered in sour cream.

bitters—An alcoholic solution flavored with bitter and aromatic herbs. Used in the making of some cocktails and mixed drinks.

bittersweet chocolate—Cocoa without any sweetener. Usually formed into solid bars or cakes.

black beans—Dried beans that are black in color. Popular South American bean. Excellent when combined with white rice.

blackberry—A bramble fruit. *(See Berries)*

blackeyed peas (beans)—A variety of cowpea. Is a traditional dish served on New Year's day. Thought to bring good luck for the coming year. *(See Cowpea)*

black mushrooms *(Ch)*—Chinese dried black mushrooms. Should be available in Oriental grocery stores. Have a flavor more distinct than fresh mushrooms. Must be soaked in liquid before using.

black radish—Globe shaped and black in color. Also called winter radish. Flavor similar to the red radish.

black walnut—An American variety of the walnut. The shells are very hard. The meat is very oily and flavorful. Used in cakes and other confections. A cooking oil is available.

blanc *(Fr)*—White. Used to describe white wine.

blanc *(Fr)*—Egg white

blancmange—A cornstarch pudding usually flavored with vanilla. Unsweetened chocolate can also be added.

blanc-mange *(Eng, Fr)*—A molded dessert. May be made of sugar, almonds, almond milk, fruits, liqueurs, milk, cornmeal, gelatin, cream and other flavorings. There is a great difference between the French and English blanc-manges.

bland—With a very mild taste or flavor.

blanquette *(Fr)*—Chicken, veal or lamb stew made with white sauce (made with cream and egg yolks). Onions and mushrooms are often added.

Blatterteig *(Ger)*—Puff paste.

ble *(Fr)*—Wheat

bleach—1) To lighten the color of something by chemical action or other means. 2) Short for household bleach.

blender—An electric machine with an upright mixing chamber. It is used for combining liquids and solids, making purees and chopping foods.

blind baked—Baked blind.

blini *(Rus)*—Pancake

blintze *(Fr)*—Stuffed pancake

blintze *(Yid)*—Main dish or dessert pancake rolled around meat, cheese or fruit filling and served with sour cream, applesauce or jam. The batter is similar to crepe batter.

blood sausage—A ready-to-eat sausage made of cooked pork meat, hog blood, other meats, spices and seasonings.

blueberries—Small blue fruit from a shrub. Can be eaten fresh or cooked. Can be added to cakes, muffins, cookies and other quick breads. Should be thoroughly drained and washed if the canned type is being used. The plant is native to the Americas.

blue cheese—A hard cheese with blue mold marbling throughout. Used in salads, sauces, snacks and as a dessert cheese. It is crumbly. Similar to Stilton, Roquefort and Gorgonzola.

blue corn—A corn raised originally by the American Indian in the southwest United States. When green, the kernels are white with a tinge of blue. When mature and dried, the kernels turn blue. Used the same as yellow and white corns.

blue point—A delicate oyster. Small in size. Originally from Long Island, New York.

Blumenkohl *(Ger)*—Cauliflower

bock *(Fr)*—Beer. Glass of beer.

bock beer—A dark and heavy beer.

boeuf *(Fr)*—Beef, ox

bohea—Black tea

Bohne *(Ger)*—Bean

bok choy—An Oriental green vegetable that is used in stir-fry dishes and as a pot herb. It is loose leafed. Sometimes called Chinese cabbage. Should be available in Oriental food stores.

bologna—A cooked or smoked sausage made of various meats and spices. It is used for sandwiches, snacks and hors d'oeuvres.

Bombay duck—A dish made with dried fish and curry.

bombe *(Fr)*—1) A bomb-shaped mold made in two halves. 2) The dessert made in a bombe mold.

bon appetit *(Fr)*—Literally, have a good meal, enjoy the food.

bon bon—Candy with a cream center and a firm outer shell. Usually the size of small walnuts.

bonbonniere *(Fr)*—A fancy dish for bonbons, a sweetmeat box.

boning knife—Strong broad backed narrow bladed knife. Used for removing raw meat from the bones. The point is generally very sharp.

bonito—A small species of tuna.

bonne bouche *(Fr)*—A toothsome morsel, tidbit

Bordeaux *(Fr)*—A red or white dinner wine.

bordelaise *(Fr)*—A brown sauce with spices, shallots and red wine. Suitable for grilled meats.

borsch or borscht *(Rus)*—A beet or cabbage soup.

Boston cream pie—A plain cake with rich pudding between the layers. Confectioners sugar is dusted over the top.

bottled water—Natural spring or filtered water that is sold in bottles. May be purchased in various sized bottles at the market. Also available in large bottles delivered to the home. Waters of this type are generally low in impurities. A soft water.

bouchon *(Fr)*—A stopper, cork

boucher *(Fr)*—Butcher

boudin *(Fr)*—Seasoned forcemeat rolled into the shape of a sausage. Blood sausage.

bouillabaisse *(Fr)*—Soup or stew made of fish, various vegetables and seasonings.

bouilli *(Fr)*—Boiled or stewed meat.

bouillie *(Fr)*—Infant's food, pap, cooked cereal.

bouillon—Clear soup or broth.

boulette *(Fr)*—Dumpling

boulettes de hachis *(Fr)*—Forcemeat balls

bouquet—1) Distinctive aroma. The aroma of a wine is called its bouquet. 2) A bunch of flowers.

bourbon whiskey—An American whiskey that is distilled from corn (at least 50%), other grains, yeasts and malts. Can be used in cooking to flavor some confections and in some marinades.

bourguigonne *(Fr)*—Meats, fish and poultry cooked in a red wine sauce with onions and mushrooms. From the Burgundy region of France.

bourse a pasteur *(Fr)*—Corn salad. A green salad.

bouter *(Fr)*—Wine that has turned sour.

bovine—Cow, beef, steer.

bowls—Those half-sphere containers that every kitchen should have an assortment of. Virtually an indispensable kitchen utensil. Sizes range from the very small to the very large. Bowls may be made of copper, stainless steel, glass, ceramic, wood or plastic. Bowls are used for mixing, cooking, storing and serving. Bowls may have sloped or straight sides.

bowl scrapers—Small hand tools used for scraping foods from their containers. Generally have a handle with a flat plastic or rubber blade at one end.

braciola *(Ir)*—Flattened piece of meat rolled around a stuffing and cooked in a wine sauce.

bramble—Any of the large family of thorny bushes producing berries. Blackberries, dewberries, boysenberries, and loganberries to name a few.

bran—The outer coating of cereal grains which is separated in milling. Used as a cereal additive and is used in some breads. Is ground for use.

brandade or brandade de morue *(Fr)*—Codfish ragout

brandevin *(Fr)*—Brandy

brandy—A spirit distilled from wine or grape and fruit juices. Used as an after dinner drink and in cocktails. Is used in various confections and other dishes. Can be used for flaming. In France several types of brandy are made: cognac, armangnac, calavados. Three stars on a label denotes the distillers' least expensive blend. VSOP (Very Special Old Pale) indicates a brandy that has been aged at least four-and-a-half years. A Napoleon brandy is at least five years old. Spanish brandy is distilled from sherry. Portugese from port wine. Several brandies are made in California.

brasero *(Sp, SW)*—Pan for holding lighted charcoal. A brazier.

Braten *(Ger)*—A roast

Bratwurst *(Ger)*—A sausage, in links, made of pork, veal and various spices. It must be cooked before eating.

braunschweiger—A variety of liverwurst.

brazier—A pan for holding burning coals over which a grill is placed for the cooking of foods. A barbeque.

Brazil nut—A large, hard-shelled triangular nut whose kernel is very oily. Used in confections and cakes. A South American tree.

bread—1) Baked food that is basically flour or meal, liquid, and leavening agents. Some breads use fats, eggs, sugar, different types of grain flour, spices, herbs and other seasonings. Some types of bread are; yeast rolls, loaf bread, cornbread, pancakes, biscuits, doughnuts, breakfast rolls, cookies and crepes.

bread box—A closed container for the storage of breads.

bread crumbs—Dried bread that has been crushed until it is very fine. Used to coat various foods before frying. Sometimes used as a topping for certain casseroles.

bread flour—Flour made from hard wheat. Good for yeast breads.

breadfruit—The fruit of this South Pacific tropical tree is edible and very nourishing. Rich in starch. The fruit can be baked whole or sliced. It is not eaten raw. The sap of the tree is used as a glue and the timber in the making of huts and canoes. The inner bark is beaten out and made into a kind of cloth. The fruit are about the size of a large grapefruit. It is now cultivated in the West Indies.

breading—Bread crumbs, flour, cornmeal, crushed cereals used alone or combined to coat various foods prior to cooking. Sometimes seasonings are added to the breading.

bread knife—A long, thin-bladed knife. The cutting edge is serrated. Used for cutting breads.

bread mix—Ingredients premixed by manufacture used in making various breads. Generally one or two additional ingredients are added by the cook. Convenient. Yeast bread, cornbread and biscuits are some of the mixes available.

bread pot—Earthenware pot used for baking breads. Made of unglazed clay and with a shape similar to a flower pot. Unused clay flowerpots can be used as a substitute. The drain hole must be covered.

bread pudding—A simple and quick dessert. Made of stale bread, sugar, milk, eggs, spices and flavorings. It is baked. Can be served with whipped cream. Raisins and other fruits can be added.

bread starter—*(See Sourdough Starter)*

bread tins—Pans used for baking yeast breads. Loaf-shaped tins are available in various sizes. Curved types for French breads and glass cylinders for breads with a crust all around. Only breads should be baked in these tins. *(See Tins)*

bream—A fresh water fish.

brecol *(Sp)*—Broccoli

bren *(Sp)*—Bran

bretones *(Sp)*—Brussels sprouts

Bretzel *(Fr)*—Pretzel

brewers yeast—A yeast used as a dietary supplement.

brider *(Fr)*—Truss

bridge mix—Mixture of various small candies and nuts. Set out for guests to nibble on at parties. Sometimes contains small pretzels and crackers. Generally sold in stores.

brie—A soft cheese. Sharp flavor and distinct odor. Surface has a red color.

brigade de cuisine *(Fr)*—The staff of the kitchen in a hotel or restaurant

brill—Flat sea fish similar to the turbot. Its flesh is light and delicate.

brine—The liquid in which foods are pickled.

brioche—A very rich basic bread dough. Used mainly for dessert type breads. May be made into various shapes and forms. Classical form is a ball with a smaller ball pressed into the top. Baked in a buttered mold and known as Grosse Brioche a tete.

brioche—A kind of sponge cake. A light roll.

brioche tin—Fluted tin with sloping sides used for baking some types of brioches.

brionne *(Fr)*—Chayote

brisket—A cut of beef used in preparing Corned Beef and Pastrami.

broccoli—A member of the cauliflower family, the unopened flower bud of this plant are eaten. May be steamed, stewed or used raw in salads. An excellent crudite. Dark green in color. Should be cooked al dente.

broccoli raab—A variety of turnip raised for its young stalks. The shoot or stalk is about 6-8 inches long when harvested. Cooked like asparagus and served with a sauce such as hollandaise or lemon and butter. Known to American-Italians as Italian stock. May be available in Italian groceries in late winter and early spring.

broccolo *(It)*—Broccoli

broche *(Fr)*—A spit

brochet *(Fr)*—A pike fish

brochette *(Fr)*—A skewer. Foods cooked on a skewer and grilled are called 'en brochette.'

brocoli *(Fr)*—Broccoli

broiler—1) That part of the kitchen stove where foods are broiled. 2) A young chicken weighing around two to two-and-a-half pounds. They are split in half for cooking. May be broiled or baked. Each half is one serving.

Brot *(Ger)*—Bread

broth—Strained liquid in which meat or vegetables have been cooked. Meat broth is often served as a consomme.

brown and serve rolls—Yeast rolls which have been cooked but not browned. At serving time rolls are put into heated oven and browned. They may be purchased in the bakery section at the grocery store.

brown betty—A pudding of bread, fruit and seasonings. It is baked and can be served warm with a fruit sauce.

brown bread—Breads made with whole wheat or graham flours.

brown rice—Unpolished rice. Natural rice that has not been processed aside from cleaning and grading.

brown sugar—Granulated sugar that has some of the molasses left in during refining. Sometimes molasses is added to the white sugar. Two types are available, light and dark. The dark has a greater amount of molasses. Used in cakes, pies, candies, sauces, other confections and some fruit dishes.

brownies—Type of chocolate cookie.

brule *(Fr)*—Any food made or served with a caramelized sugar top.

brunch—A meal between breakfast and lunch. May be a combination of foods suitable to both meals. May contain hot and cold dishes. Generally informal in nature. Popular way of entertaining on Sundays and holidays. Service is usually buffet.

brush—A tool with bristles attached to a handle. Used to apply butter, beaten eggs, water or whatever to the tops of foods. Use to grease baking pans. The kitchen should have at least two of these brushes. One for pastries and the other for meats and pans.

brussels sprouts—Small cabbage-like heads borne on an upright stalk. Generally steamed or lightly simmered. Over cooking will cause them to become mushy. Serve with butter or a cream sauce.

buckwheat—A cereal grain related to wheat. Is ground into flour and meal. Used in breads and as a hot cereal.

buckwheat cakes—Hotcakes made with flour and cornmeal.

buckwheat noodles—Noodles made with wheat and buckwheat flours. They are beige, slightly coarse and firm. Should be found in Oriental stores.

bueno apetito *(Sp)*—Literally, have a good meal, enjoy the food.

buffalo—A wild bovine usually with a shaggy coat and a hump above the shoulders. At one time roamed the plains of North America in large herds. Was a source of meat and fur for the plains Indian. In the late 1800s, the buffalo was almost killed off by the white man. Today the buffalo is raised in commercial herds. The meat is available in some specialty shops. Preparation is the same as beef.

buffet—1) Food set out on tables where the guests can serve themselves. Seating tables may be arranged beforehand or small trays with legs provided. 2) A piece of furniture usually located in the dining room. The top of the buffet can be used to set dishes of food on.

bulb baster—Hand-held tool used to baste foods. By squeezing a bulb, liquid is drawn up a tube and then is released over the food.

bun—A yeast roll.

buon' appetito *(It)*—Literally, have a good meal, enjoy the food.

burdock, domestic—Although considered a weed, this plant has many uses in the kitchen. The leaves, stalk and roots are all edible. The roots can also be made into an ale. Treat the leaves and stalks as pot herbs. It is very popular in Japan where it is called gobo.

burgundy—A dark red dinner wine.

burger—Short for hamburger.

burger press—*(See Hamburger Press)*

burner (stove)—The heating element, gas or electric, on top of the kitchen stove where pans are placed for cooking.

burritos *(Mex)*—Refried beans wrapped in a flour tortilla and either lightly fried or baked until hot and light brown. Shredded meat, cheese or chilies are sometimes added to the beans.

burro *(It)*—Butter

butcher's knife—Various sized knives that are heavier than cooks knives. Usually have larger and heavier handles. Used mainly by butchers.

butcher's saw—Similar to freezer knives. Large in size and sometimes shaped like a carpenter's saw. Used for cutting large bones.

butt—1) A wine cask. 2) The end part of a cut of meat. The thick end.

butter—Solid edible emulsion of fat obtained by churning the cream from milk. Used in cooking and as a spread for bread.

Butter *(Ger)*—Butter

butterbean—Lima bean

butter cake—Cakes made with some type of fat: butter, margarine, vegetable shortening or oil.

butterfat—The part of milk from which butter is made. The oil of the milk.

buttermilk—The liquid left after butter is churned (made). When cooking with buttermilk a certain amount of baking soda is used.

butternut—This oily nut may be eaten raw or ground into a paste. Used in various confections. Also called white walnut. It is hard shelled.

butter paddles—Small wooden paddles used to shape butter balls. Very handy tool. Keep paddles wet while making the butter balls.

butters—Fruit pulp and sugar cooked to a thick smooth paste. Spices are sometimes added.

butterscotch—1) Candy made from sugar, corn syrup and water. It is cooked until golden brown. Brown sugar may be substituted for the white. 2) The flavor and color attained in this manner.

butter warmer—Small metal or porcelain pan used to gently melt butter. These pans are usually very heavy.

buttery—A pantry or place where food is stored.

c—Abbreviation for cup

C—1) Abbreviation for Celsius or centigrade. 2) Grade of eggs, generally used commercially by bakeries, pastry makers, confectioners, etc.

cabbage—Vegetable composed of densely-packed leaves that form a round head. May be cooked or eaten raw in salads. Should be cooked al dente. Is made into sauerkraut and pickled in other ways. Light green in color.

cabbage palm—The terminal bud of some species of the palm are edible. Steamed or stewed.

cabbage rolls—Seasoned ground beef rolled in cabbage leaves then simmered in a seasoned liquid. Generally two rolls make a serving.

cabillaud *(Fr)*—Cod fish

cabillaud farci *(Fr)*—Stuffed cod fish.

cacao *(Fr, It, Sp)*—cocoa

cacciatore *(It)*—Meat or poultry that has been prepared with onions, garlic, herbs, wine and tomatoes.

cacerola *(Sp)*—Saucepan

Caesar salad—Salad composed of romaine lettuce, anchovies and various ingredients, usually assembled and tossed at the table with the last ingredient, a raw egg. Hearts of the lettuce can be left whole.

cafe au lait *(Fr)*—Coffee with hot milk.

cafe brulot *(Fr)*—Brandy is floated on top of a cup of hot coffee, then ignited; usually flamed at the table.

cafe noir *(Fr)*—Black coffee. Coffee without milk or cream.

caffe *(It)*—Coffee

caffeine—A slightly bitter alkaloid, present in coffee and tea. Acts as a stimulant.

caille *(Fr)*—Quail

caille au truffles *(Fr)*—Quails stuffed with truffles

cake—1) A dessert bread made of eggs, flour, sugar, liquid and fats. Various flavorings, fruits and nuts can be added. Baked in round, square, oblong, sheet or tube pans. Is often iced. For special occasions the top and sides may be decorated. When made in layers a sauce, icing or jam is put between them. 2) Various foods that are normally free flowing will sometimes tend to form a solid mass. This is caused by the presence of excessive moisture. Flours, powders, sugars and salts can 'cake.' Generally light stirring or sifting will return them to their proper form.

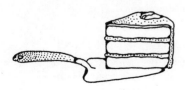

cake decorator—A hand tool used in the decoration of cakes and other confections. It consists of a hollow cylinder with a plunger that forces the icing out through decorative tips. The nozzel tips are interchangeable for different designs.

cake flour—Wheat flour that has been finely-milled to produce a very soft and white flour. Used in the making of cakes. Always sift before using. Low in gluten. Not used for breads.

cake mix—Commercially-prepared pre-mixed ingredients for cakes. Usually one or two ingredients are added by the cook. Many flavors available. Available at the grocery store.

cake tester—A thin wire with a small handle or a bunch of straws bound together. Used to test the doneness of cakes. The wire type is used over and over again. The straws are removed from the bunch for use then discarded.

cake tins—Pans with straight sides that are used primarily for baking cakes. Some are equipped with removable sides. Tins are available in round, square, rectangular or decorative shapes. They may be shallow or deep. Should be kept shiny. *(See Spring Form Pans and Tins)*

calabaza *(Sp)*—Pumpkin

calamaro *(It)*—Squid

calas—In New Orleans, a sweet rice fritter served hot with a sprinkling of powdered sugar.

calcium—A mineral found in cheeses, milk, some vegetables, essential for bone and tooth development.

calf—Veal

calories—A unit used to measure the value of foods' ability to produce heat. In controlling one's weight, the intake of calories is generally reduced.

Calvados *(Fr)*—A brandy with a delicate apple flavor. From the Normandy region of France it is made from apple cider. Served mainly as a digestif, after a meal, it can be drunk during the meal to settle the stomach.

calzoni *(It)*—A meat or cheese filled tart. Either baked or fried. Can be used as an entree or as an appetizer, depending on the size.

camaron *(Sp)*—Shrimp, crawfish

cambaro *(Sp)*—Crab

cambric tea—Weak tea with milk and sugar

Camembert—A soft cheese that is covered with mold.

camot *(Sp)*—A tuber bearing plant. The yam or sweet potato.

can—1) A metal or glass container in which foods may be preserved. 2) A container of preserved food.

Canadian whiskey—A mixed grain whiskey made in Canada. It has a flavor that is generally smoother and subtler than bourbon, scotch or rye whiskeys. Can be used in cooking the same as bourbon whiskey.

canape—A piece of bread, toast or cracker topped with cheese, meats, pates or other toppings. Generally served as an appetizer or with cocktails.

canard *(Fr)*—Duck

candied—Fruits, nuts and vegetables that have been coated with sugar or sugar syrup. This enhances the flavor and helps preserve them.

candied apples—Fresh whole apples are dipped in a flavored sugar syrup. This produces a candy coating. A small wooden stick is inserted in one end to hold while eating. Generally a fall holiday confection.

candy—Confections made with sugar, flavorings, liquids and fats. Nuts and fruits can be added.

canela *(Sp)*—Cinnamon

canella knife—Hand tool used to cut grooves in various fruits and vegetables. May be used to make citrus peel strips.

caneton *(FR)*—Duckling

canisters—Closed containers used for storing flour, sugar, coffee, tea or other dried food. Generally come in decorative sets of graduated sizes.

canned—Foods that are preserved in glass or metal containers.

canneler *(Fr)*—*(See flute)*

cannella *(It)*—Cinnamon

cannelle *(Fr)*—Cinnamon

cannellini bean—A large white bean. Popular in Italian cookery. Usually found in Italian groceries and specialty shops.

cannelloni *(It)*—Squares of pasta given a filling, rolled up, then baked with a sauce. Various types of fillings may be used. Savory or sweet.

cannelon *(Fr)*—A fluted mold. A hollow roll of puff paste. A fried or baked roll of mincemeat.

canner—*(See Pressure Cooker)*

canning—The act and art of preserving foods in cans.

cannoli—Tubes of pastry that have been deep fried then filled with whipped cream. Or in the Sicilian manner with sweetened ricotta cheese. A pudding may also be used as a filling. A simple elegant dessert.

cannoli forms—Small metal cylinders on which pastry is wrapped and then deep fried.

can opener—Hand operated and electrical devices used to remove the tops from canned goods. Some of the electrical openers have knife sharpeners built in.

cantaloupe—A melon with rough skin and orange colored flesh. Popular breakfast fruit. Is eaten raw and usually chilled.

cape cod turkey *(col)*—New England for cooked fish.

capers—The pickled flower buds of a Mediterranean shrub. Used as a garnish and in salads.

capillaire *(Fr)*—A syrup made from sugar, water and maidenhair fern.

capon—A male chicken that has been chemically castrated and raised for food. It is a large bird with tender flesh. Usually roasted. It is expensive and sometimes hard to find.

capon *(Sp)*—Capon

cappone *(It)*—Capon

cappuccino *(It)*—Espresso with cream.

capre *(Fr)*—Capers

carafe—A water or wine bottle with a flared lip.

carambola—A pulpy and acid fruit of a tropical tree. It is eaten raw in hand or in salads. Also called 'star fruit' for its shape when cut.

caramel—A chewy candy, generally square or cube shaped. Also the flavor. The flavor is produced by cooking (burning) sugar over high heat.

carbohydrates—Compounds of carbon, hydrogen and oxygen. Sugars and starches are in this group.

carbonated beverage—*(See Soda Pop)*

carciofo *(It)*—Artichoke

cardamome *(Fr, Ger)*—Cardamon

cardamomo *(It, Sp)*—Cardamon

cardoon—Possibly one of man's oldest cultivated vegetables. Seed have been found that are over 30,000 years old. The edible portion of this plant resembles celery. It can be stewed, braised, added to soups, as tempura or pickled. Popular in the Mediterranean area and in France. Probably not widely grown commercially in America. Check Italian groceries.

cari *(Fr)*—Curry

carne *(It, Sp)*—Flesh; meat

carne de puerco *(Sp)*—Pork

carne de vaca *(Sp)*—Beef

carne di manzo *(It)*—Beef

carnero *(Sp)*—Sheep; mutton

carosella *(It)*—Sicilian fennel

carota *(It)*—Carrot

carotene—Yellow to orange to red pigments found in a wide variety of plants—carrots, spinach, peas, lettuce, pumpkin, cabbages, oranges, etc. Also in egg yolks and butter. A source of Vitamin A.

carp—A variety of freshwater fish. May be cooked in several ways—poached, fried, steamed and stuffed.

carpe *(Fr)*—Carp

carre *(Fr)*—Portion of lamb, veal or pork that is cut from fleshy part of the loin between the ribs and leg. Fillet.

carrelet *(Fr)*—A flounder (fish)

carrot—A root vegetable which is red-orange in color. Size ranges from three to 12 inches. May be steamed or stewed. Cook al dente. Also used raw in salads and as a crudite. Can be added to soups and stews. Makes an attractive pickle.

carvi *(Fr, Sp)*—Caraway

carving boards—A hardwood board with a groove around the edge of the cutting surface. This groove will catch juices from meat, fruits and vegetables being cut. Should be thoroughly washed and scraped after each use. A light coating of cooking oil will help prevent the board from drying out.

carving fork—Large two-tined fork used to hold the roast or fowl while it is being carved. The tines are usually long. Often the carving knife and fork have matching ornate handles.

carving knife—Usually lighter in weight than cooks' knives. Some are flexible for carving around bones. Blades range from nine to 14 inches. Often made with a decorative handle for use at the table. Generally comes with matching carving fork.

casa *(IT, PG, SP)*—House

casaba—A muskmelon with yellow/green rind. Large with light-colored meat. Breakfast or salad melon.

case—A pastry shell

caseknife—A dinner knife

cashew (nut)—The seed of a tropical tree, the cashew apple. It is roasted before using in candies, cakes, curries and other dishes. Very rich. Good snack.

cask—A small barrel

cassava—Tropical plant from whose roots tapioca is derived.

casse-croute *(Fr)*—Snack

casse noisette *(Fr)*—Nutcracker

casserole—1) A covered utensil in which foods are baked. They can be made of earthenware, metal, glass or ceramic. When dishes are cooked in and served in them, the dish is generally described as en cocotte or in casserole. 2) A casserole is generally a mixture of vegetables, meats and liquid. Pastas and various seasonings can also be added.

cassoulet *(Fr)*—A stew made with white beans.

castana *(Sp)*—Chestnut

cast iron—*(See Ironware)*

caster sugar *(Eng)*—Fine granulated sugar.

castor sugar—Fine ground granulated sugar. Also known as bartender's sugar.

catfish—River fish found in the Mississippi basin and in some other areas. Flesh is delicate and the fish does not have many bones. Is generally crumbed and pan or deep fried.

catnip—A plant of the mint family. Cats like it very much. A tea may be made from the leaves.

catsup—A thick seasoned sauce. Americans know it as a thick tomato sauce in a bottle. Used on hamburgers, french fries, sandwiches and other foods. Catsups are also made from mushrooms, walnuts, fruits and vegetables.

cauliflower—A member of the cabbage family. The flower buds form a compact white head. This is harvested before they bloom. The head is generally steamed whole or broken into flowerettes. Can be gently stewed. Cook al dente. The flowerettes are excellent raw in salads, as crudites or pickled. *(See Purple Cauliflower)*

caviar—Salted roe of various large fish. Served as appetizers on crackers, rusks or toast. Can be eaten with chopped onions, or sour cream.

caviare *(Fr)*—Caviar

cavolfiore *(It)*—Cauliflower

cavolini *(It)*—Brussels sprouts

cavolo *(It)*—Cabbage

Cayennepfeffer *(Ger)*—Red pepper

cazo *(Sp)*—A large copper saucepan.

cebolla *(Sp)*—Onion

cebollana *(Sp)*—Chives

cece *(It)*—Chick pea

ceci—Garbanzo bean

ceia *(Por)*—Supper

cela se laisse manger *(Fr)*—That is good to eat. Is palatable.

celeri *(Fr)*—Celery

celeriac—This vegetable is related to celery and resembles it in taste. The edible portion is a large knob that grows at or just below ground level. The rough brown skin must be peeled before the knob is used. This vegetable can be braised, boiled and served with a cream sauce or with butter. Also it may be fried in butter or pureed and added to mashed potatoes. Can be used in stews or grated raw in green salads. It is rated as a standard winter vegetable in Germany and Eastern Europe. The taste is sweeter than celery with a hint of parsley.

celery—An upright plant composed of several long stalks. Generally light green in color. It is very crispy. Can be eaten alone, chopped in salads, added to stews and soups or braised and served with butter. If cooked it should be cooked al dente. Each stalk should have the 'strings' removed before using.

celery cabbage—*(See Chinese Cabbage)*

celery root—*(See Celeriac)*

cellophane noodles *(Or)*—*(See Ming Bean Noodles)*

Celsius—A temperature scale that measures the boiling and freezing points of water; same as centigrade.

celtuce—A variety of lettuce. The young leaves are used as a salad green. The stalk that appears when the plant starts to seed, can be used as a stir-fry vegetable, braised in butter or steamed. It can be cooked then pureed and made into a soup. Caution, the older leaves are rather bitter.

centeno *(Sp)*—Rye grain

centigrade—A unit of metric measure.

cepe *(Fr)*—Edible mushrooms

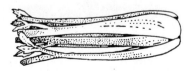

cereal grasses—Some of the cereal grasses we use as food are wheat, rye, oats, barley, rice and corn. Some grains are ground into flours for use in breads and pastries. Some are used in the manufacture of breakfast cereals.

cereza *(Sp)*—Cherry

cerise—Red, as the color of a cherry.

cerise *(Fr)*—Cherry. Also the color cherry (red).

cervelles de veau in brochette *(Fr)*—Broiled calf's brains on skewers.

cerveza *(Sp)*—Beer

cetriolo *(It)*—Cucumber

Ceylon gooseberry—A plant and fruit similar to the umokokolo.

cha *(Ch)*—Tea, the beverage

chad froid *(Fr)*—Fowl or game which has been cooked as a hot dish but is served cold. Sometimes it is glaceed or put in aspic.

chaff—The husks that have been separated from grain. Non-edible.

chafing dish—A pan mounted on a stand, used for cooking food at the table, with a spirit lamp or candle used as source of heat.

challa *(Yid)*—A bread that is usually in the form of a braided loaf. Traditionally eaten by Jewish people on their sabbath.

chalote *(Sp)*—Shallot

champagne *(Am, Fr)*—A sparkling white or pink wine. It originated in Champagne, France. A versatile wine. May be served with foods as well as a cocktail. Often served at receptions and other gatherings.

Champagner *(Ger)*—Champagne

champana *(Sp)*—Champagne

champignon *(Fr)*—Edible or inedible mushrooms.

chantilly *(Fr)*—Dessert prepared or served with whipping cream.

chantilly cream—Cream whipped with confectioners sugar and flavorings.

chapati *(Hin)*—Thin unleavened bread.

chappaties *(Ind)*—Indian pancake type bread that is served with curries. Baked on a griddle.

chapelure *(Fr)*—Breadcrumbs

chapon *(Fr)*—1) Capon. 2) Head of garlic.

chapote *(Mex)*—Mexican persimmon

chaquehue *(AmInd)*—A porridge made of blue corn meal, water and milk. Sometimes sweeteners are added.

charbon de bois *(Fr)*—Charcoal

charcoal—Pieces of partly-burned wood that are reburned to form hot coals for cooking foods. Commercially made charcoal briquettes often contain coal products to make them burn more hotly.

charcuterie *(Fr)*—1) Dressed pork. 2) Pork butcher shop. 3) Delicatessen

chard—A nutritious pot herb. Also used raw in salads and in other dishes. Has a taste a little stronger than spinach. The stems of older plants may be cooked separately.

chardonay—A white dinner wine.

charlotte *(Fr)*—(See Charlotte Ruse)

charlotte mold—Deep dish with straight or slightly sloped sides. Used for making various charlottes.

charlotte ruse—A dessert made in a deep, straight-sided mold. Can be made from eggs, milk, sugar, flavorings. The sides of the mold and bottom are usually lined with some type of sponge cake. Fruits are also used and often whipped cream and ice cream. Generally served cold.

charqui *(Sp)*—Jerked beef; beef jerky

Chartreuse *(Fr)*—An herb-flavored liqueur. Yellow in color.

chasse *(Fr)*—A liqueur taken after coffee.

chataigne d'eau *(Fr)*—Water chestnut

chateau *(Fr)*—A manor house or estate. Wines from France are labeled as to the estate from which they came. Such as Chateau-Latour is from the estate of Latour.

chateaubriand *(Fr)*—Fillet of beef, grilled and served with fried potatoes and mushrooms or truffles. The American version is served with several vegetables as side dishes.

chateaubriant *(Fr)—Same as Chateaubriand)*

chatouillard *(Fr)*—1) Potatoes cut into long ribbons and deep fried. 2) Nickname for an expert chef.

chatti *(AmInd)*—Earthenware pot.

chaudiere *(Fr)*—Boiler

chaudron *(Fr)*—Kettle or cauldron

chauffage *(Fr)*—Heating

chayote—A tropical or subtropical vine which was known to the Mayans and Aztecs before the arrival of Europeans. Almost every part of this plant is edible. It bears fruits on the vine, produces a tuber underground and the shoots can be prepared like asparagus.

The fruits can be added, raw, to salads and other dishes where a cucumber taste is desired. The fruit can also be used as a cooked vegetable and in various casseroles. May be fried or cubed, boiled and treated with a tomato sauce. Can be cooked, mashed and combined with eggs, sugar and spices to make a dessert. The tubers are boiled, sliced and fried with sugar. Similar to fried sweet potatoes. The leaves and stems are used as animal fodder. A versatile plant.

cheddar—A hearty cow's milk cheese originated by the British. Deep orange to pale orange to white in color. After a year of aging it has a strong piquant flavor. Longer aging increases its sharpness. Most popular cheese in America. Firm textured. A good cooking and eating in hand cheese. Annatto used as a coloring agent.

cheddar mill—In the making of cheese, a cutting tool used to cut curds into long rubbery pieces.

cheese—A foodstuff obtained from milk curds. Can be made from cow, goat, sheep or buffalo milk. Cheese is used as a sandwich filling, with crackers, as a dessert and in cooking. When cooking with cheese, it should not be over-cooked. Some cheeses are aged a short time while others to several years. Various spices, herbs, flavorings, wines are added to some cheeses. In America today, many traditional goat's milk cheeses are made from cow milk.

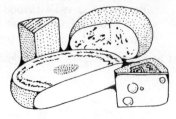

cheese cake—A type of pie made with flour, eggs, sour cream or cream cheese and flavorings. Can be served with various cooked fruits on top. A crumb crust is generally used. Serve cold. This is an open-face pie.

cheese chips—Snack chips made with cheese.

cheese dip—A dip using cheese as the main ingredient. May be hot or cold.

cheeseburger—A hamburger with the addition of a slice of cheese. The cheese is placed on the meat patty after it is turned. The cheese should melt slightly.

cheesecloth—Loosely woven material that has many uses in the kitchen. Wrap for meats to be marinated, covering mouths of jars and crocks, for straining, etc. May be laundered for reuse.

chef or chef de cuisine *(Fr)*—Head cook; master cook

chef's steel—*(See Sharpening Steel)*

Cheri-Suisse *(Swiss)*—A cherry chocolate flavored liqueur.

cherimoya—A tropical fruit that is eaten raw. It is heart shaped and scaley. Can be used in fruit salad and drinks.

Cherries Jubilee—An elegant dessert of vanilla ice cream surrounded by cooked pitted cherries and flamed with brandy. A metal or ovenproof dish should be used.

cherry—A small fruit from a tree related to the peach and plum. There are two types: sweet and the tart. Sweet cherries may be eaten raw or cooked in salads. Tart cherries are used for pies, jam, jellies, canning and confec-tions. Tart cherries are also called 'pie cherries.' A liqueur is made from the tart cherry. Colors range from pale golden to red to black. Sweet cherries are also called 'eating cherries.'

cherry pitter—*(See Cherry Stoner)*

cherry stoner—Device used to remove the pits from cherries. The hand-held type stones one cherry at a time. A larger type rests on the work surface and is capable of stoning two cherries at a time.

cherry tomato—Small tomatoes that are used whole in salads and as garnish. They are about the size of hazelnuts.

cheshire *(Eng)*—A hard cheese similar to American cheddar.

chess pie—Basically an egg custard pie. Various flavorings may be added to change the character and name of the pie.

chestnut—An edible nut from the chestnut tree. They are roasted for eating out of hand and for garnish. They can be boiled, dried and ground into a flour.

chestnut frying pan—A heavy metal skillet with holes in the bottom. Used exclusively for roasting chestnuts, especially over an open fire.

chestnut knife—Short bladed knife with a hook on the end for opening the husks of chestnuts.

chevre *(Fr)*—Goat. May also refer to cheese made from goat's milk.

chevreuil *(Fr)*—Roebuck; venison

chicco d'uva *(It)*—Grape

chicha *(Sp)*—Fermented liquor made from maize, cane sugar and water.

chick pea—1) Hard skinned round bean. May be served stewed plain or with meat seasonings. Cold, can be added to salads. There are many varieties. 2) Garbanzo beans.

chick pea flour—The dried chick pea is ground into flour. It is used in Indian cookery as a thickening agent. Also called gram flour and besan.

chicken—The most popular of the fowls. A very versatile bird. Can be baked, stewed, fried, grilled and barbequed. Cold cooked chicken is used as a sandwich filling, in salads and aspics. Makes an excellent broth to be eaten alone or used as a base for other soups and sauces. The broth has a natural gelling agent. There are four sizes of chicken: the broiler, 2-2½ pounds; the fryer 2½-4 pounds; the baking, 4 pounds and up; and the stewing, 3 pounds and up. The broiler is cut in half for cooking, the baking left whole and the stewing in various pieces. The fryer can be cut into 10 or 11 pieces. Plus the liver, heart, gizzard and neck. The frying pieces are; 2 thighs, 2 legs, 2 wings, 2 breasts, 1 back, 1 rib section and 1 wishbone (optional).

chicken ala king—Cooked, diced chicken in a cream sauce with various vegetables added. It is served on biscuits or toast points. A popular luncheon or late supper entree.

chicken fried—A small steak or other meat rolled in flour and fried in fat. A gravy is sometimes made from the pan fat.

chicken fryer—Generally a deep skillet with lid. The deep sides permit the cook to brown chicken quickly with minimal grease splatter. The pan then can be covered and the chicken permitted to steam.

chile, chili—1) A spicy pepper. Yellow or red. Used fresh or dried. 2) A dish made of ground meat and sometimes onions, tomatoes, seasonings and chili peppers. Some cooks add cooked dried beans.

chile rellenos *(Mex)*—Long chili peppers that are sometimes stuffed with meat or poultry, baked in tomato sauce with a cheese topping.

chili con carne *(Mex, Sp)*—Meat in a spicy sauce

chili verde—Chili made with hot green peppers.

chiliburger—A hamburger that is served open-faced with chili or chilibeans ladled over the top. Sometimes chopped onion and grated cheese are sprinkled on top.

chilidog—A hot dog that has chili or chilibeans ladled over the top.

chine—Backbone of the pig

Chinese artichokes—*(See Crosnes)*

Chinese cabbage—Any of a variety of long, loose-leafed vegetables from the cabbage family. Varieties include, bok choy, michihli, chihli and celery cabbage. Used in stir frys and as a potherb. Widely used in Oriental cookery.

Chinese cleaver—Same shape as a cleaver but is heavier. Used by the Chinese cook in the same manner as cook's knives.

Chinese cucumber—A long, thin, rigid cucumber. Light green in color and either straight or curved. They should be at least 18 inches long when used. The longer, the sweeter. Are mild in taste and do not cause stomach turmoil. Does not keep well. Originated in southeast Asia. Also called Armenian cucumber.

Chinese eggs—*(See Hundred Year Old Eggs)*

Chinese gooseberry—Kiwifruit

Chinese okra—Vining okra

Chinese vermicelli *(Or)—(see Mung Bean Noodles)*

chinois *(Fr)*—A conical shaped sieve.

chiodo di garofano *(It)*—Clove

chip—A thin piece of food, dried, fried or baked.

chipped beef—Dried or cured beef that has been thinly-sliced. Can be combined with a white sauce and served over toast points or biscuits.

chitterlings, chitlings, chitlins—The intestines of hogs that are cleansed, then oven baked until very crispy. A snack food. Sometimes salted.

chocolat *(Fr)*—Chocoate

chocolate—Cacao beans that have been processed and pressed into solid bars and squares. Sometimes sugar is added. Used in a variety of dishes, mostly confections.

chocolate mixing sticks—*(See molinillo)*

chocolates—Small, rounded candies of chocolate with various centers—caramel, nougat, divinity, fruits, nuts, etc.

chop—A cut of meat, pork or lamb from the tenderloin usually with the bone attached. May be grilled, baked, broiled or fried.

chopsticks—Long, thin 'sticks' used in the Orient to convey food to the mouth. They are used in place of knives and forks.

chop suey—A Chinese-American dish of vegetables and spices. The Cantonese equivalent of 'odds and ends.'

chorizo *(Sp.)*—Pork sausage

choroqi *(Or)—(See Crosnes)*

chou marin *(Fr)*—Sea kale

chou ordinaire *(Fr)*—Cream puff paste

choucroute *(Fr)*—sauerkraut

choufleur *(Fr)*—Cauliflower

choux *(Fr)*—Cabbage

choux de Bruxelles *(Fr)*—Brussels sprouts

choux rouges *(Fr)*—Red cabbage

chow *(Ch)*—Food

chow chow—Relish made from ground sweet pickles, spices and vinegar.

chowder—A soup or stew made of clams, milk and seasonings. Also called New England or Boston chowder. Manhattan clam chowder has tomatoes added. May be served with grated cheese, sprig of cilantro or of parsley. Served hot. Chowder is considered an American dish originating in New England.

chow fan *(Ch)*—Fried rice

chow mein—An American dish. Many people think of this as a Chinese dish. Vegetables and meat are cooked together and served over fried noodles. Soy sauce is used as a topping, at the table.

chub—1) A thick piece of luncheon meat or sausage. Such as a round length of bologna. 2) In Europe a fresh water fish.

chuck wagon—A wagon or vehicle equipped with the necessary foods and equipment to prepare meals out of doors. A chuck wagon always traveled with the herds of cattle to feed the workers (cowboys).

chuleta de ternera *(Sp)*—Veal cutlet

churn—Tool used to make butter. Generally a round container with some type of paddles suspended in the cream. These paddles are agitated to separate the fat from the liquid.

churrasco *(Sp)*—Meat broiled over charcoal.

churro *(Sp)*—Deep fried confections. A plain fritter dusted with sugar. A special hand tool is used to drop the batter in hot fat. In Spain, sold by sidewalk vendors.

churro press—Hand tool used to force dough out into hot oil to form churros.

chutney—Condiment made of raisins, onions, dates and seasonings. Other fruits may also be used. Served with curries and various meats.

ciboule *(Fr)*—Scallion

ciboulette *(Fr)*—Chive

cider—Juice of pressed fruits such as apples and cherries.

cilantro *(Sp)*—Fresh coriander

ciliegia *(It)*—Cherry

cimier *(Fr)*—*(See Haunch)*

cioccolata *(It)*—Chocolate

cioppino—A word that developed in San Francisco to describe a rich seafood stew.

cipolla *(It)*—Onion

cipolla porraia *(IT)*—Chive

ciruela *(Sp)*—Plum

citric acid—Sour acid obtained from lemon and limes. Used in making lemonade powder and orange and lemon syrups. It can be used in place of ascorbic acid in canning, but it tends to add a tartness.

citron—A citrus fruit. The peel is used candied in various confections and cakes.

citron *(Fr)*—Lemon

citrouille *(Fr)*—Pumpkin

citrus fruits—Fruits from a variety of thorny evergreen trees and shrubs. Grown in warm regions. Some types of citrus are orange, lemon, lime, citron, grapefruit and kumquat.

civet *(Fr)*—A ragout of hare, venison or other game prepared with wine, herbs, spices and onions.

clabber—To curdle. Milk or buttermilk that has been permitted to turn sour and thick.

clam—Shell fish that is steamed, fried or baked. Is used for stews, soups and chowders.

clambake—An outdoor meal where clams are cooked and eaten. Often a party at the beach where the clams are dug then cooked and eaten.

claret—A red table wine.

clarified butter—Butter that has been melted and the resulting oil used in cooking. The solids are strained out and discarded.

clavo *(Sp)*—Clove

clay pot—Covered pot used for cooking foods in the oven. *(See Terrine and Terrine a Pate)*

clear the palate—Term used by food and beverage tasters to explain the process of cleaning the taste buds.

cleaver—A square shaped blade with a protruding handle. Can be used the same as a cook's knife. Mainly used for splitting fowl, and breaking and cutting of small bones.

clementine—The fruit of the clementine tree. This hybrid was discovered near the beginning of the twentieth century. The origin is unknown. Similar to the Mandarin, it has a more delicate flavor and is practically seedless. It is usually served fresh.

cling-stone—A fruit, such as a peach, whose flesh clings to the seed.

cloche—Glass, silver or other metal cover under which foods are kept warm.

clotted cream—A spread for scones or a chilled dessert. Made by scalding, then cooling cream skimmed from fresh milk.

clou de girofe *(Fr)*—Clove

cloud ear fungus *(Ch)*—These rounded pieces of fungus look like charred paper. Sold dried in Chinese food stores. If possible, buy the smaller ones.

cloudberries *(Eng)*—Amber colored berries from a creeping herbaceous raspberry plant. Found in specialty shops. Usually canned. Also called Dwarf Mulberry.

club sandwich—A sandwich using three slices of bread. Sliced chicken (baked) is used for one layer of filling and sliced tomatoes and crisply fried bacon as the second. The bread is lightly toasted. Mayonnaise and butter may be spread on the toasted bread. It is cut diagonally in four pieces for serving. Of course the fillings may vary.

club steak—A small beef steak used for broiling. Sometimes the meat is tenderized with a wooden or metal mallet.

coarse—Rough, not smooth.

cobbler—Deep dish fruit pie with either one or two crusts.

cochon *(Fr)*—Pig; hog

cochon de lait *(Fr)*—Suckling pig

cocido *(Sp)*—A dish consisting of fresh and dried vegetables and meat. Can be a soup or a stew.

cocktail—Alcoholic mixed drink generally served prior to a meal. Certain food dishes are called cocktails. Such as shrimp cocktail, fruit cocktail, tomato juice. An appetizer.

cocktail party—A gathering of people for the purpose of meeting and conversing. Generally mixed alcoholic drinks and various hors d'oeuvres and canapes are served.

cocktail shaker—A metal or glass container with a removable top, that is used to mix various alcoholic drinks.

coco *(Sp)*—Coconut

cocoa—The seed, which is the fruit, of the cacao tree. The tree grows mainly in South and Central America. The seed is processed, then dried, after which it is ground into a fine powder. This powder is used to make the beverage chocolate and in baking and other confections. When the processed cocoa is pressed into solid bars it is called chocolate. In 1780, Dr. James Baker founded the first chocolate factory in America. Syrups made from cocoa may be found at the grocers.

coconut—Fruit of the coconut tree which is a species of palm. The white interior of the fruit (meat) is generally grated or shredded and used in baking and confections. The liquid (milk) inside the nut is not generally used in cooking. There is a very small amount in each nut. The meat of the coconut, when dried, is called copra and from this is pressed the oil. This oil is used in the manufacture of soap. When it is deodorized and purified it has a firm consistency. It is then called coconut butter. It is tasteless and easily digestible. In certain diets it replaces dairy butter.

coconut milk—Made by moistening shredded coconut with cow's milk. Used in curry sauces and some other dishes.

cocose *(Fr)*—Coconut butter

cocotte *(Fr)*—See Casserole)

coddle—Eggs that are baked in the oven until the whites are just set.

coeurs de palmier *(Fr)*—Palm hearts

coffee—Beverage made from the ripe, roasted and ground fruit of the coffee shrub. Several methods are used in brewing coffee—steeping, boiling, percolating and dripping. Utensils for making coffee range from the simple percolator to the automatic drip-alator to the complex espresso machine. Usually served hot, some people add cream and/or sugar. Coffee may also be poured over ice and served cold. As an iced beverage, sometimes a slice of lemon or orange or sprig of mint is added. Spices can also be added, but sparingly. Coffee also comes in a powdered form that is called 'instant.' It is made by adding very hot water. Brewed coffee is sometimes used in breads, cakes and confections.

coffee cake—Sweetened and spiced bread served as an accompaniment to coffee or tea. May be in the form of rolls or loaves, simple or elaborate.

coffee cream—The cream from milk used in coffee. There is a packaged product which is half cream and half milk.

coffee creamer—A prepared substitute for cream. It may be purchased dry, frozen or liquid form. Most of them contain a certain portion of milk, generally in the form of milk solids.

coffee filters—Paper discs or cups that are placed in the coffee basket. The coffee is placed on top of the filter. Filters help remove the bitter oils when the coffee is brewed. A clean (new) filter should be used each time a pot of coffee is brewed.

coffee grinder—*(See Coffee Mill)*

coffee mill—Grinder used to grind whole coffee beans. Hand operated and electric types available.

coffins—*(See Pastry Coffins)*

cognac—The finest of brandies. From the area of Cognac in southwestern France.

cohombro *(Sp)*—Cucumber

coing *(Fr)*—Quince

Cointreau—A French-made orange flavored liqueur.

Coke—A trademark name for a carbonated soda. In some areas refers to any cola drink or carbonated beverage.

col *(Sp)*—Cabbage

cola—A soft drink that is carbonated.

colander—A bowl-shaped utensil that is perforated. Is used for draining foods. Are made of metal or plastic.

colby cheese—A hard cheese, pale orange in color. The best is in the stores three to four weeks from making. Mild flavor with tiny holes. Is moister than other cheddars. When aged a year, it develops a sharp flavor.

cold cuts—Sliced luncheon meats, also cold sliced meats, chicken and turkey.

cold duck—A sparkling red wine. An aperitif or cocktail.

cold pack—In canning, the process of packing the fruits or vegetables in the cans cold and then adding the hot liquid. They are then processed.

cole slaw—Salad made of sliced or chopped cabbage. Onions, celery, carrots and apples can be added. Served with a dressing. Chill.

colewort—A cabbage that is loosely headed.

coliflor *(Sp)*—Cauliflower

collards—A leafy green used as a potherb. High in nutritional value.

collops—A slice or small portion of food, especially meat.

colorimeter—Device used to measure the sugar content of a liquid.

coloring—Changing the color of foods by adding artificial food coloring.

coltello *(It)*—Knife

comino *(It, Sp)*—Cumin

common salt—Same as salt, cooking.

compote—Fruit cooked with sugar. A savory ragout. The container in which a compote is served.

concombre *(Fr)*—Cucumber

condensed milk—Milk that has had a large portion of the water removed. Sugar is then added. It is packed and sold in cans.

condensed soup—Soup that has been cooked by the manufacturer then half of the liquid is removed. It is then canned. Prepared for eating by adding (generally) a can of liquid. Sometimes these soups are used in casseroles and stews.

condiment—A seasoning added to a dish (usually by the diner) after cooking. This can include salt, pepper, mustards, sauces, etc.)

condimento *(It, Sp)*—Condiment, seasoning

condire all'indiana *(It)*—The blended spice mixture curry.

conejo *(Sp)*—Rabbit

coney island—A frankfurter and roll sandwich with chili. Originated at Coney Island, a resort at Brooklyn, New York.

confectioner's custard—*(See Pastry Cream)*

confectionery mold—Various shaped molds used when making candies.

confections—Any type of sweet; cake, cookies, candies, pies, tarts.

confectioners sugar—Very finely-ground sugar. Has the consistency of flour. Sift before using. Also known as dessert sugar and powdered sugar.

confiserie *(Fr)*—Candy, confection

confit *(Fr)*—Preserved, candied

confite *(Sp)*—Candy

confiture *(Fr)*—Jam, preserves

confituriere *(Fr)*—Jam dish. Dealer in preserves.

coniglio *(It)*—Rabbit

connoisseur—A person who is qualified to judge a subject.

consomme *(Fr)*—Strong clear soup made from meat or from meat and vegetables. Served very hot, sometimes with a dab of sour cream or slice of cheese toast floating on top.

consomme de tete de veau *(Fr)*—Mockturtle soup

convection oven—*(See Oven, convection)*

cookbook—A book that gives directions on how to prepare various dishes. The cook should have at least three cookbooks—a general cookbook, one on breads and one on home preserving. There are specialized books for pies, cakes, candies, cassroles, vegetables, meats, poultry, crock pots, microwave, diets and many more. Books on ethnic cooking the world over are readily available.

cooked meringue—Egg whites beaten with powdered sugar over heat. Has a higher ratio of sugar to egg whites than other meringues. Can be baked for garnishes or added to frostings, puddings and such.

cookie—A sweet cake, generally flat and baked.

cookie press—A tool with chamber which holds the cookie dough. Has changeable cutters. Dough is forced out by pressing the plunger.

cookie sheet—*(See Baking Sheets)*

cooking banana—Another name for the plantain.

cooking salt—*(See Salt, cooking)*

cooking sherry—A sherry that is neither dry nor sweet. *(See Sherry)*

cooking wines—1) Wines that are used in cooking. 2) There are available in the markets bottles labeled "cooking wine." These wines generally have had various seasonings added. The cook should use these with caution as the flavor of the wine is often very weak.

cookout—A meal that is cooked outside. The event itself.

cook's knife—Very sharp. Blade is straight and curves up about halfway to the point. This permits a rocking motion when chopping. Blade size ranges from four to 10 inches.

cook's palette knife—*(See Spatula)*

cookstove—An appliance used for cooking food. Usually has heating units on the top and an oven below them. Below the oven a broiler. Electricity, natural gas and kerosene can be used as the heating fuel. Before the advent of modern fuels, wood and coal were used.

cooky—Cookie

cooler—1) An insulated box used to keep foods and drinks cold. Portable coolers are used on picnics and other outings. Ice is put in the box along with the food and drink. 2) An iced drink. Usually in a tall glass with much ice.

copra—Dried coconut meat from which is pressed the oil. *(See Coconut)*

coq *(Fr)*—Cock, rooster

coq de bruyere *(Fr)*—Grouse, black game

coquelicot *(Fr)*—A field variety of poppy.

coquetier *(Fr)*—Egg cup

coquillage *(Fr)*—Shellfish

coquille *(Fr)*—Shell, scallop, ragout

coquilles de moules *(Fr)*—Scalloped mussels.

coral—In a lobster the unimpregnated eggs. Bright red in color.

cordero *(Sp)*—Lamb

cordial—A liqueur that is sweet and aromatic. Can be drunk before or after any meal. There are many flavors.

cordon bleu *(Fr)*—A first-rate cook. Expert chef.

corer—Hand tool used to remove the cores from various fruits and vegetables.

Corianberjame *(Ger)*—Coriander

coriandolo *(Iy)*—Coriander

coriandre *(Fr)*—Coriander

coriandro *(Sp)*—Coriander

corkscrew—Device used to remove the corks from bottles. Many types available from the very simple to the elaborate wall mounted type.

corn—A cereal grain that produces its seed (kernels) in rows on a long cylinder called a cob, or an ear of corn. May be cooked on the cob, cut off the cob and stewed or dried and ground into corn meal. Also the dried kernels can be made into hominy. Corn should be cooked al dente. On the cob it is a popular dish for picnics and other outdoor meals. To eat on the cob, it is held in the fingers and the kernels bitten off. Small handles can be inserted in the ends to help keep the fingers clean. Melted butter, salt and pepper can be spread on the ear.

corn chips—Snack chips made from ground corn.

corn holders—Small handles that are inserted in the ear of corn. These are used to hold the ear while eating. May be made of metal, wood or plastic.

corn on the cob—Method of cooking corn. The ears are shucked and boiled or steamed. The shuck can be left on and the ear steamed or cooked over hot coals. Be sure to remove all silks before cooking. Should be ligtly cooked. Corn loses its flavor and becomes rather tough if overcooked. Serve with butter, salt and pepper.

corn pone—Oval shaped cornbread cakes. May be formed by hand and fried or dropped by spoonfull into hot oil. Bacon drippings ideal fat to use. Chopped onions can be added to the batter.

corn salad—A variety of valeriana. Used as a salad green. Sometimes corn salad is used by people who cannot eat lettuce. It is grown commercially in America. In Europe it grows wild. can be cooked as spinach. Also known as lamb's lettuce.

corn spoon—*(See Spoon Bread)*

corn syrup—A sugar syrup made from corn. Widely used in baking and other confections.

cornbread—A bread made with cornmeal. Can be baked or fried in small cakes. Usually served hot.

corndog—A wiener (frankfurter) wrapped in cornmeal dough, then baked or lightly fried. Sometimes at refreshment stands; a small wooden stick is pushed into one end to hold while eating.

corned beef—Beef preserved in a salt brine with spices. Generally the brisket is used. After pickling the meat is boiled. Sometimes with onions. When done it is allowed to drain and cool. It slices easier when cool. Serve with cabbage, potatoes and carrots which have been cooked in the pot liquid. A spicy mustard is an excellent accompaniment. Corned beef is a good sandwich filling.

corned beef hash—Cold boiled potatoes, cooked corned beef and chopped onions mixed together. Formed into patties they are lightly fried in a small amount of oil.

cornet *(Fr)*—A cone shaped pastry.

cornflour *(Eng)*—Cornstarch

cornichon *(Fr)*—A gherkin. Cucumber or vegetable pickled in vinegar and spices.

Cornish hen—A small breed of fowl. Usually baked whole or in halves. The whole or half serves as a portion.

cornmeal mush—Made from cornmeal, water and seasonings. Can be served as a breakfast cereal. Formed in a loaf and chilled then sliced it can be fried. Serve with butter and syrup as desired.

cornnuts—Snacks made of kernels of corn that have been fried and seasoned.

cornstarch—A thickening agent derived from corn. Should be mixed with a little liquid before adding to the mixture being cooked. During cooking, the liquid should be stirred constantly. Cornstarch does not cloud like flour.

cornsticks—Cornbread that is baked in special pans that are shaped like small ears of corn.

cornucopia—A container shaped like a goat's horn and is filled with various items to denote plenty. Used as an attractive table decoration. Many are made of silver and porcelain.

cos—*(See Romaine)*

cosaque *(Fr)*—Cracker bonbon

coscoussier—A special two compartment pan used to cook the North African dish 'couscous.'

cotelette *(Fr)*—Cutlet; a chop

cotelettes d'agneau *(Fr)*—Lamb chops

cotelette de filet *(Fr)*—Loin chop

cotelette en papillote *(Fr)*—Cutlet cooked in a paper wrap.

cotes de boeuf *(Fr)*—Ribs of beef

cotogna *(It)*—Quince

cottage cheese—A soft cheese made from soured milk curds. Is eaten fresh or may be used in salad dressings and various sauces. With other ingredients is used to stuff crepes and cannelloni. Is not generally used in cooked dishes.

cottage pudding—Plain cake served with a sauce.

cotto salami—Precooked salami with whole peppercorns.

cotton candy—A flavored spun sugar confection that is made with the aid of a special machine. Generally found at carnivals, fairs and other amusement areas. Usually pink in color.

cottonseed oil—Oil refined from the cotton seed. It is used to make margarines, cooking and salad oil. The seed can be made into a high protein flour. America is the largest world producer of cottonseed oil.

coupe-legumes *(Fr)*—Vegetable cutter

coupe pate *(Fr)*—Pastry cutter

coupes glacees *(Fr)*—Sundaes

coups *(Fr)*—1) Champagne glass; a stemmed bowl; a cup. 2) A dessert served in this type of glass. Can be ices, creams or fruits.

courge *(Fr)*—Gourd; pumpkin; squash

courge a la noelle *(Fr)*—Squash; vegetable marrow

courgette *(Eng, Fr)*—Zucchini

court bouillon *(Fr)*—Cooking broths made of water, milk, herbs, vegetables, wine or vinegar. There are different types of court bouillon. Mostly used for the cooking of fish and shellfish.

couscous—North African dish cooked in a special two-piece pan called a coscoussier. Meat and vegetables are placed in the lower half and semolina in the upper part. A pierced lid is placed on top. The semolina is cooked by the steam rising up through the meat and vegetables.

couteau *(Fr)*—Knife

couteau de cuisine *(Fr)*—Kitchen knives

cover—1) The implements set out, on the eating table, for each diner. The three implements the diner uses—knife, fork, spoon. Can also mean all implements, plates, glasses, napkins, condiment containers, and decorations that are put on the table before the diners are served. The place where the diner sits. 2) Lid for a pot, pan or dish.

cover plate—A large plate, usually decorative, that is placed at each cover (place), at a formal or semi-formal dinner. The first courses, on their own plates are placed on the cover plate. Food is not placed directly on the cover plate.

cow—A four-footed bovine. The word cow refers to both the meat and milk animal. *(See Milk Cow and Beef)*

cowpea—One of man's oldest cultivated vegetables. Originally from India they made their way to America around 1700, arriving here from Africa aboard the slave ships. The bean may be eaten as a string bean, shelled green or used as a dried bean. There are many varieties including black eyed pea (bean), pink eyed crowder and brown crowder. In the late 1700s, they were called pease, callicance or corn field pease.

cozy—A padded cloth cover used to put over a teapot or dish to keep them hot.

crab—A desirable shellfish. It is a crustacean. May be steamed and eaten from the shell or the flesh can be used in casseroles and salads.

crabe *(Fr)*—Crab

crab pick—Small thin tool used to remove meat from the crevices of the crab shell.

Cracker Jack—Trade name for a popcorn, caramel and nut confection.

crackers—Small, thin, dry bakery product made with various flours, liquids, fats, seeds, nuts, cheeses, flavorings and seasonings. Eaten as a snack and as a base for canapes and hors d'oeuvres. Available in a variety of shapes and sizes.

cracklin bread—Cornbread with pork cracklings added before baking.

cracklings or cracklin's—Skin of the hog cooked until most of the fat is removed and they are crispy. Used as a snack or in cornbread. Can be salted.

cracknel—A hard, brittle biscuit

cranberry—Fruit of a small shrub. It is made into a sauce, jelly or juice. Is a traditional condiment served with roast turkey. It grows in boggy regions of North America and Europe. Cranberry is a native of America.

crayfish—A freshwater crustacean similar to the lobster but smaller.

cream—1) The fatty part of cow's milk. It will rise to the top of fresh milk when allowed to set several hours. Butter is made from this cream. 2) Cream can be beaten until it is light and fluffy. A small amount of sugar and flavoring is generally added. The whipped cream is used as a dessert topping and folded into various dessert dishes. Bowls and beaters should be cold for beating.

cream cheese—A soft cheese made from fresh milk with added cream. Used in salad dressings, sandwich or cracker spread and some pies and cakes. Traditionally served with bagels.

cream cheese *(Eng)*—Cottage cheese

cream horn mold—*(See Horn mold)*

cream of tartar—A powder that is used in cooking, especially when beating egg whites. Is an ingredient of baking powder.

cream puff paste—A basic pastry dough made of flour, liquids, fats, eggs and salt. A soft dough, it is piped or dropped by spoon in the desired shape and size. All types of pastry shells, plain and fancy, are made from this dough. Good for cream puffs and eclairs.

cream puffs—Small cakes that after baking are filled with whipped cream. May be made from plain cake muffins or from cream puff paste shells.

cream sherry—A sweet and heavy sherry. A dessert wine. Also served as an aperitif or for occasional sipping.

creme *(Fr)*—Dairy cream. Custard.

creme a la glace *(Fr)*—Ice cream

creme anglaise *(Fr)*—A simple vanilla flavored custard. Served alone or used as a base for other desserts such as mousses.

creme chantilly *(Fr)*—Whipped cream

creme d'arachides *(Fr)*—Peanut butter

creme de cacao *(Fr)*—A chocolate flavored liqueur.

creme de cassis *(Fr)*—A liqueur flavored with black currants. From France.

creme de menthe—A peppermint flavored liqueur. Green or white in color.

creme de noyaux *(Fr)*—A liqueur flavored with almonds and hazelnuts.

creme de vanille *(Fr)*—A vanilla flavored liqueur.

creme de violette *(Fr)*—A liqueur flavored with violets.

creme fouetee *(Fr)*—Whipped cream

creme fraiche *(Fr)*—Heavy cream with a small amount of buttermilk added. Usually one cup cream to one tablespoon buttermilk. Used in various sauces.

creme glacee *(Fr)*—Ice cream

creme patissiere *(Fr)*—*(See Pastry cream)*

creme St. Honore *(Fr)*—Pastry cream or custard made of eggs, flour and milk. As is, it is used for garnishing and coating sweet dishes. With the addition of various flavorings it may be served as a dessert custard.

Creole—Foods from the mid-south United States. These foods are probably the result of the combination of early settlers who were French and Spanish and the native Indians and blacks. Many of these foods are very spicy.

crepe *(Fr)*—A thin pancake. Usually made with more eggs and milk than flour.

crespelle *(It)*—Italian pancake. Made the same as crepes.

cresson *(Fr)*—Cress; watercress

crevette *(Fr)*—Shrimp; prawn

Crisco—A trade name for a solid vegetable shortening.

crisp—Brittle

crock pot—An electrically heated counter top ceramic pot used to cook foods very slowly. It is especially good for soups, stews and dried beans.

croissant *(Fr)*—Pastry roll shaped like a crescent.

croquante *(Fr)*—Crisp tart. Crisp almond cake.

croquembouche *(Fr)*—Dessert made of small filled cream puffs. The small puffs are coated with a sugar glaze and placed in a special conical mold to set. When unmolded the 'tree' may be decorated with candied fruits or nuts.

croquembouche tin—A tall conical metal tin used to assemble a croquembouche. A conical potato ricer may be substituted by lining it with greased parchment paper.

croquette—Meat, fish or vegetables formed into a roll, ball or patty and fried in hot fat.

crosnes—A tuber similar to the Jerusalem artichoke. Preparation is the same. In America they are also called knotroot, Japanese/ Chinese artichokes and in Oriental markets choroqi.

croustade *(Fr)*—A kind of pastry or bread shell in which various mixtures can be baked and served. An unsliced loaf of bread is often hollowed out and used as a croustade.

croute *(Fr)*—Piece of toast; crust

crouton—Small cube of toast or fried bread. Used as a garnish in soups and salads. Often flavored with herbs.

Crowley's cheese—A colby cheese made in Vermont

crudities—Small slices or pieces of fresh fruits and vegetables that are served with a dip at informal gatherings. A finger food. Should be well chilled.

cruet—A small glass stoppered bottle for holding oil or vinegar.

cruller—A sweet cake made with eggs and fried in deep fat.

crumb crust—A crust made of crushed graham crackers, nuts or coconut mixed with fat and pressed into the pie pan. Can be baked blind or not depending on the pie being made.

crumber—*(See Silent Butler)*

crumbs—Small fragments of bread, crackers or cake. Can be used as breading.

crumpet—A small, thin, round, un-sweetened cake that is cooked on a griddle.

crumpet rings—Small metal rings used to contain the batter from spreading on the griddle. The ring is placed on the griddle and the batter poured into it. The ring is removed when the crumpet is turned.

crystal—The glasses used to drink from. Any dish, glass or serving container that is made from crystal glass.

cubed steak—A small piece of beef that is pounded with a meat mallet or put through a special machine. This breaks up the tendons and fat. This process is used on the tougher cuts of meat.

cubed sugar—White sugar that has been formed into small cubes. One cube equals about one tea-spoon.

cucumber—A green elongated vege-table that grows on a vine. It is eaten raw, in a vinegar marinade and made into pickles. Rarely cooked.

cuisine *(Fr)*—The kitchen. Manner of cooking. The dishes themselves.

cuisine bourgeoise *(Fr)*—Plain cooking; home cooking

cuisse *(Fr)*—Rump of beef. Leg—as of goose.

cuissot *(Fr)*—Haunch—as of venison.

cuit a point *(Fr)*—Cook to a turn. Cooked just right.

cul-de-four *(Fr)*—Bottom of the oven.

culinaire *(Fr)*—Culinary

culinario *(It, Sp)*—Culinary

culinary—Relating to cookery.

culotte *(Fr)*—Rump—as of beef

cumin *(Fr)*—Cumin

cumino tedesco *(It)*—Caraway seed

cuoco *(It)*—Cook

cup—1) Small round container used for drinking. Generally used for hot beverages. 2) A standard measure—eight ounces liquid.

cupboard—Generally shelves in the kitchen where pots, pans, dishes, foods and other supplies and equip-ment are stored. May also be a separate piece of furniture.

cupping—Word used by professional tea taster to describe the act of tasting tea.

curacao—A liqueur distilled from dried bitter green oranges. They are grown on the island of Curacao in the Netherlands Antilles. The flavor is of oranges and should be used with care. The flavor is strong.

curcuma *(Fr, It)*—Turmeric

curcuma *(Sp)*—Turmeric

curd—The coagulated part of milk. Is used to make cheese.

curd *(Eng)*—Cooked custard. Can be fruit flavored. Spread for breads and toasts.

curdle—To thicken. Coagulate. When milk turns sour it will curdle. Also some cream sauces that use milk and lemon juice have a tendency to curdle.

curds—Cauliflower flowerettes

currants—The dried seedless berry of the currant plant. Used in cakes and cookies. *(See Spice Section)*

curry—A combination of spices used to season a dish by that name. About 15 to 20 different spices and herbs are ground and mixed together to form the curry powder. Principal ingredients are anise, allspice, bay leaves, cinnamon, caraway, cumin, garlic, ginger, mace, chilies and paprika. Each manufacturer has their own recipe.

curry stone—A mortar stone that is flat with a slight depression in the center. A pestle rod is pulled over the spices to pulverize them. Popular in India.

custard—A dessert consisting of milk, eggs, sweeteners and various flavorings. It is cooked on top of the stove or in the oven. Sometimes the flavored custard after cooking is put into a baked blind pie shell. It can be topped with whipped cream or meringue. Coconut and bananas are often added.

custard marrow—Name given to the chayote by some European gourmets.

cutlery—Cutting and eating tools. Knives, forks and spoons.

cutlet—Small cut of meat from area near the rib; usually applies to veal.

cutting board—A piece of hardwood either round, square or oblong, which is used as a base for cutting and chopping various foods. They are also made of plastic.

dab—1) A flat fish with soft flesh that is easily digestible. 2) A small piece of something, such as butter.

daikon—Japanese white radish which is quite long. May be eaten raw, stewed as turnips or used in stir fry dishes. Is an interesting addition to green salads.

dairy—A farm that specializes in producing milk. Also a store that sells dairy products.

dal *(Hin)*—A kind of pea.

dalbhat *(Hin)*—Cooked dal and rice.

dandelion—A weed whose toothed leaves can be eaten in salads when they are young and tender. May be cooked as spinach. A wine is made from this plant.

Danish pastry—A dessert pastry that uses yeast as the leavening agent. Fat, butter or margarine is rolled into the folded dough. Used for many rolled and filled pastries. Similar to puff paste.

Danziger-Goldwasser *(Ger)*—A liqueur containing bits of gold leaf.

dariole *(Fr)*—Flowerpot-shaped tins that can be used for baking cakes and breads. Can also be used for molding puddings. Various sizes available. The small molds are idea for individual servings.

dark beer—A dark-colored beer. Is generally sweet and heavy.

darne *(Fr)*—A slice of fish

dash—A very small amount. Generally the amount one can get from a salt shaker by turning over briefly one time. About a half-of-a-pinch.

dashi *(Ja)*—A soup stock made of kelp, water and bonito.

date—The edible fruit of a tall palm tree. The dried and preserved fruit is used in the making of various confections. Also as a snack. The tree is native to the Middle East. It is grown commercially in Arizona and California.

datte *(Fr)*—Date

Dattel *(Ger)*—Date

dattero *(It)*—Date

datil *(Sp)*—Date

daube *(Fr)*—A way of stewing and seasoning certain braised dishes. The dish itself.

decaffeinated—A process used to remove the caffeine from coffee and tea. There is some flavor loss.

decanter—A tall, often decorative, bottle from which wine and other spirits can be served.

decorating knife—A short-bladed knife with about an inch at the end that is straight and sharp. The remaining blade is serrated and unsharpened. Used to make vegetable decorations.

deep fryer—A utensil capable of containing a large amount of fat. Three or more inches deep. The utensil may be heated on top of the stove or it may have a built in electric heating coil. The electric type generally have a thermostat to control the temperature of the fat. Usually have a removable cooking basket. Some commercial fryers are equipped with a tight-fitting cover to permit deep frying under pressure. Widely used in take out and fast food restaurants that specialize in chicken.

deep pit barbeque—Method of cooking meat by burying it in the ground with hot coals. Large pieces of meat (generally beef quarters or hog halves) are coated with the sauce, wrapped in cloth soaked with sauce, then wrapped in burlap and tied. A layer of rocks is placed over the coals. The wrapped meat is placed on this and the pit filled with dirt. This method takes several hours, roughly eight to 24. Well worth it. Popular in the south and southwest.

degustation *(Fr)*—*(See savoring)*

delayer *(Fr)*—To dilute, thin

deli—Delicatessen

delicatessen—Store where ready to eat salads, cooked meats and desserts are sold. Usually to take out.

demi—Half

demi-glace *(Fr)*—Brown sauce that has added to it either white stock or sherry wine.

demijohn—A large glass or ceramic bottle that is wrapped in a straw basket. Generally used for wine.

demitasse—Small cup used to serve after dinner coffee.

Denver omelet—An egg omelet with chopped onions, green peppers and ham as the filling. The omelet can also be used as a sandwich filling.

depecage *(Fr)*—Jointing. Separating the joints of meats and fowls.

depouiller *(Fr)*—*(See Ecumer)*

dessert—The last course of a meal. Generally is some type of sweet, cake, pie, pudding or ice. Can also be fresh fruits and cheeses.

dessert spoon—A round-bowled spoon for eating desserts.

dessert sugar—*(See Confectioners Sugar)*

dessert wine—Wines that are served as a dessert or with the dessert course.

deviled eggs—Stuffed, hard-boiled eggs.

dextrose—Scientific name for glucose.

diable sauce—A brown sauce with shallots, wine and cayenne pepper. Served with grilled fowl and left-over meats.

digestif *(Fr)*—Generally a liqueur or wine served at or near the end of a meal. It is supposed to aid in the digestion of the food eaten.

digestive biscuits *(Eng)*—Graham crackers

Dijon—Name of a mustard from the capital of Burgundy, France.

Dill *(Ger)*—Dill

dim sum *(Ch)*—Appetizers. Squares of pastry with a filling. Are usually steamed.

dinde *(Fr)*—Turkey hen

dindonneau *(Fr)*—Young turkey

dinner rolls—Any small yeast roll that is served with the evening meal.

dinner wine—Wines that are served at meals.

dip—Thick sauce into which crackers, potato chips, fruits and raw vegetables are dipped then eaten. Often mayonnaise and sour cream are used as the base. Various herbs, spices and other seasonings are added for a flavorful dip. Used as an appetizer or snack

Dirty rice *(Cr)*—A rice dish made with chicken livers and gizzards cooked in oil with celery, onions and green pepers. Cubed eggplant may also be added. It is cooked in chicken broth and takes on a darkish color.

di sagala *(It)*—Rye whiskey

dish—1) Container for holding food for serving. 2) The food served in a dish. 3) Food that is prepared in a certain manner

dishcloth—A piece of material, unbleached muslin is good, that is used in the kitchen for drying dishes, pots and pans. Can also be used to wipe up spills and clean the hands. *(See Dish rag)*

dish rag—Piece of cloth used to wash dishes, pots and pans. Also for wiping up spills and cleaning countertops and appliances. *(See Dishcloth)*

dishrag plant—*(See Luffa)*

dish ring—A round ring of ceramics or metal that is placed under hot dishes. A trivet.

dishwasher—A kitchen appliance that is used to wash and dry soiled dishes, pots, pans, tableware and utensils.

distilled water—Water that has been filtered to remove many of the imputities. Tasteless. May be purchased in bottles.

divinity—A candy made of sugar, egg whites and flavorings. Nuts, candied and dried fruits are sometimes added.

dolce *(It, Fr)*—Cake

dolciumi *(It)*—Candy

dollop—A small amount

dolma—Vegetable shells (such as eggplant, zucchini, cucumber, cabbage and grape leaves) stuffed with meat, rice and seasonings.

Dom Perignon *(Fr)*—Name of the monk who discovered the process for making sparkling champagne. He was from the Abbey of Hautvilliers near Epernay, France. His name was given to Moet et Chandon champagne.

double boiler—Two saucepans, one of which fits into the other. The bottom pan has water in it. This water is heated. The other pan is set on top of it and the cooking is accomplished in this manner. This type of pan is used when direct heat is not desired for cooking.

double cream *(Eng)*—Heavy cream

dough—A mixture of flour and other ingredients that is capable of being kneaded and rolled. Some types of dough are—pastry, bread, pie, tortilla, pasta.

doughnuts—Small, round cakes with a hole in the center. Can be baked or deep fried.

dough scraper—A rectangle of stiff metal (about 4x5 inches) with a wooden or plastic covering attached to one side. Used for cutting dough, scraping dough boards and anywhere a stiff scraper is needed.

dragoncello *(It)*—Tarragon

Drambuie—A Scottish liqueur flavored with honey and using scotch whiskey as the base.

drawn butter—Same as clarified butter.

dredger—Small containers that have the appearance of large salt shakers. Used for sprinkling flour and sugar.

dressing—1) The process of preparing poultry for cooking. 2) A sauce poured over salads. 3) Stuffing used to fill the cavities of fowl. Also this mixture cooked by itself. This stuffing is generally made of stale bread.

dried beans—Several varieties of beans are raised for their seed. The seed is dried, usually on the plant. The dried beans are cooked in water or other liquid until tender. Seasonings and other ingredients may be added. Serve hot as a side dish. Cooked, dried beans can also be used in salads. Mashed, the cooked bean can be made into an excellent dip or used as a sandwich filling. Dried beans may be soaked in water overnight or several hours before cooking. *(See Measurement Section)*

drink mix—Mixture of powdered ingredients that when mixed with soda or water and the particular alcoholic beverage will produce a cocktail or mixed drink.

drippings—The fat that cooks out of a piece of meat as it is roasted. Used to make sauces, gravies and especially with beef roasts, Yorkshire pudding.

droga *(It)*—Spice

droghiere *(It)*—Grocer

drop dumplings—Made from a dough that is sticky and are dropped by spoonfuls into boiling liquid. This type does not have a filling, but may have pieces of meat, vegetable or fruit in them.

dry milk—Milk that has had the water removed, leaving a dry powder. It is reconstituted by adding water.

dry roasted—Anything roasted without the benefit of additional fat or liquid.

dry sherry—A dry (unsweet) wine that is mostly used as an aperitif or with snacks. Chill in the bottle.

dry soup mix—A mixture of dried vegetables, herbs and seasonings used to make soup. Most are made by adding hot water.

du jour *(Fr)*—On restaurant menus this literally means what is prepared that day. Such as soup du jour means the soup they are serving that day. An item that is not always the same from day to day.

duck—A domestic and wild fowl. Usually cooked by roasting. When baked, the skin should be very crips. The duck is cut into four pieces for serving. Two breast and two leg portions. The eggs are used for frying and cooking. The eggs have a rather strong taste.

duck press—A kitchen tool whose only purpose is to remove the juices from ducks.

dulces *(Sp)*—Sweetmeats, bon bons or candy pieces.

dulse—A sea algae that when dried and powdered may be used as a substitute for salt. The dried leaves can be added to salads after being soaked in water. Should be found in health food stores.

dumpling—A small piece of dough cooked by boiling or steaming. They may be filled or not. Meat, fruits and vegetables can be used as fillings. Fruit encased in pastry and baked is also called a dumpling.

durum flour—A hard, wheat flour used in the making of pastas and as a livestock feed.

dutch oven—A heavy, covered pan used for roasting meats on top of the stove or in the oven. This type of pan can also be used for making stews, soups and other dishes. Roasts cook quickly in this type of pot.

duxelles *(Fr)*—Mushrooms, shallots and herbs cooked together till they are reduced to a paste. Used as a garnish and in sauces, stuffings and with meats.

dwarf cape gooseberry—Ground cherry

dwarf mulberry—*(See Cloudberries)*

earthenware—Dishes and cooking vessels made of fire hardened clay. These are generally glazed, at least on the inside.

Easter eggs—Generally hard boiled eggs that are decorated with various colors and designs. Used during the Easter season.

eau *(Fr)*—Water

eau de selz *(Fr)*—Soda water; sparkling water; seltzer water

eau-de-vie *(Fr)*—Brandy; spirits

eau rouge *(Fr)*—Red wine and water.

eau sucre *(Fr)*—Water sweetened with sugar.

eau vive *(Fr)*—Spring water

eaux minerales *(Fr)*—Mineral water

ebouillanter *(Fr)*—Scald

ecailler *(Fr)*—*(See Scale, Fish)*

ecalure *(Fr)*—Peeling of fruits and vegetables.

echalote *(Fr)*—Shallot

eclair—An oblong pastry that is baked then filled with pudding or whipped cream and given a sugar icing.

ecole *(Fr)*—School

ecorce *(Fr)*—Rind

ecumer *(Fr)*—To skim cream from milk.

ecumoire *(Fr)*—A skimmer.

edam—A hard cheese. Round with a red rind. Mild.

eel—A snake-like fish. The best eels are from fast flowing waters. They can be fried, stewed or roasted. They should not be killed until just prior to cooking.

egg—Rounded shell product of the domestic chicken. One of the most versatile ingredients in cookery. Eggs are prepared alone and used in breads, cakes, souffles, puddings and sauces. Eggs of other fowl are also eatable. *(See Hints Section)*

egg cup—Dish to hold the boiled egg upright when they are served in the shell.

egg custard—Simple egg and milk custard baked in a pie shell or in individual cups. Generally vanilla flavored.

egg flower soup *(Ch)*—Soup with a base of chicken broth. A beaten egg is swirled in prior to serving.

egg foo yung *(Ch)*—Small egg pancakes that are stuffed with vegetables, bean sprouts and sometimes meat and fish. They are fried in oil

egg noodles—*(See Noddles, Egg)*

egg poacher—Pan for poaching eggs. Has individual cups to hold the eggs over simmering water. A lid is placed on top for cooking.

egg rolls *(Ch)*—Small egg pancakes, fried and stuffed with bean sprouts, vegetables or meats.

egg separator—Small device used to separate the egg white from the yolk. It is round with slots to permit the whites to slip through.

egg timer—A device used to time the boiling of eggs. Some timers are of the hour glass type, with sand passing from one section to the other. Others have a calibrated dial and are wound by hand. Electric timers are available.

eggnog—Holiday beverage made with eggs, milk, sugar, spices and a liquor. Generally whiskey, rum or brandy is used. Served hot or cold. Can be made without liquor.

eggplant—A large, pear-shaped fruit from a plant related to the potato. It is treated as a vegetable. Usually dark purple in color with a shiny skin. It is cooked in a variety of ways. Fried, stewed with tomatoes or stuffed and baked. *(See Japanese Eggplant)*

eggs Benedict—Dish consisting of an English muffin, poached eggs, Canadian bacon or ham and a hollandaise or cheese sauce. Served open-faced. Popular brunch, lunch or late supper entree.

eggshell cutter—Tool that slices the top off boiled eggs. Permits the egg to be served with the top neatly removed. Can be classified as a scissor.

egrugloir *(Fr)*—Salt grinder

Egyptian onions—An onion which forms its bulbs on top of the blades. These may be stewed and served in a cream sauce. Pungent. The blades are also eaten. A self renewing plant for your garden.

Ei *(Ger)*—Egg

Eierpflanze *(Ger)*—Eggplant

Eis *(Ger)*—Frozen water; ice

ejotes *(Sp)*—String beans

elderberry—The fruit of this plant is used to make jams and pies. Wines can be made from the berries and blooms. The blossoms can be dipped in batter and fried as fritters.

electric carving knife—Two thin serrated blades are placed together and attached to an electric motor. Slicing is achieved when the blades are oscillated against each other. Generally used for plain carving. When dull the blades are usually replaced.

electric mixer—A tool with a small motor and removable beaters. Used for beating, mixing and whipping. There are two types—the hand held (portable) and a larger one that sits on a stand.

elixir—A flavored alcoholic liquid used for medicinal purposes.

emince *(Fr)*—Various dishes made with leftover meat.

Emmenthal cheese—Same as swiss cheese.

empanada *(Sp)*—Meat tart. Foods cooked in a pastry covering. To coat with batter or breadcrumbs.

emparedado *(Sp)*—Sandwich

emulsifier—An agent added to two dissimilar substances, such as water and oil, so that they are combined into one mass.

en brochette *(Fr)*—On a skewer

en daube *(Fr)*—Meat, poultry or fish stew made with wine, herbs and vegetables.

en papillote *(Fr)*—Method of baking and serving food, such as fish. The food is wrapped in parchment or brown paper. To serve, a slit is made in the top of the wrapper.

enchilada *(Mex)*—Dish of tortilla, chili, meat cheese and spices.

encurtido *(Sp)*—A cucumber pickle

endive—A small leafed salad green. Rather pungent in flavor.

eneldo *(Sp)*—Dill

English chops—Veal or lamb chops cut with a portion of the kidney attached.

English muffins—A coarse chewy yeast muffin. They are cooked on top of the stove on a griddle or skillet. Split with a fork. They then may be toasted or not. Serve with butter, jams or jelly. Can be used as a base for creamed dishes such as chicken ala king and eggs Benedict.

English sugar pea—Snow pea; garden pea.

English suet roll pudding—*(See Roly-Poly Pudding)*

English walnut—A thin-shelled variety of walnut widely used in baking and confections. A cooking oil is pressed from the kernels. Also known as Persian walnut.

enoki *(Or)*—A type of mushroom.

ensaimade *(Sp)*—A yeast bread made with honey and nuts. Often shaped like a rope and formed into snail-like curlicues. Called Conch rolls in Mexico.

ensalada *(Sp)*—Salad

entrecote *(Fr)*—Tenderloin

entree or entree—1) Can refer to the main course of an informal luncheon or dinner. 2) Dish served before and/or after the main course at a formal dinner. 3) Entrees can be meat, vegetable or salad.

entremets *(Fr)*—Side dishes or dishes usually following the main course. Dishes are generally small in portion. Can also refer to desserts.

epergne—A table centerpiece of glass, porcelain or metal, usually ornate. Can be filled with fruits, flowers or other decorations. Can be used to serve stewed fruit or ices.

eperlan *(Fr)*—European smelt (fish)

epice *(Fr)*—Spice

epigramme *(Fr)*—Ragout of lamb; small cutlet.

epinard *(Fr)*—Spinach

erable a sucre *(Fr)*—Maple sugar.

erba *(It)*—Herb

Erbse *(Ger)*—Pea

Erdapfel *(Ger)*—In Austrian German, potato

Erdbeere *(Ger)*—Strawberry

Erdnussbutter *(Ger)*—Peanut butter

escallop—Variation of Scallop, both definitions.

escalope de veau *(Fr)*—Veal cutlet

escargot *(Fr)*—Edible snail.

escarole—A variety of endive. Has broad leaves.

Escoffier, Auguste (1847-1935)—Great French cook, the supreme chef. Considered by many to be the final authority on classical French cooking. Creator of Peach Melba in 1893 in honor of the Australian singer Nelli Melba. His culinary writings are authorities on French cooking. Among his works are *Guide Culinaire* and *Ma Cuisine.* American title of *Guide Culinaire* is *The Escoffier Cook Book.*

espagnole sauce *(Fr)*—The basic brown sauce which can be used to make other brown sauces.

esparrago *(Sp)*—Asparagus

espedia *(Sp)*—Spice

espinaca *(Sp)*—Spinach

espresso *(It)*—1) Coffee brewed by a steam process. It is very dark and strong. Usually made from a black roasted bean. 2) A coffee-flavored liqueur.

essence—A liquid extracted by distillation. Various fruits, nuts, vegetables, meats and spices are distilled to obtain a very strong flavoring.

Essig *(Ger)*—Vinegar

estouffade *(Fr)*—Dish that is slowly stewed. A clear brown stock used to dilute sauces and moisten braised meats.

estragon *(Ger)*—Tarragon

estragon *(Fr)*—Tarragon

estragon *(Sp)*—Tarragon

esturgeon *(Fr)*—Sturgeon (fish)

etouffe *(Fr)*—Method of cooking food in a pot with a tightly fitting lid. Little or no liquid is added.

etuver *(Fr)*—Method of cooking food in a covered pan without liquid. Usually a small amount of fat is used.

evaporated milk—Milk that has had over half of the water removed. Can be diluted with water or used as is. It is packaged in cans.

ewer—A vase shaped container for liquids. Ewers used at the table are sometimes ornate and decorative. Some have a handle and pouring lip.

expresso coffee—*(See espresso)*

extract—The concentrated juice of a fruit, vegetable, meat or spice. The flavor is very pronounced. Extracts are generally thought of as being liquid flavorings such as vanilla, mint, walnut cinnamon, etc.

extractor—Appliance for juicing fruits & vegetables

extrait *(Fr)*—Extract

F—Abbreviation for Fahrenheit, relating to a temperature scale at which freezing point for water is 32 degrees F and boiling point is 212 degrees F.

faah jiu *(Ch)*—Anise-pepper

faggot—Bundle of herb stalks tied together to flavor a dish during cooking and removed before serving.

fagiolino *(It)*—String bean

fagiolo *(It)*—Bean

fagiolo bianco *(It)*—Lima bean

faisan *(Fr)*—Pheasant

fan *(Ch)*—Rice

fannie daddies—The Cape Cod name for fried clams.

farce *(Fr)*—Forcemeat

farcir *(Fr)*—To stuff, as a chicken.

farina—Fine cereal grains used as a breakfast food and sometimes in puddings.

farina *(It)*—Flour

farinaceous—Starchy

farine *(Fr)*—Flour

farine de pois chiches *(Fr)*—Chick-pea flour.

farmer's cheese—A soft, white, natural cheese. Very perishable.

faro *(Bel)*—A slightly fermented beer. It is fairly sour and sometimes sugar has been added.

Fasan *(Ger)*—Pheasant

fast foods—Foods that are served in eateries that specialize in preparing foods very fast. Some of them specialize in a certain type of food—hamburgers, hotdogs, tacos, fish and chicken.

Fastnache Krapfen *(Ger)*—A rich doughnut that is often served in some German homes, as a traditional pre-lenten delight.

fat—Oil, grease, shortening, butter, margarine.

fatback—The fatty strip from the back of the hog. Usually cured by salting. Use in larding, as a case for meat terrines and to cover various meats when roasting.

fausse tortue *(Fr)*—Mock turtle

fava bean—A versatile vegetable that is not widely grown in America. Most are raised for cattle feed. The ancient Egyptians, Romans and Greeks used this vegetable as a food. Its flavor is a blend of lima bean and garden pea. They can be treated like string beans or hulled, when green, as garden peas. The young pod may be stir fried, steamed or simmered. The dried bean can be popped like popcorn or roasted as you would peanuts. In the Middle East, the dried beans are pickled. Should be available in stores selling Oriental foods.

Feige *(Ger)*—Fig

Fenchel *(Ger)*—Fennel

fennel—There are three types of fennel. One is an herb and two that are cultivated for their leaves, stalks and stems. a) Common fennel—*(See Spices and Herbs Section);* b) Sicilian fennel—The young stems are used like celery and asparagus; c) Florence fennel—Has thick basal stalks and a bulbous base. Both may be eaten raw, steamed, stir fried or creamed.

fenouil *(Fr)*—Fennel

feta—A natural cheese made from goat's milk.

fettucini *(It)*—A wide noodle.

feuillete *(Fr)*—Puff pastry

feve *(Fr)*—Lima bean

feve de marais *(Fr)*—Broad bean

fig—Pear-shaped fruit from a tree related to the mulberry. A warm region tree. Used as fresh fruit and is dried. Can be made into jams and preserves. Pick when ripe as the fruit does not ripen after it is picked.

figue *(Fr)*—Fig

filberts—*(See Hazelnut)*

file powder—Ground sassafras leaves with a small amount of thyme, used in New Orleans-style dishes. Also called "Gumbo file."

filet mignon—Round cut of beef from the tenderloin, porterhouse or sirloin. Usually wrapped in bacon and grilled.

fillet—Long thin piece of boneless meat or fish.

filleting knife—Thin backed, strong and very sharp. Should have a flexible blade.

filling—Anything that is surrounded by a crust, bread, cake or other food. Such as the fruits put into a pie, the pudding between the layers of a cake, the mixture that tomatoes are stuffed with, the stuffing of a chop.

filo leaves—*(See Phyllo Dough)*

fines herbes—A mixture of parsley, chervil, tarragon and chives in equal amounts. This is the combination called for in many French recipes. Used in various dishes.

finger bowl—Small bowl of water furnished each diner for the cleansing of their fingers. Sometimes the water is lightly scented or a small flower may be floated. The finger bowl should be used before the dessert is served and after eating the dessert.

finger food—Foods that are eaten with the fingers.

finjan *(Or)*—An Oriental coffee cup without a handle.

finnan haddie *(Sc)*—Smoked haddock

finocchio *(It)*—Fennel

Fior de Alpe—An Italian liqueur flavored with herbs and a rock candy base.

firkin—Small wooden sack for tallow, butter, etc.

first fruits—The first fruits and vegetables that are harvested in the season.

first joint—The leg of a chicken.

Fisch *(Ger)*—Fish

fish—An edible water breathing animal. Low in fat.

fish cakes—Various types of cooked fish are combined with other ingredients, shaped in small cakes and lightly fried in fat.

fish kettle—A special pan with a removable grid so the fish may be lifted out. It is oblong in shape and permits the cooking of a fish whole.

fizz—1) The sound of a carbonated drink. The sound is the bubbles bursting when they come to the top. 2) A mixed drink using carbonated soda water.

flageolet(s) *(Fr)*—Kidney bean(s)

flambe *(Fr)*—Some dishes are sprinkled with a spirit (alcoholic beverage) and set aflame, usually done at the table.

flan—Type of cake pan. It is a straight sided, round, metal tin.

flan *(Fr)*—1) An open tart with various fillings, fruit, creams, meat, fowl. The flan cakes are baked blind or filled then baked.

flan *(Sp)*—Custard

flan rings—Forms of metal that are round, square or rectangular. Used to support the sides of the pastry when making pastry cases. The rings are placed on the baking sheet and the pastry formed around them.

flan tins—Two-pieced tins used for making flan cases. They are available in various sizes and shapes.

flanchet *(Fr)*—(See Flank)

flank—Cut of beef between the fatty section and the breast.

flannel cakes—Pancakes with cornmeal added to the batter. Cooked in the manner of hotcakes.

flask—A flat bottle of metal or glass, sometimes with a cover. Designed to carry in the pocket or purse. Generally used for alcoholic beverages.

flatware—Tableware such as platters, plates, knives, forks, spoons and other items used on the table.

flavoring—Any substance, liquid or solid, that is used to enhance the taste of a dish. These can be extracts, herbs, spices or essences

flesh—The edible portion of meats, fruits, vegetables, poultry and nuts.

fleur de farine *(Fr)*—Wheaten flour

flip—An alcoholic drink containing egg, sweetener and spices and a spirit such as sherry, brandy or whiskey.

float(s)—1) An alcoholic drink where one liqueur is floated on the top of another. 2) Short for Ice Cream Float.

floating island—Spoonsful of meringue (baked or not) placed on top of dessert sauces and puddings.

Florence fennel—The thick leaf stalks of this vegetable are eaten along with the bulbous base. Can be used raw, steamed, creamed or stir fried.

florentine *(Fr)*—Food prepared with spinach.

flour—Finely-ground and sifted meal of various cereals, especially wheat and rye. Used to make breads, cakes, pastries, cookies and other confections. Also used to coat various foods before cooking. Is used as a thickening agent in sauces and gravies.

flour mill—A hand or electric operated device for grinding various grains into flour and meal. The grain is pulverized between two stones. The grinding stones are made of stone or metal. Stones should not be washed. Can also be used for grinding cornmeal and the hulling of sunflower seeds.

flour sifter—Device used for sifting dried foodstuffs such as flours and meals. Generally made with one or more screens through which the material passes. Has some type of agitator.

flowering kale—A member of the cabbage family the flowering kale can have pink and white, green and white, or yellow and white heads. Very attractive in the garden and in cabbage salads.

flummery—A molded semolina pudding garnished with fresh berries or other fruit.

foie *(Fr)*—Liver

foie de veau *(Fr)*—Calf's liver

fois gras *(Fr)*—Goose liver paste

fondant—Creamy sugar mixture that is used as the base for certain candies and icings. May be stored in the refrigerator for later use.

fonds *(Fr)*—Stock

fondue—Melted cheese with or without spices or spirits. Generally served in a fondue pot at the table or on the buffet. An informal dish. Cubes of bread are dipped into the cheese for eating.

fondue pot—Small pan in a rack with a spirit lamp underneath to supply heat. Heated oil is placed in the pot. Pieces of food on small fondue forks are immersed in the oil to cook. This pot is used at the table where each diner can cook their own food. Also used to hold and keep the rarebit, dips and various fondues hot.

food coloring—Edible liquid colors that are added to various dishes to enhance their color. Generally available in red, green, yellow and blue. Use sparingly. Remember blue is not a common color in foods.

food dryer—A box-shaped device with an internal heat source. Used to remove moisture from various foods. Dried foods can be stored for a very long time.

food mill—Hand or electrical device used to pulp and separate the flesh from the seeds and peel. Used with various fruits and vegetables.

food processor—An electric kitchen tool. Many different types. Most are capable of slicing, chopping, shredding, mixing, pureeing. Some models can mix and knead breads, make ice cream and juices. A useful and handy tool for the kitchen.

fool—Dessert of mashed fruit mixed with cream or custard, served cold.

forcemeats—Mixtures of various ingredients used to garnish dishes, making of pates, stuffing meats and poultry. Can be made with or without meat.

Forelle *(Ger)*—Trout

foret *(Fr)*—A small steel point which is sometimes used by waiters to uncork bottles.

fork—A tined tool for eating and cooking. This implement came into use much later than the knife and spoon. Early forks had only two prongs or tines. There are several types of forks—dinner, salad, dessert, cooking.

formaggio *(It)*—Cheese

fortified wine—Wines that have had alcohol added to stop the fermentation. These wines have about twice the alcohol content of other wines. Port and sherry are two of the best known fortified wines.

fortune cookie—Crisp, bland, folded cookie with a slip of paper inside with your printed 'fortune' on it. Usually served in Chinese restaurants at the end of the meal. The slip of paper is placed on the warm baked cookie then the cookie is folded. The cookie must be broken to get at the 'fortune.'

fouet *(Fr)*—A whisk

four *(Fr)*—Oven

four spices—*(See Quatre Epices)*

fourchette *(Fr)*—Fork

fourneau de cuisine *(Fr)*—Kitchen stove

fowl—Chicken, turkey or any bird eaten.

fragola *(It)*—Strawberry

fraisage *(Fr)*—Kneading of dough

fraise *(Fr)*—Strawberry

Framberry—A raspberry-flavored liqueur from France.

framboise *(Fr)*—Raspberry. There is a liqueur called Framboise.

frangipan cream—A cream used in preparing various sweets, desserts and cakes. Basically a pudding.

frankfurter—A wiener; hot dog

frappe—Liquor, liqueur or flavored syrup poured over shaved ice. Usually served in a wide-mouthed, stemmed glass. A small spoon or short straws are placed in the glass.

freeze dried—The process by which food is frozen and the moisture is removed. The remaining powder or particles are generally reconstituted by adding a liquid.

freezer—An appliance for the freezing and storage of frozen foods. Two types are made, one is the chest type, the other upright like a refrigerator.

freezer knife—Heavy knife with sawtoothed cutting edges. Produces a wide cut. Used for cutting frozen foods.

french—1) A vegetable or fruit cut into thin strips. 2) A slice of meat that is flattened.

French bread—A water bread baked so as to give the long loaves a crunchy crust.

French fries—Strips of potatoes deep fried in hot fat until golden brown. Crunchy on the outside and soft inside.

French fryer—*(See Deep Fryer)*

French pattern knife—*(See Cook's Knives)*

French salad dressing—1) American variety is made of mayonnaise, catsup and various spices and herbs. 2) French (true) variety is made with oil, vinegar, spices and herbs.

French toast—Slices of white bread dipped into egg and milk mixture, then fried in butter. Served with syrup, jam, jelly or powdered sugar.

French tortilla *(Sp)*—Omelette

fresa *(SP)*—Strawberry

friandise *(FR)*—Sweetmeats, sweets, delicacies.

fricassee—Chicken or veal cut up and stewed in a sauce. Any dish prepared in this manner.

fried rice—Rice dish where the rice is lightly browned in fat then a liquid is added to complete the cooking. Seasonings, onions, peppers, mushrooms, waterchestnuts, chopped or sliced meats can be added. Broth or consumme can be used as the liquid.

frier—*(See fryer)*

frijol *(Sp)*—French bean

frijole *(Mex)*—Bean, usually the dried bean.

fritella *(It)*—Pancake

fritta *(It)*—Omelette

fritter—A spoonful of batter, often containing pieces of meat, vegetable or fruit, that is deep fried. Served hot as an appetizer or as a side dish.

friture *(Fr)*—Frying; anything fried; fry; fried fish.

frog legs—A delicacy. The legs are prepared the same as fried chicken. The flesh has a taste similar to chicken.

frokost *(Dan)*—Breakfast

fromage *(Fr)*—Cheese

froment *(Fr)*—Wheat

fromentee *(Fr)*—Porridge made from wheat flour.

frosted mug—A glass mug with a handle that is chilled or frozen before using. Root beer and beer are often served in this manner.

frosting—A light creamy substance that is used to cover the sides and tops of cakes and other confections. Often made of egg whites and sugar, butter and sugar or solid shortening and sugar. Appropriate flavorings are added.

frozen custard—A form of soft ice cream that is available in drive-ins and fast food eateries. It is made and dispensed from a special machine. Often served in cones made of a baked crust.

frozen foods—Most fruits, vegetables, poultry and meats can be frozen for future use by storage in home freezers. Or, can be purchased in frozen form ready-to-eat or with minimal cooking.

fructose—The natural sugar found in fruits and honey.

fruitcake—A traditional Christmas cake. This is a heavy cake made with flour, shortenings, eggs, liquids, candied fruits, nuts and spices. Can be baked several weeks before using and treated with brandy, wine or fruit juices while it ripens. One type is not baked. Graham crackers are used in place of flour, eggs and shortening.

fruit leather—A rolled confection. Dried or fresh fruit is cooked with sugar, pureed, then spread thinly and dried. The dried fruit (leather) is then rolled up for storage. May be sliced or pieces torn off to eat. Excellent hikers and campers food. When dried properly can be stored a lengthy time.

fruit sec *(Fr)*—Dried fruit

fruit sugar—Fructose

fruits—Generally the edible and sweet body of seed plants.

fruits confits au vinaigre *(Fr)*—Pickled fruits

fruits rafraichis *(Fr)*—Fruit salad

fruits secs *(Fr)*—Dried fruit

fruit wines—Wines that are distilled from various fruits and flavored with the essence of fruit. Many flavors available.

frumento *(It)*—Wheat

fry basket—A meshed basket that is used when deep frying foods.

fryer—A young chicken. Ideal size for frying.

frying pan—A skillet with a long handle

fudge—A rich chocolate candy that often has nuts, raisins, dried fruits and coconut added.

fumet *(Fr)*—1) Aroma, scent. 2) The concentrated essence from fish or game that is made by slow cooking.

fungho *(It)*—Mushroom

fusil *(Fr)*—Sharpening steel; whetstone

galatine *(Fr)*—A chicken that has been boned, stuffed, cooked in stock, pressed, cooled in aspic and served cold.

galette *(Fr)*—A flat, thin cake; a pancake

galettoire *(Fr)*—Griddle

Galliano *(It)*—A liqueur flavored with herbs and flowers. Used in the mixed drink Harvey Wallbanger.

game—Wild animals or fowl which are hunted for food.

gambretto *(It)*—Shrimp

gammelost—A hard cheese made from sour skimmed milk. Has a distinct odor.

gamy—A food that is over ripe, near spoiling. High.

ganado *(Sp)*—Cattle

garbage disposal—An electric grinder attached to one of the drains in the kitchen sink. Used to grind food scraps and flush them down the drain.

garbanzo *(Sp)*—Chick pea

garbures *(Fr)*—A thick vegetable soup. A hodge-podge of ingredients.

garbure au gras *(Fr)*—A thick vegetable soup with meat.

garbure au maigre *(Fr)*—A thick vegetable soup without meat.

garden cress—Watercress

garden pea—*(See Pea)*

garlic press—Hand-held device used to extract the juice from garlic cloves.

Garnele *(Ger)*—Shrimp

garni *(Fr)*—Garnished

gatha *(Arm)*—A rich, fragile pastry generally served with tea or coffee. Similar to tea breads and cookies.

gateau *(Fr)*—Cake

gaufre *(Fr)*—Waffle; wafer; honeycomb

gavage *(Fr)*—Forced feeding or fattening—as of poultry.

gazpacho *(Sp)*—A soup/salad of fresh vegetables including tomatoes, cucumbers, sweetpeppers and slices of bread moistened with water. Also may contain various spices, salad oil, vinegar and vegetable juices. Served cold.

Geflugel *(Ger)*—Fowl

Gefrorene *(Ger)*—Ice cream

gelatin—Substance used to solidify various liquids and juices. Also used in some puddings.

gelatina *(It)*—Jelly

gelatina *(Sp)*—Gelatin

gelatine *(Fr)*—Gelatin

Gelbwurz *(Ger)*—Turmeric

gelee *(Fr)*—Jelly

Gelee *(Ger)*—Jelly

Gemuse *(Ger)*—Vegetable

genepi *(Fr)*—Sweet absinthe made from alpine wormwood.

genievre *(Fr)*—Juniper. Gin.

genoese *(Fr)*—A very rich cake

genoise—A cold mayonnaise.

Gerat *(Ger)*—Utensil

German pancakes—White potatoes that have been grated, mixed with eggs, flour, spices and seasonings, then shaped into patties and fried in hot fat. Patties should be thin and crispy.

Gernurznelke *(Ger)*—Clove

gherkins—Small, sweet pickles

ghiaccio *(It)*—Frozen water; ice

gibier *(Fr)*—Birds and wild animals that are eaten.

giblets—The edible internal organs of fowls.

gin—A neutral grain spirit flavored with juniper berries. Not often used in cooking.

gingembre *(Fr)*—Ginger

ginger ale—A non-alcoholic carbonated beverage flavored with ginger.

gingerbread—Cake highly seasoned with ginger.

gingerbread man—Soft cookies made from ginger-flavored dough. Cut out to resemble little men. Usually decorated after baking.

gingersnap—A thin, crisp cookie flavored with ginger. Also used to thicken sauerbraten gravy.

ginkgo nut—This nut from the Maidenhair tree is used in Chinese and Japanese cookery. Should be found in specialty shops.

girdle *(Scot)*—Griddle

gjedost—A hard cheese made from goat milk.

glace *(Fr)*—1) Ice cream; 2) Frozen water, ice

glaces aux fruit *(Fr)*—Fruit-flavored ices.

glaciere *(Fr)*—1) Ice box; refrigerating machine; icehouse. 2) Sugar dredger.

glair—A glaze made from egg whites.

glogg—A hot wine and brandy punch with various spices. A traditional Scandinavian Christmas holiday drink. There are several variations.

glucose—A sugar in its natural state in various plants.

gluten—A protein substance that is present in flour. It causes the dough to be sticky and elastic. This elasticity is achieved by kneading the dough.

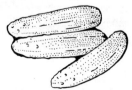

gnocchi—A small drop dumpling. Can be made from wheat flour, semolina or potatoes. Sometimes cheese is added to the dough. Generally water is used as the poaching liquid.

gnoccho *(It)*—Dumpling

goat—A meat and milk animal similar in size to the sheep. The meat is often barbequed. The milk is drunk fresh and can also be made into cheese.

gobbler *(col)*—A turkey

gobo *(JP)*—Domestic burdock

godiveau *(Fr)*—A kind of forcemeat ball.

goober *(col)*—Peanut

Good King Henry—A potherb native to England. The young leaves are cooked as greens. Shoots and flower heads can be prepared as asparagus.

goose—A barnyard fowl raised for its eggs, meat, feathers and down. Cooked the same as duck.

gooseberry—An acid berry from a shrub related to the currant. It is used in jams and pies. It is not eaten raw. A wild variety has its fruit covered with sharp needles. It is used to make jelly only.

gorgonzola—A semi-hard cheese. Blue/green mold throughout.

gorp—A confection made by grinding equal parts of peanuts and raisins together. A hand-cranked food chopper should be used.

gouda—A hard cheese. Round and flat. Mild.

gougeres *(Fr)*—Cheese puffs served as an appetizer.

goulash *(Hun)*—A beef stew seasoned with Hungarian pepper.

gourmet—1) The highest degree of food preparation. The preparation of which brings out the food's most natural and palatable tastes. Simplicity and care is the guide. (A dish that is elaborate and contains many ingredients is not necessarily gourmet.) 2) Products which are superior. 3) Service that is exceptionally superior.

gousse d'ail *(Fr)*—Clove of garlic

gousse de vanille *(Fr)*—Vanilla bean

gout *(Fr)*—Flavor; taste

graham crackers—Crisp, sweet crackers made from graham flour. Often used to make crumb crusts. A snack cracker.

graham flour—Flour milled from the whole grain of wheat.

grain—Seed of any of the cereal grasses. Used to make flours, meals, breakfast foods and cooked whole in some dishes. *(See Cereal Grasses)*

grain de poivre *(Fr)*—Peppercorn

graine *(Fr)*—Seed

granada *(Sp)*—Pomegranate

granadilla fruit—*(See Passion Fruit)*

Granatapfel *(Ger)*—Pomegranate

granchio *(It)*—Crab

Grand Marnier—An orange-flavored liqueur

grano *(It)*—Wheat

granturco *(It)*—Corn

grape—Fruit of a vine. There are mainly two types of grapes)—table and wine. Table grapes are eaten as snacks and used in some food dishes. Some table grapes are made into juice. The wine grapes are used for wine. Raisins are made from a sweet seedless white grape.

grapefruit—A citrus fruit used fresh, canned and as a juice. Used to some extent in cooking. The peel may be candied for use in various confections and cakes. The zest is used fresh, dried or candied.

grapefruit knife—A short, narrow-bladed knife that is serrated on both sides. The blade is curved. This permits cutting around the halved grapefruit separating the flesh from the membrane.

grappefruit *(Fr)*—Grapefruit

gras *(Fr)*—Fat; fleshy; plump

grasshopper pie—One crust pie made with creme de menthe, creme de cacao, whipping cream and other ingredients. Usually poured into a chocolate wafer crumb crust. Served cold. Elegant dessert.

grater—A hand tool used for grating various foods.

gratin pan—Generally shallow pans, round or oval, with handles. Used to bake and serve in. Made of porcelain or metal with or without a lid.

gratinee *(Fr)*—Dishes that have been sprinkled with buttered bread crumbs then browned in the broiler or oven. This gives the dish a light crust. Breaded. Au gratin.

Graves—A dry, white, dinner wine.

gravy—Seasoned juices from cooked meat that can be thickened to make a sauce. Also the fat that meats have been pan fried in, may be thickened with flour and liquid added to produce a sauce. Gravy is used on various vegetables and meats.

grease—Any type of cooking fat.

grease gravy—*(See Red-Eye Gravy)*

great northern beans—Same as the navy bean and northern bean.

green—Fruit or vegetable that is not ripe.

green bean—*(See String Bean)*

green pepper—Any of the sweet green pepprs.

green shrimp—Live shrimp. Usually packed in ice for shipment. Shrimp turn pink when cooked.

greengrocer—The store or person who sells fresh fruits and vegetables.

greens—*(See Pot-Herbs)*

grenade *(Fr)*—Pomegranate

grenadine—A pomegranate-flavored sweet syrup. Used in punches, alcoholic drinks and in cooking.

grenadins *(Fr)*—Small slices of fillet of veal. Can also refer to beef cut in this manner.

gribiche *(FR)*—A cold sauce that is served with cold fish.

griddle—Heavy, flat pan used for cooking pancakes, crepes, hotcakes or toasting buns. Can have a low rim or not. May be round, square or rectangle, usually with a handle. Can also be used for toasting sandwiches, crumpets or English muffins.

griddle cakes—Same as hot cakes.

Griess *(Ger)*—Semolina

grille *(Fr)*—Broiled

grinder—A mechanical device used to grind fruits, vegetables and meats into various-sized particles. Many attach to the work surface. Various shaped and sized cutting discs may be used. Electric-powered grinders are available as well as grinder attachments for food processors and electric mixers. Generally not used for nuts.

grissine—Salty bread sticks.

grist—Grain to be ground or grain already ground.

grist mill—Mill that grinds various grains.

grits—Coarsely-ground hulled grain. Short for hominy grits.

groats—Crushed grain usually oats. Also a cooked breakfast cereal.

grog—Hot drink containing rum or other spirit, sugar, lemon and water. An English admiral named Vernon had the nickname of Old Grog. About 1740 he ordered his men to put water in their ration of rum. The men called this drink grog.

groseille *(Fr)*—Currant

groseille verte *(Fr)*—Gooseberry

Grosse Brioche a tete *(Fr)*—*(See Brioche)*

ground cherry—A fruit related to the tomatillo. It is sweeter. Is used to make pies and preserves. When ripe it is yellow in color. Sometimes called 'strawberry tomato' and 'dwarf cape gooseberry.'

ground nut—Peanut

ground pea—Peanut

grub *(sl)*—Food

gruel—Thinnish cooked paste made from oats, corn, wheat or other grain. Served as a breakfast cereal.

gruyere—A hard cheese. Nut-like flavor.

guacamole *(Mex)*—An appetizer or dip made of mashed avocados, chopped onions and tomatoes, and various spices. Can be served on crackers or with tortilla chips. Can be used as a garnish for soups, salads and cold dishes.

guarapo *(Sp)*—Fermented drink made from sugar cane. Cane juice.

guava—A native South American fruit that is pear-shaped. Used in making jellies and jams. Some varieties can be eaten raw and made into juices. Some varieties have the flavor of lemon, strawberry or chocolate.

guisado *(Sp)*—Stew

guisante *(Sp)*—Pea

gum acacia—Same as gum arabic.

gum arabic—A water soluble gum from acacia plants. It is used in the making of confections such as marshmallows and jujubes. It is a gelling agent. *(See Gelatin)*

gum tragacanth—Same as gum arabic.

gumbo—1) A thick soup made with meat or seafood, vegetables, seasonings and always okra. 2) Okra

gumdrops—Candy made of gelatin, sugar, water, flavorings and molded in a dome shape.

Gurke *(Ger)*—Cucumber

H

haba *(Sp)*—Bean, especially lima bean.

hachis *(Fr)*—Minced meat; hash

Hafer *(Ger)*—Oats

haggis *(Scot)*—Traditional Scottish dish. Made by stuffing a sheep's stomach with the minced internal organs of the sheep, spices and other ingredients. It is then boiled. Traditionally whiskey is served with haggis.

half glaze—*(See Demi-Glace)*

halva, halvah—Confection consisting of crushed sesame seeds, honey or other syrup.

ham—The rear leg of the hog. Can be eaten fresh but generally they are cured by smoking or by using salt, sugar, spices or a combination of all. Can be sliced and slightly fried or baked whole then sliced. A versatile meat. Can be served hot or cold. Is also made into sandwiches and casseroles.

hamburg parsley—The leaves of this root vegetable can be used as flavoring and garnish as you would parsley. The white roots, resembling a parsnip, can be used in stews, soups and cooked with meat. Can be cooked, mashed with spices and sugar, formed into patties and fried in fat.

hamburger—A sandwich consisting of a beef patty that has been grilled or fried. It is placed between the halves of a hamburger bun. Usually mayonnaise, mustard or other sauce is spread on the bun. Onions, lettuce, tomato, pickle and relish are often put into the sandwich. The bun is often heated or grilled. A very popular American sandwich.

hamburger bun—A round, yeast bun. Used for hamburgers and cheeseburgers.

hamburger press—Small tool used to form ground meat into patties.

hand cheese—Soft cheese made from sour milk. Has a sharp and pungent odor and taste.

hanging—Method of tenderizing meat and game by leaving it to hang for a period of time. Generally it is hung in a cold walk-in box.

hard boiled—The degree of doneness of an egg that is cooked, in the shell, by boiling. The white and yolk are very firm.

hard cheese—Cheese that is cut with a knife or slicer. Can be grated. Some cheeses are permitted to become very hard (dry) so that they may be grated into a powder.

hard cider—Cider that has been fermented so that it becomes alcoholic.

hard sauce—Sauce made of confectioner's sugar, butter, cream and flavorings. Used on cakes and other confections.

hard water—Water that has a large amount of salts, minerals and impurities present. Not a desirable water to cook with.

hard wheat flour—Flour milled from a hard wheat. It has a high gluten content to produce great elasticity. Used for puff pastes, breads, Danish and strudel doughs.

hardtack—A coarse hard biscuit. Was used on oldtime sailing vessels as a food staple.

hare—Rabbit

hareng *(Fr)*—Herring

hareng frais *(Fr)*—Fresh herring

hareng fume *(Fr)*—Smoked herring

haricot *(Fr)*—Bean

haricot de mouton *(Fr)*—Mutton stew

haricot vert *(Fr)*—String bean

harina *(Sp)*—Flour

Harvey's sauce *(Eng)*—There are many recipes for this sauce which dates to the 17th century. Mainly it is based on mushroom and walnut catchups. Various spices are added. Has the appearance and consistence of Worcestershire sauce. Generally it is not hot.

hasarde *(Fr)*—Relating to food that is tainted or spoiled.

Hasenpfeffer *(Ger)*—Stew made of hare with pepper and vinegar.

hash—Dish of precooked vegetables and meats that have been seasoned, chopped together and often fried in fat. Can be formed into patties.

hash brown potatoes—Cold boiled potatoes that are grated or chopped and lightly fried. An accompaniment to breakfast eggs.

hasty pudding—Cornmeal mush

haunch—The hindquarters of the ox and certain wild animals, such as venison and roebuck

haut gout *(Fr)*—Highly flavored; seasoning

haws—1) The fruit of the hawthorne tree. Several varieties can be made into jellies and preserves. 2) Rose hips.

hazelnut—The cooked meat from the hog's head is combined with seasonings and pressed into a loaf. Generally served sliced, cold.

health foods—Foods that are considered by many to be more healthful than most foods sold in grocery stores. Generally they are organically grown and have few if any additives. These foods and supplements range from organically grown fruits, vegetables, meats, grains for flour, dairy products, nuts and syrups to vitamins, minerals and protein supplements. Beverages such as herbal teas and carob are also considered health foods.

heartnut—A Japanese walnut variety. The nuts are heart-shaped and with a flavor ranging from mild to one similar to the butternut.

hearts of palm—*(See Palm Hearts)*

heat diffuser—Device that is placed over the burners on a stove. Helps to spread the heat evenly.

Hefe *(Ger)*—Yeast

helado *(Sp)*—Ice cream

hen, baking—The adult female chicken. The large ones are ideal for baking whole. Smaller hens may be stewed. This type of chicken is the most economical for making broth.

hen, laying—A female chicken bred to produce eggs in large quantities. Usually has little flesh.

herbalist—One who collects herbs. A dealer in herbs.

herbe *(Fr)*—Herb; grass

Herkimer cheese—An aged cheddar

hibachi *(Ja)*—A small charcoal brazier.

hielo *(Sp)*—Frozen water, ice

hierbabuena *(Sp)*—Mint

highball—An alcoholic drink that is served in a tall glass with ice. Generally two ingredients are used—the spirit and the mix. Sometimes garnished.

higo *(Sp)*—Fig

higo chumbo *(Sp)*—Prickly pear

hinojo *(Sp)*—Fennel

hips—Short for rose hips.

hoagie—Same as a Poor Boy sandwich.

hoecake—A cornmeal cake usually cooked on a griddle.

hog—A meat animal from which is produced bacon, ham, roasts, chops and sausage.

hojaldre *(Sp)*—Puff paste

hojuela *(Sp)*—Pancake

hollandaise sauce—A hot, tart sauce made with egg yolks, butter, lemon juice and seasonings. Served on eggs, fish and vegetables.

Holland gin—A gin imported from Holland. It is more aromatic and sweeter than American dry gin.

homard *(Fr)*—Lobster

home brew—Beer that is made at home

hominy—Dried corn that has been processed to produce a plump kernel. Served as a side dish.

hominy grits—Hominy that has been flaked and dried. It is cooked with water or milk and seasoned with butter, salt and pepper. Serve as a side dish. Often gravy is served over the grits.

honey—Sweet syrup produced by the honey bee. The bee gathers nectar from the blooms of various plants. Nectar from different plants will have different flavor. When possible, honey should not be cooked very long. High heat will affect the flavor. It is best to add honey to a cooked dish after it is removed from the fire. CAUTION: Do not feed honey to children under one (1) year of age. The digestive system of infants cannot handle botulism spores found in honey.

hongo *(Sp)*—Mushroom

Honig *(Ger)*—Honey

hooch *(sl)*—Whiskey; liquor

hoop cheese—A dry, crumbly fresh cheese.

hop—The ripe dried fruit of this vine is used in the flavoring of malt liquors, beers and in medicine.

horn of plenty—*(See Cornucopia)*

horn mold—Metal cones on which puff pastry is wrapped then baked. Molds may also be used for shap-ing certain types of cookies after they are baked.

hors de saison *(Fr)*—Appetizers served at the beginning of a meal or with cocktails before dinner. Also served at cocktail parties and other gatherings.

hors d'oeuvre *(Fr)*—Appetizers served at the beginning of a meal or with cocktails before dinner. Also served at cocktail parties and other gatherings.

hot cakes—Flat cake made from a thick batter. Cooked on a griddle. About four to six inches in diameter. Is browned on both sides. A breakfast and late supper dish. Usually served with butter, syrup or jelly.

hot cross buns—Yeast rolls with currants. A cross is made on top, after baking, with confectioner's icing.

hot dog—Wiener or frankfurter served in a long bun, hot or warm, with various condiments. Sometimes chili is added. Very popular for picnics and other outdoor events.

hothouse—A building for raising fruits and vegetables out of season. Quality is generally high. These fruits and vegetables are generally high in cost.

hothouse lamb—A baby lamb. Up to three weeks old. Usually has been fed its mother's milk only. Expensive.

hot pack—In canning, the fruit or vegetable is heated in liquid before packing and processing.

hot-pot—Meat and vegetable stew.

houblon *(Fr)*—Hops

house boat *(sl)*—A banana split

household bleach—A commercial product used to lighten the color or stains from clothing, sinks and other items. Used mainly in the laundry. CAUTION: It will bleach almost anything.

house wine—The wine served in restaurants by the glass or carafe. It is not vintage. Many restaurants offer three wines, a red, a white and a rose.

huevo *(Sp)*—Egg

huevos rancheros *(Mex)*—Eggs cooked with cheese, chilies, tomatoes and spices.

huile *(Fr)*—Oil

huile d'olive *(Fr)*—Olive oil

huile de palme *(Fr)*—Palm oil

huitre *(Fr)*—Oyster

humble pie—A deep-dish pie made of the inner organs of the deer.

Hummer *(Ger)*—Lobster

hundred-year-old eggs *(Ch)*—Fresh hen eggs that have been coated with a mixture of salt, ashes and lime. They are let set for a month and a half or longer. The whites become firm and the yolks are partly firm. Whites become yellowish green and the yolks a greenish cast. Very strong smell and sulfuric taste. Found in specialty stores.

hure *(Fr)*—Head of a boar, salmon or other animal.

hush puppies—A fried bread or fritter made of cornmeal, eggs, onions, liquids and seasonings. May be dropped in deep fat for fritters or in shallow fat for bread cakes.

husk—The outer covering of an ear of corn. It is generally removed before cooking. The dried husks are used for wrapping tamales. Many cereal grains have husks.

husk tomato—Ground cherry

hydrometer—Instrument used to measure the density of liquids. *(See Colorimeter and Salometer)*

hydroponics—The growing of plants in a liquid. Generally water with nutrients added.

ice—Frozen water

ice box—1) An upright wooden chest that holds a block of ice. Used for cooling foods. 2) Colloquial for refrigerator.

ice bucket—An insulated container with a lid. Used to hold ice cubes. Can be used at the bar or drink table.

ice chest—*(See Cooler)*

ice cream—Frozen dessert of milk, eggs, sugar and flavorings. Commercially made ice cream must contain at least 10 percent milk fat and 20 percent milk solids by weight. Often made at home.

ice cream bar—A frozen confection of ice cream or sherbet, that is coated with chocolate and sometimes nuts.

ice cream cone—A holder for ice cream. Made of a baked waffle-like batter in the shape of a cone or tube.

ice cream float—A glass of soda pop with a scoop of ice cream.

ice cream freezer—A tool for making ice cream at home. It consists of a metal cylinder, with stirring paddles (dasher) that fit inside, and a cover. The unit fits inside another cylinder with a geared box on top. Ice and salt are placed around the inner cylinder. This is rotated by hand or a small electric motor. It is rotated until the cream is frozen. The cream will not be hard but very firm.

ice cream sandwich—A frozen confection consisting of a small slab of ice cream that has a piece of cake or cookie on each side.

ice cream scoop—Hand tool used to remove ice cream and other frozen ices and milks from their containers. Helps to form them into balls. Can also be used to shape meatballs, mashed potatoes and for serving certain foods.

ice cream soda—Ice cream in a tall glass with plain soda water added. The ice cream is slightly mashed.

ice crusher—Hand-held or countertop tool used to crush ice to varying degrees of fineness. Electric crushers are available.

ice milk—A frozen confection similar to ice cream. Commercially made ice milk must contain two-seven percent milk fat and at least 11 percent milk. The remaining liquid can be water or juices.

ice pick—Long, sharp, steel rod with a handle enclosing one end. Used to break up and chip blocks of ice. Use with caution. When not in use, a cork should be stuck on the pointed end.

ices—Frozen dessert of water, fruit juices, sugars and flavorings.

icing—Frosting

icing sugar *(Eng)*—Confectioners sugar

icing syringe—*(See Cake Decorator)*

idili steamer—A three-tiered rack that is placed over water for the steaming of foods. From southern India.

inciser *(Fr)*—*(See Incise)*

Indian corn—Maize

Indian doughpress—Device for forcing chickpea dough out, in decorative strips, directly into the hot oil.

Indian pudding—Pudding made from cornmeal, molasses and spices.

indoor grill—A gas or electric grill either a part of the kitchen stove or a separate appliance. Used for grilling meats and other foods.

infuser *(Fr)*—*(See Infuse)*

Ingwer *(Ger)*—Ginger

insalata *(It)*—Salad

instant coffee—The essence of coffee that is dried to a powder or granular form. It is recombined by adding hot water. Instant coffee may also be used as a flavoring.

instant flour—A flour that will combine with cold water easily. Higher priced than regular flour.

instant potatoes—Potatoes that have had the moisture removed. Available as flakes or granules. Milk or water is added to make mashed potatoes. Handy to have on the kitchen shelf for emergencies.

instant rice—Rice that has been treated by the manufacturer so that it may be cooked in a very short time.

instant tea—The essence of tea dried so that it becomes a powder. It is recombined by adding hot or cold water.

Irish coffee—Alcoholic drink made of Irish whiskey, hot coffee, sugar and with whipped cream on top. Very popular on St. Patrick's Day.

Irish mist—A liqueur made of Irish whiskey and honey.

Irish potato—A white potato used mainly for stewing, mashing, salads and frying.

Irish stew *(Ir)*—Mutton stew in white stock with potatoes and sliced onions.

Irish whiskey—A whiskey that is made in Ireland. The taste is less distinct than scotch whiskey and the color is lighter than bourbon whiskey. May be used the same as bourbon in cooking.

iron ware—Cooking utensils made of iron. Generally heavy. A good conductor of heat. Their color, black, is a natural color. After washing they should be given a coating of vegetable oil to prevent rusting. Green beans tend to darken when cooked in this type of pan. Also known as cast iron.

Italian bean—Same as romano bean.

Italian celery—Florence fennel

Italian marrows—Zucchini

Italian meringue—Meringue made of egg whites and hot sugar syrup. Used as cake icing and frosting for petit fours and other sweets.

Italian stock—*(See Broccoli Raab)*

Izarra *(Fr)*—A liqueur flavored with aromatic herbs.

J

jackfruit—A southesast Asian fruit from a tree of the breadfruit family. It is eaten raw, in fruit and vegetable salads.

jagging iron—Toothed wheel set in a handle and used for decorating pastries.

jalea *(Sp)*—Jelly

jalousies *(Fr)*—Little cakes made of flaky pastry, almond paste and apricot jam.

jam—Pulp of fruits cooked with sugar until very thick. Use same as jelly.

jambon *(Fr)*—Ham

jambonniere *(Fr)*—A special pan for braising and cooking ham.

jamon *(Sp)*—Ham or bacon

Jam(s)wurzel *(Ger)*—Yam(s)

Japanese artichokes—*(See Crosnes)*

Japanese cucumber—Same as Chinese cucumber.

Japanese eggplant—An eggplant that is long like a cucumber. Use same as the globe eggplant.

Japanese mortar—Mortar bowl lined with sharp ridges. Good for crushing seeds.

jar—A container, usually of glass, that is used for canning. Generally equipped with a screw-type lid.

jarabe *(Sp)*—Syrup

jardiniere *(Fr)*—Dish composed of various vegetables cut into cubes and combined with a thick sauce.

java *(sl)*—Coffee

Jell-O—A trademark name for a flavored gelatin. Available in many flavors. Is pre-sweetened.

jelly—Clear fruit juices that have been cooked with sugar and often citric acid, to produce a gelatin. Eaten with bread, rolls and used in prepared sweets.

jelly *(Eng)*—A sweetened fruit flavored gelatin.

jelly bag—Cloth bag with handles used to strain fruit juices. Can also be used for straining broths. Bags should be washed alone and in hot water only. No soap.

jelly beans—A small gelatinous candy with a hard covering. Shaped similar to an egg. Are available in a variety of flavors and colors.

jelly pan—*(See Preserving Pan)*

jelly roll—A thin sponge cake coated with jelly and then rolled up. Slice to serve.

jerez *(Sp)*—Sherry

Jerezwein *(Ger)*—Sherry

jerky—Any meat that has been dried.

Jerusalem artichokes—A root vegetable from a plant related to the sunflower. They may be prepared in the same way as potatoes. They are also good cut up raw in salads. Crispy, crunchy and starchless. Also called sunchokes.

jicama *(Mex)*—An edible brown root shaped somewhat like an irregular turnip. It is used mainly in salads but it can be cooked. The vegetable is widely used in Mexico and South America. Has a taste similar to water chestnuts but a little sweeter. Should be available in Mexican grocery stores and in the larger supermarkets in the west and southwest.

jigger—A measure for liquor. Usually one ounce

joe *(sl)*—Coffee

johnnycake *(ErAm)*—A type of cornbread. A two to one ratio is used for the cornmeal and flour. Both sweet and sour milk are used along with eggs, fat, leavening and salt. It is baked and served hot.

joint *(Eng)*—A roast

jook *(Ch)*—Rice porridge

jug—A round container with a small neck and opening. Usually has a handle. Used for liquids.

juice—That liquid part of fruits and vegetables. Also the drippings from a roast or baked fowl.

juicers—Various shaped tools used to extract the juice from citrus fruits. Hand and electric types are available.

jujube—1) Small shrub that produces a shiny reddish-brown fruit about the size of a date. Can be used fresh or dried for use in various confections. 2) A small candy made of sugar and gelatin. Sometimes flavored with the jujube fruit or other fruit flavors.

julep—Mint julep drink

julienne—Food cut into long thin strips.

jus *(Fr)*—The liquids squeezed out of foodstuffs. Also the juice that is cooked out of meats (pan drippings). Serve as is or used to make the sauce. Gravy.

jus de fruits *(Fr)*—Fruit juice

K

k—Abbreviation for kilo

kabob, kebob—Cubes of meat, vegetables or fruit put on a skewer and cooked on a grill. Can also be baked.

kaffe kaka *(Sw)*—Tea ring with cardamon seeds.

kahab *(Hin)*—Roasted meat; a roast

Kaffee *(Ger)*—Coffee

Kahlua—A Mexican liqueur flavored with coffee.

Kakao *(Ger)*—Cocoa

Kalbfleisch *(Ger)*—Veal

kale—A headless cabbage. The elongated leaves are used as a potherb.

kaltschall *(Rus)*—A fruit salad moistened with liqueur, wine or syrup.

kangaroo—This Australian mammal is edible. Kangaroo tail soup is a delicacy in Germany.

Kaninchen *(Ger)*—Rabbit

Kapun *(Ger)*—Capon

kari *(Fr)*—Curry

kari a l'indienne *(Fr)*—Indian curry

Karotte *(Ger)*—Carrot

Kartoffel *(Ger)*—Potato

Kase *(Ger)*—Cheese

kasha *(Rus)*—A cooked buckwheat dish.

katsuobushi *(Ja)*—Bonito

kava—A shrub from Polynesia. Member of the pepper family. A beverage is brewed from it.

Kaviar *(Ger)*—Caviar

kebab *(Tur)*—Kabob

kedgeree *(Ind)*—1) Mix of rice, beans, lentils, seasonings and sometimes smoked fish. 2) Cooked, flaked fish, rice, hard-boiled eggs and seasonings heated in cream.

keg—A cask or barrel of less than 10 gallons.

kei apple—*(See Umkokolo Fruit)*

Kellner *(Ger)*—Waiter

kelp—Various coarse brown sea-weeds. It is dried and powdered, and can be used as a salt substi-tute. Should be found in health food stores.

kernel—The seed

ketchup *(Eng.)*—Catsup

Key lime pie—A lime-flavored custard pie. Key is a variety of lime from Florida.

Kicherebse *(Ger)*—Chickpea

kickshaw—A tidbit; trivial appetizer

kidney beans—A dark red colored dried bean. Used in chili, salads, in casseroles and as a side dish.

kielbasa—A smoked, spiced sausage. Can be steamed, sauteed or baked.

kilkis *(Rus)*—Small fish that is pre-served like an anchovy.

kilo—Short for kilogram.

kilogram—Unit of metric measure. Equals 1,000 grams or 2.2046 lb.s

kimali burek *(Tur, Rus)*—Pancake stuffed with forcemeat or other filling rolled up and fried.

kim chee *(Kor)*—Spicy pickled cab-bage. Can contain other vegetables. Heavy on the garlic and hot peppers.

kipfels *(Tur)*—A sweet roll with various fillings.

kippers—Herrings which are split open and smoked. May be grilled or broiled. Served with melted butter.

kirsch—A liqueur made from ripe wild cherries. Made mainly in eastern France and Germany. Used in pastries and confections. Also called Kirschwasser.

Kirsche *(Ger)*—Cherry

kissel *(Rus)*—Dessert of berries and cream baked in a charlotte mold. May be served hot or cold.

Kishka *(Yid)*—Beef or fowl casing stuffed with a savory filling.

kissing crust—The pale, soft crust resulting when one loaf touches another in baking.

kitchen salt—Same as cooking salt.

kitchen shears—*(See Shears)*

kitchen stove—The appliance where most of the cooking is performed. Equipped with burners on the top and an enclosed area known as the oven. Below the oven is generally a sliding drawer where the broiling is done.

kitchen ware—Utensils and tools that are used in the kitchen.

kiwi—Kiwifruit

kiwifruit—A small, egg-shaped, furry, brown fruit. Has a greenish flesh with a taste similar to strawberries. Native to New Zealand. Now grown commercially in California. It is eaten raw. Can be made into preserves.

knife—Hand tool used for cutting and slicing. One edge of the blade is generally sharp. Kitchen knives should be of the highest quality. Store in a rack—not in a drawer. Always keep kitchen knives sharp. Some type of hand-held sharpener is best. Electric sharpeners tend to harm the cutting edge. See listings for individual types of knives.

knife rest—A small utensil on which the knife is rested to prevent the soiling of the tablecloth. Usually found at the formal dinner.

knob celery—Celeriac

Knoblauch *(Ger)*—Garlic

knotroot—*(See Crosnes)*

Koch *(Ger)*—Chef; cook

kochen *(Ger)*—To boil; cook

Kochin *(Ger)*—Cookery

Knodel *(Ger)*—Dumpling

Kohl—Cabbage

kohlrabi—This vegetable forms a bulb at the base of the stalks. This is the portion that is eaten. Can be used in place of turnips, raw in green salads or as a stir fry vegetable. Can be used on the appetizer tray with other fresh vegetables and fruits.

Kokosnus *(Ger)*—Coconut

kombu *(Ja)*—Kelp

kosher *(Heb)*—Food prepared in accordance with Jewish dietary laws.

kosher salt—An even and coarse salt used by many cooks and those who observe Jewish dietary laws. Usually not as strong as table salt.

kraut—Short for sauerkraut.

Kraut *(Ger)*—Herb

Kringle *(Dan)*—A rich rolled yeast pastry that uses beaten egg whites and chopped nuts as the filling. It is baked in a roll and decorated with chopped nuts.

Kruzkummel *(Ger)*—Cumin

Kuchen *(Ger)*—Cake

kulich *(Rus)*—A cake of risen dough decorated with artificial roses. A traditional Easter dinner bread.

Kummel *(Ger)*—1) Caraway seed; 2) A liqueur flavored with caraway seed.

kumquat—A fruit with a spongy rind and acid pulp. A member of the citrus family. Cultivated widely in China and Japan. The rind and pulp are edible. Can be eaten raw or made into marmalade, jelly or crystallized. The rind is spicy and the pulp sweet.

Kurbis *(Ger)*—Pumpkin

kvass *(Rus)*—A mildly alcoholic beverage similar to beer.

lactic acid—An acid present in sour milk and certain other fermented substances. In primitive times meat was preserved by immersing it in sour milk.

lactose—The sugar in milk.

ladle—A tool with a cup-shaped bowl on one end of a long handle. Used for dipping liquids.

lady—The stomach of the lobster.

lady fingers—Small, finger-shaped cakes, which can be served plain or used to line molds before adding various creams or puddings.

lager beer—A light beer that is usually stored for several months before using.

lagniappe *(Fr)*—Something given extra, such as an extra doughnut when buying a dozen. The extra dough-nut is the lagniappe. Something served with a dish that is. not normally a part of the dish. Also a gratuity for service.

lait *(Fr)*—Milk

lait de coco *(Fr)*—Coconut milk

lait de poule *(Fr)*—Eggnog

laitue *(Fr)*—Lettuce

lamb—A young ovine (sheep) that is widely used as a food. *(See Baby, Hothouse, Spring and Summer Lamb. Also see Mutton and Sheep.)*

lamb, baby—A 4 to 6 week old lamb. Ideal weight about 15 pounds.

lamb, cuts of

BRAINS—Delicate as all brains. Can be braised, fried, or creamed.

BREAST—Can be cut into riblets or deboned and rolled for a roast. The meat is also ground.

CHOPS—Those cut from the loin are called loin chops. Those cut from the rack are called rib chops. Loin chops should be cut thick. May be grilled, baked or pan fried. Caution—Do not overcook.

CHUCK—A roast cut from the shoulder.

CROWN ROAST—Cut from the rack. An attractive roast but with little meat. Should be roasted.

FLANK—Stringy cut of meat. Sometimes a portion of the flank is cut with the loin chop. Ground to make patties.

FORESHANKS—The front legs. May be braised whole or cut into pieces. They are fatty and contain a fair amount of meat.

LEG—The rear legs. May be cut whole or into two roasts.

LIVER—Has a sharp distinctive odor. Cook as beef liver.

LOIN—Can be left whole for a roast or cut into chops. The tenderest cut of lamb.

RACK—This is the entire rib foresaddle. Often roasted whole. Rib chops are cut from this section.

SADDLE—Rear legs left attached to the rump. Usually roasted.

SKIN—The skin is tanned to produce a very soft leather.

Lambick *(Bel)*—A Belgian beer that is high in alcoholic content and is rather sour in taste.

lambs fry—The internal organs of the lamb. Also, lamb testicles.

lamb's lettuce—*(See Corn Salad)*

Lamm *(Ger)*—Lamb

langosta *(Sp)*—Lobster

langouste *(Fr)*—Spiny lobster

lapin *(Fr)*—Rabbit

lapin au kari *(Fr)*—Curried rabbit

Lapland cakes—Breakfast muffins using whipped cream and beaten egg whites as the leavening agents.

lard—Fat of the hog produced by rendering the fatty parts. Used in cooking as a fat. Ideal for some pastries.

lard *(Fr)*—Bacon; pork; fat

larder—A place where food is stored. A pantry or cupboard.

larding needle—Long, thin, hollow rods used for placing strips of fat in meats.

lardoire *(Fr)*—Larding needle.

lasagne *(It)*—Wide strips of pasta. The dish of this name consisting of the pasta, meats, cheeses, tomato sauce and spices. It is a baked dish. En casserole.

latte *(It)*—Milk

lattuga *(It)*—Lettuce

Lauch *(Ger)*—Leek

laural *(Sp)*—Bay leaf

laurier *(Fr)*—Bay leaf

lazy susan—A round serving dish that is divided into several compartments. The dish sits on a device that permits it to be revolved.

lb—Abbreviation for one pound.

leaf lard—Lard made from the fat surrounding the kidneys of the hog. A very fine lard.

leather—*(See Fruit Leather)*

leavening agent—Those ingredients that cause breads and cakes to rise during baking. Soda, baking powder and yeast are leavening agents. Stiffly beaten egg whites are used in souffles and some cakes and puddings. Whipped cream is sometimes used as a leavening agent.

Lebkuchen *(Ger)*—Gingerbread

leche *(Fr)*—Sliver of food.

leche *(Sp)*—Milk

lechuga *(Sp)*—Lettuce

leek—An edible non-bulbous root vegetable. The taste is milder than onion, to which it is related. May be used in place of onion. Only the white portion is used. The green blades are not edible. A necessary ingredient in vichyssoise. Very good with salsify in a cream soup.

lefse *(Nor)*—A potato bread that is baked on a griddle without any grease.

legume *(Fr)*—Vegetable

lekvar *(Heb)*—Prune jam

lemon—A citrus fruit used mainly as a flavoring agent and to make lemonade, a beverage. Colored portion of skin is used as zest. The peel can be candied and along with the juice and zest used in various confections and cakes.

lentil—The dried seed of a legume. Used in soups, as a side dish and for sprouting.

lentille *(Fr)*—Lentil

letchi *(Fr)*—Litchi nut

lettuce—Any of a variety of plants whose leaves are used in green salads and on sandwiches. Some are leaf and others form some form of head. Iceberg and butter are headed. Romaine, bibb and curly endive are leafed. Some varieties may be braised in butter.

levadura *(Sp)*—Yeast

levulose—Fructose

levure *(Fr)*—Yeast

Leyden—A hard cheese with cloves and cumin seed added.

lichee—*(See Litchi Nut)*

licorice—Flavoring made from the dried root of a leguminous plant. Used as a flavoring for various confections. Also, the candy made in this flavor.

Liederkranz—A cheese similar to Camembert and Limburger. This is an American trademark name. The cheese is quite strong in odor.

lievito *(It)*—Yeast

lievre *(Fr)*—Hare

lifters—*(See Turners)*

lima *(Sp)*—Lime

lima bean—A flat green-white bean. Only the seed is eaten. It is used either fresh or dried. The dried lima is excellent cooked with ham hocks or bacon.

limande *(Fr)*—The dab (fish)

limburger—Soft cheese with a very strong odor. Should be kept in an airtight container.

lime—A citrus fruit used mainly as a flavoring agent. Often added to punches and alcoholic drinks. Makes an excellent pie. Lime juice will act as a cooking medium on certain fresh fish.

limon *(Fr)*—Lime

limon *(Sp)*—Lemon

Limone *(Ger)*—Lime

limone *(It)*—Lemon

linen—Tablecloths and napkins.

linguine—A long, flat, narrow pasta.

liqueur—Alcoholic beverages flavored with aromatic substances such as fruits, spices and herbs. Many are of a sweet nature. Can be served as an aperitif or digestif. Some are used in cooking mostly in confections. Also called a cordial.

liquor—Any distilled spirit.

lista *(It)*—Menu

lista de platos *(Sp)*—Menu

litchi—The fruit of this plant. It is very sweet with a slight acid flavor. Can be eaten raw or used in confections. The dried litchi is used like nuts. Are available canned or dried.

liter, litre—Unit of metric measure. To convert quarts to litres, multiply number of quarts by .95. *(See Weights & Measures)*

liverot—Soft cheese similar to brie. Strong flavor.

lobster—An edible marine crustacean. The meat from the claws and tails are both eaten. Generally is cooked by plunging into boiling water. The shell will turn bright red. Used in salads, casseroles and various seafood dishes. Can be eaten from the shell.

lobster bisque—A rich, creamy lobster soup.

lobster cracker—Plier-shaped hand tool used to crack lobster and crab shells. Some are designed with points on the handles for pulling the flesh from the shell.

Lobster Newburg (Fr)—Lobster prepared in a cream sauce with spices and wine.

lobster pick—(See Crab Pick)

Lochan Ora (Sc)—A Scottish liqueur flavored with honey and oranges. Scotch whiskey is used as the base.

loganberry—A hybrid berry resulting from the crossing of the raspberry and blackberry. Eaten fresh or can be made into jam or jelly.

loin chop—A cut of meat from the loin of the animal, Bone is usually left attached.

London broil—Beef steak cut from the flank. Can be marinated for tenderizing. When serving, cut on the diagonal.

longe (Fr)—Loin

long flake—A crust where the particles of fat are fairly large and elongated in the dough. The fat particles are not allowed to combine with the flour. The crust will come apart in large flakes or will crumble after baking.

longhorn—A hard cheese; a type of cheddar

loquat—A fruit from a tree that is native to eastern Asia. When very ripe it can be used in fruit salads, fruit drinks or eaten in hand.

Lorbeerblat (Ger)—Bay leaf

louche (Fr)—Soup ladle

love apple—Tomato

low fat—Any food that is low in fat content—either naturally or made so.

lox—Smoked salmon. Traditionally served with bagles and cream cheese by Jewish cooks.

luffa—A vine with a long green fruit. When small the fruit can be eaten like cucumbers or fried as zucchini. Permitted to grow to maturity, the fruit is dried and the interior used as a scrubbing sponge. Also known as dishrag plant.

lug—A unit of measure. A lug box holds 26 to 29 pounds of goods. Used in the western United States.

lukewarm—A temperature of 100 to 110 degrees fahrenheit.

lunch meat—Any of a variety of cooked seasoned meats that are in loaf or roll form. Used for sandwiches and snacks. Bologna, pimento loaf and liverwurst are lunch meats.

lychee nuts—(See Litchi)

lye—A very strong alkaline solution that is used in the making of soap. Used in canneries for peeling certain fruits and vegetables. Can be used as a cleaning agent. If used in the home, extreme caution should be taken.

Lyonnais—Food cooked or fried with onion.

lyophilisation—Freeze drying

M

macadamia nut—A highly prized nut that when roasted is used in confections and as a snack. A native of Australia, this tree also grows in Hawaii and the warmer southern and central United States. The flavor is similar to the Brazil nut.

macaroni—Pasta made in the form of slim tubes. Available in various diameters and lengths. Elbow macaroni is short, curved pieces. Salad macaroni is short pieces. Is dried before using.

macaroon—Pastry or cookie made of ground almonds, sugar and egg whites. It is baked until it is very dry. Shredded coconut may be used.

macedoine *(Fr)*—A mixture of cooked or raw fruit or vegetables. Can be served hot or cold. A salad.

machhli *(Hin)*—Fish

macis *(Fr, It, Sp)*—Mace

mackerel—A long, slim, saltwater fish.

Madeira—A dessert wine that is sweet and amber in color.

madelaine *(Fr)*—A rich cake of flour, sugar, eggs, brandy and grated lemon peel. Also a small sponge cake.

Madere *(Fr)*—Madeira wine

madrilene *(Fr)*—Consomme

maggiorana *(It)*—Sweet marjoram.

magnum—A bottle of two quart capacity. Usually used for liquor or champagne. Also any very large bottle.

maguey—*(See Agave)*

maiale *(It)*—Pork

Maigram *(Ger)*—Marjoram

maigre *(Fr)*—Made without flesh meat or meat juices; lean; thin.

maionese *(It)*—Mayonnaise

mais *(Fr)*—Corn

Mais *(Ger)*—Corn

mais *(It)*—Corn

maison *(Fr)*—Food prepared to the chef's own recipe.

maitre d'hotel—1) Dishes in which parsley provides the prime flavor. 2) A sauce of melted butter, chopped parsley, lemon juice and seasonings. 3) Generally, the person in charge of a restaurant. Also identified as "maitre d'."

maiz *(Sp)*—Corn

maize—Native American Indian corn. A cereal grass.

mallet—*(See Pounder)*

Malsadas *(Por)*—Deep fried pastry that can be glazed or sprinkled with sugar.

malt—The dry powder obtained by steeping grain, especially barley, until it is sprouted. It is then dried and ground into a powder. Used in brewing beer and the distilling of various whiskeys. Also, with dry milk, as a flavoring agent in various food preparations.

malted *(sl)*—A malted milk shake.

malted milk shake—A milk shake with malt flavoring added.

maltose—A sugar obtained from starch.

mamey—A tropical American fruit. It is eaten raw and in salads.

manche *(Fr)*—Shank of meat.

manchette *(Fr)*—Paper frill used to cover the projecting bone of cutlets and joints.

manchon *(Fr)*—1) Petit fours made of almond paste, rolled, baked briefly then rolled again and filled with a flavored butter cream. 2)Small flaky pastries baked in a muff shaped mold.

Mandarine—A tangerine-flavored liqueur from France.

mandarin orange—*(See Tangerine)*

Mandel *(Ger)*—Almond

mandorla *(It)*—Almond

mandorla indiana *(It)*—Cashew

mango—1) An oblong, green, tropical fruit. Looks like a large pear. When ripe the skin turns an orange-yellow with a rosy blush. The flesh is orange in color and a little acid in taste. They are eaten raw and can be made into jams, pickled and into chutney. 2) *(col)* A sweet green pepper.

mango squash—Name given to the chayote in South America.

mangue *(Fr)*—Mango

manicotti *(It)*—Pasta tubes filled with chopped ham and cheese.

manier *(Fr)*—Working a mixture by hand.

manihot—*(See Cassava)*

manteca de cerdo *(Sp)*—Lard (fat)

mantequilla *(Sp)*—Butter

manzana *(Sp)*—Apple

mao tai *(Ch)*—A Chinese brandy

maple stick—A rectangular yeast bread about four-inches long. It is deep fried, then coated with maple flavored icing. Raised doughnut dough can be used.

maple sugar—Maple syrup that has been permitted to crystalize.

maple syrup—A sweet syrup made from the sap of the maple tree.

Used on breakfast breads and in some confections.

maraschino—A sweet cherry preserved in sugar. Used as a decoration and in confections, fruit salads and cakes. Also a liqueur made from cherries.

marasquin *(Fr)*—A liqueur made from crushed black cherries.

marble cake—Cake made of two colored batters. The batters are swirled, after pouring into the pans, to achieve a marble effect. Chocolate and yellow are the usual combination used.

marble cheese—Off white and orange cheddars mixed to produce a marbled effect. Colby is sometimes used. A Canadian favorite. A hard cheese.

marbling—The fat that is present in animal flesh. The fat aids in keeping the flesh moist and flavorful during cooking.

marchpane—Marzipan

margarine—Table spread made from various oils and emulsifiers. Used as a substitute for butter. Can also be used in cooking.

mariculture—The harvesting of food stuffs from the oceans and seas.

marinade—The liquid or sauce used for marinating.

marinara—A marinade generally with a tomato base.

marine farming—*(See Mariculture)*

marjolaine *(Fr)*—Marjoram

marmalade—A thick preserve, generally made from oranges, grapefruits or lemons.

marmite—Any of several sizes of covered cooking pots. Usually used in the oven and made of earthenware.

marron *(Fr)*—A type of chestnut used in pastries and confections.

marrow—Soft interior of beef bones. Very rich.

marshmallows—A confection made of egg whites (albumen) sugar and other ingredients. Used in pastries, as a topping for some dishes and toasted on a stick at camp fires. Can be cut in small pieces and added to fruit salads and ice creams.

marzipan—Confection made of almond paste, sugar and egg whites.

masa *(Sp, SW)*—Dough; cornmeal

mashers—Various hand-held and countertop tools used to reduce foods to pulp. Used for making mashed potatoes, purees, pastes and pates.

massepain *(Fr)*—Marzipan

mastiha *(Gr)*—A liqueur falvored with mastic. *(See mastic, chapter III)*

mate *(Sp)*—South American tea.

matelote *(Fr)*—Fish stew flavored with red wine.

matzo, matzoth *(Yid)*—Flat piece of unleavened bread.

matzo balls—Matzos crushed, moistened and formed into small balls, then added to soup.

mayo *(sl)*—Restaurant jargon for mayonnaise.

mayonesa *(Sp)*—Mayonnaise

mayonnaise—Sauce made of eggs, lemon juice, oil and seasonings. Used on vegetables, in dips and as a sandwich spread.

Mayonnaise *(Ger)*—Mayonnaise

mazagran *(Fr)*—Iced black coffee served in a glass.

mazorca *(Sp)*—An ear of corn. (Maize)

mead—Alcoholic drink made of water, honey, malt and yeast.

meal—1) Food; to partake of food; a repast. 2) Edible ground grain.

meat—Flesh of the beef. Flesh of any animal eaten.

meat chopper—Similar to the cleaver in shape but heavier. Used for splitting heavy bones.

meat loaf—Ground beef shaped into a loaf and baked. Generally spices, eggs and onions are added. For a richer loaf pork sausage is added. Can be wrapped in puff paste and baked a la Wellington.

meat pie—Savory dish made of cubed meat, vegetables, spices, herbs and seasonings. Can be baked in a deep dish with both top and bottom crusts.

meat press—A closed container with a covering that can be forced down on the meat.

meat tenderizer—1) A chemical sprinkled on meats to make them more tender. Using too much will cause the meat to become mushy. 2) Tool used to tenderize meats. *(See Pounder)*

medaillon *(Fr)*—Medallion

medallion—Various foodstuffs which are cut into round or oval shapes.

medium—Degree of doneness in cooking meats. Beef flesh will have a slight pink color.

medium flake—A crust where the particles of fat are relatively small and elongated in the dough. The fat particles are not allowed to combine with the flour. The baked crust will come apart in medium sized flakes or it will crumble. Very good crust.

Mehl *(Ger)*—Flour

mejorana *(Sp)*—Marjoram

mela *(It)*—Apple

melagrana *(It)*—Pomegranate

melange *(Fr)*—Mixture

melanzana *(It)*—Eggplant

melasse *(Fr)*—Molasses

melba—Fruits served on a bed of ice cream.

melba toast—A thin toast, very dry. Good to serve with meat pates, dips, caviar and other spreads.

melocoton *(Sp)*—Peach

melon—Any of several gourds that are edible. Used as a breakfast and salad fruit.

melon *(Sp)*—Melon

melon baller—Small hand-held tool used to scoop small balls from the flesh of melons. Several sizes available.

Melone *(Ger)*—Melon

melone *(It)*—Melon

membrillo *(Sp)*—Quince

menta *(It)*—Mint

menta *(Sp)*—Spearmint

menta piperita *(It)*—Peppermint

menta romana spicata *(It)*—Spearmint

menthe *(Fr)*—Mint

menthe poivree *(Fr)*—Peppermint

menu—In an eatery the list of dishes available. Dishes are listed in a prescribed order—appetizers, soups, salads, meats, vegetables, desserts, cheeses, breads and beverages.

menu gibier *(Fr)*—Small game

meringue—Stiffly-beaten egg whites with sugar and flavorings. Used as a topping for cakes, pies, cookies and other sweets. Sometimes lightly browned before serving. Also used to make meringue baskets and vacherins. *(See Swiss Meringue, Italian Meringue and Cooked Meringue)*

merlan *(Fr)*—Whiting fish

mescal *(Mex)*—Alcoholic beverage distilled from various species of agave and maguey plants.

Messer *(Ger)*—Knife

metate *(Sp)*—Primitive stone handmill used for grinding various dried grains.

Mexican ground cherry—Tomatillo

microwave oven—An electric counter top oven that cooks food by radiation. Cooking time is drastically reduced. Also an excellent way to warm up leftovers, breads and rolls. CAUTION—Never put anything of metal in the microwave.

miel *(Fr, Sp)*—Honey

miele *(It)*—Honey

mignonette *(Fr)*—Coarsely-ground pepper

mijoter *(Fr)*—To simmer

Milch *(Ger)*—Milk

milk—The liquid produced by the mammary glands of certain animals. The milk of the cow is widely used. Can be drunk as a beverage plain or flavored. Widely used in cooking. The cream from milk can be used as a whipped topping or churned to produce butter. The whole milk and whey are used to make various cheeses. Homogenized milk will not sour; it spoils.

milk cow—That breed of female bovine which produces milk for human consumption.

milk shake—Creamy drink made of milk, ice cream and flavorings. Mixed in a blender. Very thick. A snack food.

milkfat—*(See Butterfat)*

mill—Small machine used to pulverize (grind) foodstuffs such as coffee, peppers, breadcrumbs, grains and spices. Hand operated and electric types are available. Generally a specific mill is used for each food.

mille-feuille *(Fr)*—A flaky pastry with various fillings between the layers. A napoleon.

millet—A cereal grain widely used in Europe. Used as a breakfast cereal. Cooks easily. In baking it may be used to replace sesame or sunflower seeds. Can be ground into a meal.

milosti *(Cz)*—A deep fried, rich pastry, served hot.

milt—Fish roe

minced meat *(Eng)*—Ground meat

mincemeat—A chopped mixture of apples, raisins, spices and rum or brandy. The American type has meat added. The English type does not. The mincemeat should be allowed to ripen for at least a month before using. It is made into pies, tarts and is used in cakes, omelettes, cookies and other dishes.,

minestrone—Spicy thick soup with vegetables and pasta.

minerals—Homogenous crystalline substances needed for a healthy diet. Minerals are generally obtained from the earth and in the plants we eat. May be artificially added to the diet in the form of tablets made for this purpose.

mineral water—Water from natural springs. May be purchased in bottles. The water from different springs can have a different taste.

minestra *(It)*—Minestrone

mint—An aromatic shrub with fragrant foliage. Used to make various flavorings, such as spearmint and peppermint.

mint jelly—Apple jelly flavored with fresh mint and colored green. Good accompaniment for roast lamb.

mint julep—An alcoholic drink made of whisky or brandy, sugar, fresh mint and ice. Served in a tall frosted glass or a silver mint-julep cup.

mints—Small mint flavored candy rounds used to freshen the breath after a meal.

minute steak—A small thin steak that can be cooked quickly. Can be purchased or the cook can make them.

Minze *(Ger)*—Mint

mirepoix *(Fr)*—A cooked mixture of chopped vegetables and sometimes meat. Used to coat various cuts of meat. Also in certain sauces such as Espagnole.

mirliton—Name given to the chayote in Louisiana and Mississippi.

miroton *(Fr)*—Beef collops smothered in onions.

Mississippi Mud cake—A popular chocolate cake in the southern United States. Some recipes call for marshmallows and nuts in addition to the cocoa.

mitten, cooking—A large padded mitten used for holding hot pots, pans and dishes.

mocha—A type of coffee bean from Mocha, a port in Yemen. Can be brewed alone, but it is more commonly blended with other coffee varieties. Mocha is also a flavoring.

mock turtle soup—Soup made with calf's head, spice and other ingredients. Has the taste and look of green turtle soup.

moelle de boeuf *(Fr)*—Beef marrow

Mohn *(Ger)*—Poppyseed

Mohrrube *(Ger)*—Carrot

moist cooking—Foods that are cooked with a liquid. Especially roasts and fowl. Water, broth, stock or juices can be used.

moka *(Fr)*—Mocha

molasses—A dark syrup made from the juice of sweet sorghum cane. *(See Sorghum, sweet)*

mold—1) Any of a variety of hollow containers in which various preparations are put to solidify. These containers are made of various materials. 2) Surface growth of fungus on food.

mole *(Mex)*—Spicy sauce made with unsweetened chocolate.

molinillo *(Sp)*—Wooden sticks that are used to stir chocolate milk. By gyrating the sticks between the palms of the hands, the chocolate milk is made frothy. Can be used in the pan, cup or glass.

mollusk—Any of several aquatic invertebrate which includes clams, snails, squids and oysters.

mollusque *(Fr)*—Mollusk

monkey bread—A yeast bread that is seasoned and baked in a special ceramic container.

monkey bread pot—Special pot used to bake monkey bread. Is usually made of ceramic and is shaped like a flower pot.

monkey nuts *(Eng)*—Peanuts

monosodium glutamate—A flavor enhancer. Flavorless. MSG.

Monterey Jack cheese—A cheddar cheese. Firm with tiny holes. Used in cooking, snacks and as a sandwich filling.

morel—An edible mushroom.

morille *(Fr)*—Morel

Mornay sauce *(Fr)*—Basically a white sauce that has various ingredients added, depending on what type of food it is being used on. Always contains one or two types of cheese.

morsel—A small piece of food.

mortadella *(It)*—Bologna

mortadelle *(Fr)*—Bologna

mortar—A tool consisting of a bowl and a pestle. Used to pulverize and crush various things. Can be made of wood, marble, stone or metal. Used to crush various spices and herbs. Can also be used on garlic and like items. Mortars made of wood will pick up flavors.

mortier *(Fr)*—Mortar

mortifier *(Fr)*—*(See Hanging)*

morue *(Fr)*—Codfish

Moscovite *(Fr)*—A dessert similar to Bavarian cream, except it is made in a hexagonal mold. An iced bombe.

Mosel wine *(Ger)*—A white wine from the Mosel Valley in West Germany.

mostarda *(It)*—Mustard

mostaza *(Sp)*—Mustard

mother—The slimy thick substance that forms in vinegar. Is not harmful.

mould—Same as mold

moule *(Fr)*—Mussel

moule *(Fr)*—Mold

Mouli—Brand name for several types of hand-held graters.

moulin *(Fr)*—(See Mill)

mountain oysters—The testicles of calves, sheep, boars and other animals. Often breaded and pan fried. Also called Rocky Mountain oysters.

moussaka *(Ger)*—Baked dish of ground lamb or beef, sliced eggplant and topped with cheese.

mousseline *(Fr)*—Various dishes with whipped cream added. Also sauces enriched with whipped cream. In confectionery refers to pastries and certain cakes of a delicate nature.

mousses—Generally a cream dessert that is chilled or frozen in a mold. Also can apply to some hot dishes.

moutarde *(Fr)*—Mustard

moutardelle *(Fr)*—A kind of horseradish.

mouton *(Fr)*—Mutton; sheep

moyeu *(Fr)*—Old word that means the yolk of an egg.

mozzarella—A hard cheese. Bland in taste. Used in cooking especially on pizzas.

MSG—Monosodium glutamate

mud *(sl)*—American slang for coffee.

muffin tin—Special baking pan for cooking muffins. Comes in various sizes.

muffineer—A closed container with small holes in the top. Used for sprinkling confectioners sugar and flour.

muffins—Small round cakes baked in a special baking pan.

mug—A cup shaped container for drinking. Usually used for hot liquids. Can have a handle.

mulberry—Fruit of this tree. Shaped like blackberries and about the same size. Used to make jams and jellies. A syrup is also made which has a slight tart flavor.

mulberry wine—A dark red-black wine made from the fruit of the mulberry tree. Used as an aperitif or cocktail. Quite often homemade. White wine can be flavored with the mulberry.

mulled cider—Apple cider with sugar and spices, simmered and served very hot.

mulligatawny hotpot—Highly spiced dish of chicken, curry powder and rice. May also contain other spices.

munchies *(sl)*—Literally, snacks of various kinds.

mung bean noodles *(Or)*—Noodles made with mung bean flour. Are white, thin and brittle. Become transluscent when soaked.

mung bean sprouts—Mung beans that are sprouted. Eaten raw or used in stir-fry vegetables.

mung bean threads *(Or)*—Same as mung bean noodles.

Munster—A semi-hard cheese with aniseed or caraway mixed throughout.

mure *(Fr)*—Mulberry

muscade *(Fr)*—Nutmeg

mush—Cornmeal gruel. *(See Cornmeal Mush)*

mushroom—A fungus that is used extensively in cookery. They can be eaten raw in salads, braised in butter, in soups, stews, dips and sauces. If gathering wild mushrooms, use extreme caution as many varieties are poisonous.

mushroom brush—Small brush used to clean mushrooms. A small paint brush may be substituted.

mushroom fluter—Small hand tool used to make grooves in the mushroom caps.

Muskatblute *(Ger)*—Mace

Muskatnuss *(Ger)*—Nutmeg

muskmelon—Melon with green or orange flesh. Is eaten raw and is quite sweet.

muslin—A thin cotton fabric which can be used for straining liquids and as a cover for the pastry board.

mussel—Any of a variety of bivalve mollusks. The flesh is whitish and has a very delicate taste. May be steamed in the shell or the flesh can be deep fried or sauteed.

mustard—The seed of the mustard plant has various culinary uses. Whole seeds are used in pickling. Used crushed in some dishes. Can be ground into a paste for use as a condiment.

mustard greens—The young leaves of some mustard plants are used a potherb. It is often one of the first vegetables in the spring.

mustard, prepared—*(See Prepared Mustard)*

mustard spinach—A mustard green. Its name probably comes from its resemblance to some variety of spinach. Does not taste like spinach.

mutton—Meat of older sheep. Generally sheep that are over two years of age. The older the sheep the coarser the flesh.

mycologist—One who studies/collects fungi-mushrooms.

myost—A semi-hard cheese made from whey. It is mild and sweetish.

nabo *(Sp)*—Turnip

nachos *(Mex)*—Snacks; hors d'-oeuvres. Tortilla chips with cheese sauce.

nalesniki *(Rus)*—Mixture of white cheese and butter used to stuff pancakes that are made without sugar. They are then dipped in butter and deep fried.

nam pla *(Viet)*—*(See Nuoc Nam)*

napkin—Square of cloth or paper used to wipe lips and fingers while eating. It is laid in the lap to catch any food scraps or dribbles.

napoleon *(Fr)*—A rich pastry with a cream filling.

nappe *(Fr)*—Food lightly covered with sauce.

naranja *(Sp)*—Orange

nasturtium—The flowers and leaves are similar to watercress in flavor. Can be used in green salads. Be sure the leaves are young and tender. *(See Chapter III)*

nasu *(Ja)*—Japanese eggplant

natural cheese—Soft cheeses made from fresh milk. They are not aged or fermented. Cottage, pot, ricotta, feta and neufchatel are some of the natural cheeses. Perishable. Should be served from the refrigerator.

natural foods—Generally foods prepared or preserved without the addition of preservatives. May also refer to organic and health-type foods.

navarin *(Fr)*—Mutton or lamb ragout made with small onions and potatoes.

navet *(Fr)*—Turnip

navy beans—Small, dried, white beans.

Neopolitan bread *(It)*—A rich pastry with lemon rind and grated almonds. Served with tea or coffee. Armenian Gatah is similar.

neopolitan ice cream—Three alternate layers of different flavored ice creams are formed into a block. To serve, the block is sliced from the end so that each slice has some of each flavor. Generally the flavors used are vanilla, chocolate and strawberry.

near beer—Beer with a very low alcohol content. There are some brands with no alcohol.

nectarine—A fleshy fruit similar to the peach but smooth skinned. Is eaten fresh and in fruit salads.

negus—Wine with sugar, lemons and nutmeg.

neige *(Fr)*—Snow

Nelkenpfeffer *(Ger)*—Allspice

neroli *(Fr)*—Oil extracted from orange blossoms and used as a flavoring in confections and in some liqueurs.

nesselrode *(Fr)*—A pudding made with cream, chestnuts, candied and dried fruits and other ingredients, then frozen.

neufchatel—A soft, natural cheese.

neve *(It)*—Snow

New Zealand spinach—A potherb that is high in potassium. Can be used the same as spinach. Not a member of the spinach family.

Newburg sauce—A sauce generally used for seafood, consisting of butter, cream, egg yolks and wine.

nibbles—Small snacks, such as roasted nuts, pretzels, popcorn, pickles, crackers, etc.

nicoise *(Fr)*—Foods prepared with tomatoes and garlic. A style from Nice, France.

Nierenbaum *(Ger)*—Cashew

nieve *(Sp)*—Snow

nippy—Something that is biting and pungent in taste.

noce *(It)*—Nut

noce di cocco *(It)*—Coconut

noce moscata *(It)*—Nutmeg

nogada *(Mex)*—Pecan candy

noisette *(Fr)*—Hazelnut

noix *(Fr)*—Nut; walnut

noix d'acajou *(Fr)*—Cashew

noix de coco *(Fr)*—Coconut

nokkelost—A hard cheese made from skim milk with various spices added.

nonpareil—A chocolate candy. It is small and flat and covered with white sugar pellets.

nonparielle *(Fr)*—Small capers pickled in vinegar.

noodles, egg—Pasta made with eggs and flour. Rolled in long flat strips and dried. Are cooked in stock, broth or water. Should be cooked al dente. Can be served with a sauce or butter and seasonings. Meats and/or chopped vegetables are often added to create a main dish. Small appliances are available to make fresh egg noodles.

Normandy sauce—Fish-flavored cream sauce, used on filet of sole and other fish.

northern beans—Small, white, dried beans.

Norwegian omelette *(Fr)*—Baked Alaska

nougat—Candy made with roasted almonds or walnuts and syrup or honey. A solid but soft candy. Can be used as centers for dipped chocolates.

nouilles *(Fr)*—Egg noodles

nova—Smoked salmon; lox

noyer *(Fr)*—Walnut tree

nubbin—A small ear of corn, often an imperfect one.

nuez *(Sp)*—Nut

nuez moscada *(Sp)*—Nutmeg

nuoc nam *(Viet)*—A fermented fish sauce. Should be available in Oriental groceries.

Nub *(Ger)*—Nut

nut—Fruit with the meat enclosed in a hard shell. *(See individual listings, i.e., walnut, almond, filbert, etc.)*

nutcracker—A tool for opening nut shells.

nutmeg grater—Special designed mill for grating whole nutmegs.

O

oatmeal—A breakfast cereal made from oats. They are cooked and served hot with sugar and cream, if desired. The oats are rolled to form small flakes and used in various cookie and cake recipes.

oats—A cereal grain. Mainly an animal grain eaten by man as a breakfast cereal. *(See Oatmeal)*

oca—Wood sorrel

octopus—An edible marine mollusk. The flesh must be beaten before cooking.

oenophile—A connoisseur or lover of wine.

oeuf *(Fr)*—Egg

oeufs brouilles *(Fr)*—Buttered eggs

oeufs frais *(Fr)*—New laid eggs.

oeufs a la coque *(Fr)*—Boiled eggs

oeufs a la neige *(Fr)*—Whisked eggs

oeufs a l'indienne *(Fr)*—Curried eggs

oeufs poches *(Fr)*—Poached eggs

offal—Various edible parts of meat animals, such as ears, tongue, tail, kidneys, liver and heart.

oignon *(Fr)*—Onion

oil—Greasy liquid obtained from plants. Can be made from corn, olives, sunflower seed, safflower seeds, palm, poppy, peanut, mustard, almond, walnuts, hazelnuts and grapeseeds. Used in cooking.

oke—Short for okolehao

okolehao—A liquor distilled from sugar cane molasses and other ingredients. Native to the Hawaiian Islands. Dark in color with a smoky flavor and smell. Occasionally found in the United States.

okra—The pods of a tall growing plant. The pods are picked while young. Can be stewed plain, with onions and tomatoes or breaded with cornmeal and fried. A necessary ingredient of several Creole dishes, namely gumbo and jambalaya. When stewing, the pods should be pricked and a little vinegar added to the water. This will prevent the thick scum from forming. Very small pods can be pickled.

old fashioned oats—Regular oatmeal

oleomargarine—Margarine

olio d'oliva *(It)*—Olive oil

oliva *(Sp)*—Olive

olive—One of the oldest known fruits. Native to the Mediterranean. Grown commercially in California. The fruit is generally cured in a salt brine. Canned ripe olives are black in color and are rather bland in taste. The canned green olives have a dull color and are rather salty and pungent. Green olives are often stuffed with pimento pepper. Used on the relish tray, in salads and in various hot dishes. Are available whole, pitted, sliced and chopped.

olive oil—A fine salad and cooking oil derived from olives. There are three grades of oil. EXTRA VIRGIN - green color with a strong olive flavor. VIRGIN - lighter in color and milder in taste. PURE - light green or yellow to clear in color and with a mild taste. This is the most common grade.

Olivenol *(Ger)*—Olive oil

olla *(Mex)*—A stewpot

omelet—Eggs beaten with water or milk and cooked until set. Usually in a frying or omelet pan. Some cooks prefer to cook them without stirring, others stir. Cooked on one side only. When done, the omelet is folded over to form a half circle. Various fillings can be added before folding. Sometimes a sauce is also served over the omelet.

Omelett *(Ger)*—Omelet

omelette *(Fr)*—Omelet

omelette a la Norvegienne *(Fr)*—Baked Alaska

onion—A root herb. Probably the most widely used of the herbs. Eaten in several forms. The small immature bulb, with the green blades, are eaten in salads, as they are and in some cooked dishes. The green blades can be chopped and used as a topping or as a garnish. The mature bulb, called a dried onion, is used in many cooked dishes and in green, meat and pasta salads. The dried onion can be sliced and the rings dipped in batter and deep fried or the rings can be sauteed and used as a topping for hamburgers and liver. Dried onions are available in the powder or flaked form. Onion juice is also available.

onion fork—Tool with several sharp tines that is inserted in the dried onion. This holds it steady while it is sliced.

onion rings—Large dried onions are peeled then sliced into fairly thick slices. The rings are separated, dipped into batter and deep fried until golden brown. Used as an edible garnish.

open faced sandwich—*(See Sandwich)*

opossum—A wild North American marsupial, sometimes tree dwelling. It is hunted for its culinary value and pelt. It can reach the size of an adult rabbit. The flesh is commonly made into a stew. The pelt is used for clothing.

orange—A citrus fruit used fresh and as a juice fruit. Principal varieties are the Navel, used mainly for eating; and the Valencia, used mainly for its juice. Either one can be used in cooking although the Valencia is superior. The white inner membrane of the Navel tends to impart a bitter taste when bruised, as in juice extraction. The colored portion of the skin is used as zest. The peel can be candied and used in confections and cakes.

orangeade—A beverage flavored with oranges. Served cold. Carbonated soda may be used instead of water.

orange pekoe—A black tea. The most widely used tea in America.

organic—Food grown and prepared without the use of chemicals or artificial preservatives.

oregano *(Sp)*—Wild marjoram

orejones *(Sp)*—Dried fruit

orge *(Fr)*—Barley

orgeat *(Fr)*—Syrup made from water, sugar and almonds. Sometimes orange flower water is used.

oriental cucumber—Chinese cucumber

ortolan—A small bird that in Europe is much prized as a culinary treat.

oseille *(Fr)*—Sorrel; Sorrel leaves

osso-bucco *(It)*—Veal shanks cooked in white wine.

ostra *(Sp)*—Oyster

ostrica *(It)*—Oyster

ostrich—A flightless bird of Africa and Arabia. Its wings are tender enough to eat.

ounce—A unit of weight. Sixteen ounces equal one pound.

out-of-hand—Foods that can be held in the hand while eating.

ouzo *(Gr)*—An alcoholic beverage distilled from wine or grain. Flavored with aniseed.

oveja *(Sp)*—A sheep

oven, convection—Basically the same as a conventional oven. Has the ability to circulate the hot air around the items being cooked. Cooking is faster. Usually made as a portable counter top appliance.

oven, conventional—An enclosed space that may be heated to various controlled temperatures. Most ovens are contained in the kitchen range, and are heated by gas or electricity. Oven should be checked periodically for correct heating.

over easy—Method of cooking eggs. The eggs are fried on one side then gently turned over and cooked briefly.

ovine—Sheep; lamb

ox—The adult castrated male of the common cattle. Cooking is the same as beef, but caution should be taken as the meat tends to be tougher.

Oxford sauce *(Eng)*—Cold sauce generally served with venison. Made of jelly, wine, shallots, the gratings and juice of oranges and lemons, mustard and ginger.

oxtail soup—Soup made from braised beef tails.

oxymel *(Fr)*—Syrup made of honey and vinegar.

oyster—A shell fish. Can be eaten raw from the shell, steamed, broiled, breaded and sauteed, in stews, dressings. A versatile shellfish. Available fresh or canned.

oyster cracker—A small round puffed cracker that is usually served with oyster stew.

oyster knife—A very short-bladed knife with a sharp point. Is used to open oyster and clam shells and for cutting the muscle.

oyster plant—*(See Salsify)*

oz—Abbreviation for ounce.

paella *(Sp)*—A rice, seafood and poultry casserole seasoned with saffron and other spices.

paella pan—Large shallow pan, with handles, used for making and serving paella in.

pai *(ErAm)*—Pie

pailles de parmesan *(Fr)*—Cheese straws

pain *(Fr)*—Bread

pain de fruits *(Fr)*—Fruit mold

pain de seigle *(Fr)*—Rye bread

pain d'epices *(Fr)*—Gingerbread. Or a bread made with honey and rum. Fruit can also be added.

pains *(Fr)*—Dishes, hot or cold, made of forcemeat formed in special molds. If hot, is cooked in a bain marie. If cold, put into an aspic lined mold and chilled.

pale ale *(Eng)*—A light English beer.

palette knife—*(See spatula)*

palm hearts—The tender shoots of palm (hearts) are used in the same manner as asparagus.

Pampelmuse *(Ger)*—Grapefruit

pan—Any container used to cook in.

pan *(Sp)*—Bread

panada—1) A kind of soup made of bread, stock, milk or water and butter. 2) A paste of flour, bread and toast used as binding for meat and fish forcemeats.

panais *(Fr)*—Parsnip

pancake—A flat cake made from a thin batter that is poured on a hot griddle and browned on both sides. Similar to a crepe but thicker. A breakfast or late supper dish. Usually served with butter, syrup or jelly.

pancetta *(It)*—Porkbelly; bacon

pandowdy—A fruit dessert topped with a rich biscuit dough. Similar to cobbler. Baked in a deep dish.

pane *(It)*—Bread

paner *(Fr)*—To crumb. Coat with bread crumbs.

panino imbottito *(It)*—Sandwich

pan nero *(It)*—A chocolate bread. Can be served cold with coffee.

pantry—Area adjacent to the kitchen where foods and utensils are stored. In a large pantry, the breads and pastries can be prepared here and taken to the kitchen for baking.

panure *(Fr)*—Fine bread crumbs. Used to sprinkle over dishes to be baked.

papaya—A yellow-skinned American tropical fruit. Its seeds are black. They are edible and have a peppery taste. It is almost always eaten raw. The ripe mashed flesh is sometimes used as a facial moisturizer.

papaw—The custard-like fruit of this tree should be picked when ripe. It is usually eaten raw. Native to the eastern and northern United States.

papillote *(Fr)*—Buttered or oiled paper used to enclose various foods for grilling or baking.

paprica *(It)*—Paprika

paprika *(Fr, Ger)*—Paprika

paprikash—Food seasoned with paprika.

paraffin—An odorless substance obtained from oil. It is used to seal jars of jams and jellies. Also used in making candles. It is melted before using. CAUTION—very flammable.

parfait—Dessert served in special glasses, generally tall. A parfait can be of puddings, ice creams, sherbets, gelatins and whipped creams. Usually two or more flavors or substances are used to make an attractive dessert.

paring knife—Short bladed knives used in preparing various foods. Blades are about three inches in length, permitting close control when preparing small fruits and vegetables. A knife of many uses.

Parker House rolls—Yeast rolls that after forming are creased along the center and folded in half. Then baked.

parmesan—A hard cheese that is ground for use at the table as a topping. Mild flavor. Available ground.

parmentier *(Fr)*—Method of preparing certain dishes which always includes potatoes.

parsley—A biennial plant which is used as a flavoring in cooking and the sprigs of leaves are used for garnishing. Several varieties available. Some varieties have a root that is eaten.

parsnip—An edible root that can be prepared like potatoes. Also may be added to soups and stews.

pasa *(Sp)*—Raisin

pashka *(Rus)*—A molded dish made of cottage cheese, sour cream, butter, sugar, flavorings, lemon rind, almonds and raisins. It is chilled. Unmolded it is decorated with nuts, raisins and candied fruits.

passarelle *(Fr)*—Dried Muscat grapes.

passe-puree *(Fr)*—A puree presser

passion fruit—The edible fruit of the giant granadilla or passion fruit tree. A dessert fruit. Can be used in fruit salads or eaten alone.

passoire *(Fr)*—A colander or strainer

pasta *(It)*—Dough from which spaghetti, noodles and other shaped forms are made. General name for such dishes. Dough is usually made of eggs, flour and sometimes a very small amount of oil.

pasta afoglia *(It)*—Puff paste

pasta d'arachidi *(It)*—Peanut butter

pasta machine—A hand operated or electric machine used to form various pastas.

pastel *(Sp)*—Pie, cake

Pastete *(Ger)*—A savory pie.

pasteque *(Fr)*—Watermelon

pastille—A small round candy or medicine drop.

pastrami—Cut of beef that is highly seasoned and smoked. Usually a shoulder cut is used. Can be used as an entree, cold on the buffet or picnic table and as a sandwich filling.

pastry—1) Any dough that is used for pies, tarts and other pastries. Generally made with flour, water and some type of fat. Usually butter or a mixture of butter and solid shortening. Lard is very good for pie pastry. Butter makes a flaky crust. 2) Any of a variety of sweets using pastry dough as the case.

pastry bag—A cloth or plastic bag into which various sized nozzles may be attached. Icings, soft doughs and pureed foods are placed in the bag. By exerting pressure on the bag, the food is forced out thru the nozzle creating various designs and shapes. Used for decorating of dishes, cakes, pastries and for dispensing cream puff pastry. Parchment paper can be cut and formed into a disposable pastry bag.

pastry blender—Hand tool. Several wire strands are curved and attached to a handle. Used to blend solid fats into flour.

pastry brush—Various sized brushes used to apply washes to doughs, tarts, pies, cookies, breads and cakes. Also for dusting of flours, sugars and spices. May be made of hog bristles, nylon strands or feathers.

pastry coffins—Pastry shells for meat dishes.

pastry cream—A custard made of sugar, eggs, flour, milk and flavorings.

pastry crimper—Small tongs used to make decorative edges on tarts, pies and other pastries. The ends are flat. Not a common kitchen tool.

pastry cutter—Tool used to cut pastry. Generally they are small, round, metal wheels attached to a short handle. The wheel can be either plain or crimped.

pastry flour—A medium gluten flour. Good for pie and tart doughs as it will absorb a large amount of fat.

pastry prickers—Small devices used to prick holes in pastry before baking.

pastry stamp—Tool used to press delicate designs onto the surface of cookies, pastries, pates, pies and other dishes the cook wishes to decorate. Some are equipped with changeable design plates.

pastry tube—Similar to a cake decorator, but having larger nozzle tips. Used to apply decorative borders and designs to meat and vegetable dishes. Pureed foods are used. Also used when dispensing cream puff paste or similar material.

pastry wheel—*(See Pastry Cutter)*

pasty—In general, filled tarts that are baked. Fillings can include ground meat, cooked vegetables or a combination of both.

patata *(It, Sp)*—Potato

pate *(Fr)*—1) A pie, patty or pasty. 2) Meat ground fine and formed into various shapes. Served with crackers or toast. Used as an hor d'ouevre. 3) A crust or pastry dough.

pate a chou *(Fr)*—Cream puff pastry.

pate brisee *(Fr)*—Puff paste

pate feuilletee *(Fr)*—Puff paste

patent clam shucker—A thin blade mounted on a base. Will open and cut through the clam when the blade is depressed.

patisserie *(Fr)*—Pastry; pastry business.

patisserie au fromage *(Fr)*—Cheese cake.

patissier *(Fr)*—Pastry cook

patty tins—Small shallow tins used for baking patty shells.

pave *(Fr)*—Specifically a square or oblong shaped solid. Cold sweet or meat mousses are often formed in this manner. Also this can refer to a layered cake.

pavot *(Fr)*—A garden variety of poppy.

pawpaw—*(See Papaw)*

paysanne *(Fr)*—Meat or poultry braised with vegetables. Peasant cooking.

pea—The edible seed of a bushy legume. The peas may be eaten fresh or dried. It has a very delicate flavor. Cooking should be al dente. Butter, salt, pepper or nutmeg can be added after cooking. Split pea soup is made from the dried seed. One variety is called snap pea. The pod and seed are both cooked and eaten. This snap pea may also be used as a crudite. Very good as a stir fry vegetable.

peach—A sweet, juicy fruit. Two types, the cling and the freestone. The flesh of the cling adheres to the seed whereas the freestone comes free from the seed. Used as a fresh fruit, with cream and in fruit salads. Makes excellent pies and cobblers. Can be canned and sometimes frozen. Frozen peaches tend to become dark colored when thawed. Makes an excellent jam alone or with pineapple. Also can be dried and used in fried pies and to make peach leather.

peach liqueur—A peach flavored liqueur.

peacock—At one time this fowl was highly esteemed by gormands. Today it is rarely cooked. If it is cooked, follow the directions for pheasant.

peanut—The seed of an annual herb enclosed in a dried fibrous shell. A native to South America, it is grown in most temperate regions of the world. After shelling, the nuts are roasted and can be served as a snack or ground into a thick butter. Peanut butter is popular as a sandwich spread and is used in certain sauces and widely used in cookies and other confections. A very fine oil is made from the peanut, rivaling olive oil for use in cooking and salads.

peanut brittle—A brittle candy made of sugar, water and peanuts.

peanut butter—A spread made from ground peanuts.

pear—A fleshy fruit from a tree related to the apple. An excellent fruit fresh, cooked or canned. Excellent dessert when poached in sugar syrup with brandy or vanilla. Does not freeze. Dries well. Some varieties are Bartlett, Anjou, Bosc, Seckel. The Asian varieties are generally round, crisp and mild tasting.

pear tomato—A small tomato shaped like a pear. Red and yellow varieties available.

pearl barley—Barley which has had the husk and germ removed.

pearl tapioca—Thickening agent, finely-ground. Same as tapioca.

pease *(Er.Am)*—Cowpea

peau *(Fr)*—Skin; peel

pecan—A rich and flavorful nut. Can be eaten from the shell or used in various confections. Shells are thin and easy to crack.

peche *(Fr)*—Peach

peck—Unit of measure equal to eight quarts.

pectin—The mucilaginous substance occurring naturally in certain fruits and vegetables. The fruit's skin is especially rich in pectin and should be used. It is from this substance, that when sugar is added, fruit juices can be made into jelly. Today, when making jellies and james, we add a commercial pectin to insure the setting.

peel—The skin of a fruit or vegetable.

peelers—Hand-held tool used for peeling potatoes, carrots, celery and other fruits and vegetables. Can also be used to curl chocolate and to make carrot curls. Many types available.

peeling—The skin of a fruit or vegetable.

peg rolling pin—Rolling pin with small barbs on the surface. Pricks the dough as it is rolled.

pekoe tea—A black tea. *(See orange pekoe tea)*

pelican—A large, web-footed water fowl. Although its meat is oily and tough it is eaten in some countries. There are both fresh water and salt water types.

pelmeni *(Rus)*—Meat filled ravioli generally served in soup. Can be boiled plain and served with a dollop of sour cream.

pemmican—Dried meat that is powdered and mixed with fat. It can be eaten as is or boiled. The North American Indian is credited with developing this dried food. It is generally formed into small cakes. Hikers and campers find this a handy food to carry.

penuche—A fudge-like candy that is made with brown sugar. Sometimes nuts are added.

pepe *(It)*—Pepper

pepe di Caienna *(It)*—Red pepper

pepitas *(Mex)*—Toasted squash seeds. Served as an appetizer and in various dishes. Generally available in markets that sell Mexican foods.

pepper mill—Device used to grind peppercorns. Fresh ground pepper is at its height of flavor.

pepper pot—1) A small table dish with spoon. Used to hold ground pepper. 2) A highly seasoned West Indian or Philadelphian stew.

peppermint—An aromatic plant that is very pungent. The leaves are used as a flavoring, either fresh or dried. An essence is made from the plant. Also a candy flavored with peppermint.

peppermint schnapps—A strong gin, flavored with peppermint.

pepperoni—A dry sausage of beef and pork seasoned with ground red pepper.

peppers—Several varieties of plants that bear both sweet and hot fruits. Both kind can be used in stews, soups and other cooked dishes. The sweet type can also be used fresh in salads and on the relish tray. The sweet bell shaped pepper is often stuffed with a meat mixture and baked. Both are used in various pickled relishes. Also known as bell pepper, sweet pepper and chili or hot pepper. *(See Pepper, Black & White and Chilies in the Spice Section)*

pepper shaker—Small cylinder with removable lid that is pierced with holes. Used to dispense ground pepper.

pera *(It, Sp)*—Pear

percolateur *(Fr)*—A percolator type coffee maker.

perdrix *(Fr)*—Partridge

perejil *(Sp)*—Parsley

Pernod—A French liqueur with a distinct licorice taste. Occasionally used in cooking.

Perrier—Brand name for a highly effervescent water imported from France. Very popular in the United States.

persian walnuts—Same as English walnuts.

persil *(Fr)*—Parsley

persiller *(Fr)*—To sprinkle a dish with chopped parsley.

persimmon—This orange colored fruit is usually eaten raw. It can be used in some breads and cookies. The ripe fruit can be frozen and will retain its flavor when thawed. The Japanese variety, because of its sweetness, can be dried. If possible buy fruits that are bright in color and are very firm. Let ripen in a warm room. They should be soft when ripe.

pesca *(It)*—Peach

pescado *(Sp)*—Fish

pesce *(It)*—Fish

pestle—Rod used in a mortar to crush and pulverize. Can be made of hardwood, marble, stone or metal.

Petersilie *(Ger)*—Parsley

petit dejeuner *(Fr)*—Breakfast

petit lait *(Fr)*—Whey

petit souper *(Fr)*—An informal supper

petit verre *(Fr)*—A small glass, especially of liqueur.

petits fours—Small iced cakes

petits pois *(Fr)*—Small garden peas

petoncle *(Fr)*—Scallops

Peychaud's bitters—A bitters usually found in the state of Louisiana. Is slightly more pungent than Angostura bitters.

Pfannkuchen, Apfel *(Ger)*—A pancake with diced apples that is baked in a large skillet. Cut in wedges it is served with sugar and lemon juice sprinkled over it.

Pfeffer *(Ger)*—Pepper

Pfefferkuchen *(Ger)*—Gingerbread

Pfirsich *(Ger)*—Peach

Pflaume *(Ger)*—Plum

Pflaumenkuchen *(Ger)*—Plum tart

pheasant—A game bird that is also raised commercially. Can be roasted or braised and cooked in a cream sauce.

phyllo dough (leaves)—An extremely thin pasta dough. It is generally purchased ready to use. Used to make various confections, and meat and vegetable tarts and dishes.

piccalilli—Relish made of chopped vegetables, spices and vinegar. Sometimes sugar is used.

pickle—Cucumbers preserved in various brines; salt, sugar or vinegar. Often spices, herbs and other flavorings are added. Used as a condiment.

pickle fork—Small, often decorative, forks used to spear pickles from the jar or serving dish.

pickling spices—A blend of whole and broken spices, herbs and seeds. Can be purchased or the cook can create his own.

pie—Fruit, nut, custard and cream pies are considered an American innovation. They are baked in a shallow, round pan. Pie crust crust dough is used to line the pan and sometimes is used as a top covering. Most fruit pies have a top crust. Custard, nut and cream pies do not. Cream pies are generally put in a baked blind crust. Often topped with meringue and lightly browned. Fruit and nut pies are often served with whipped cream or ice cream. Some crusts are made of crushed graham crackers or cookies, nuts or coconut. Apple pie is often served with a slice of good cheddar cheese. Pies are widely eaten for dessert and for snacks.

pie bird—A small, ceramic bird, generally with an opened up-reached mouth, that is placed on the bottom of a two crust pie. The beak breaks through the top crust. This permits the steam to escape, helping to keep the juices from boiling out. A pie funnel.

pie crust—A dough made of flour, salt, water and fat. Lard is an excellent fat. Used mainly for pies, cobblers and fruit tarts. Some recipes call for the addition of eggs, sugar or spices. May also be called pastry dough. There are four types of crust—short flake, medium flake, long flake and crumb. *(See the individual listings)*

pie dishes—Deep containers used for baking meat and fruit pies. Made of ceramic, glass or metal. The American cobbler is made in this type of dish.

pie funnel—Device placed in a two-crust pie. It sits on the bottom crust. It supports and pierces the top crust permitting steam to escape. *(See Pie Bird)*

pie pans—*(See Pie Tins)*

pie plant *(ErAm)*—Rhubarb

pie plates—*(See Pie Tins)*

pie safe—A tall cabinet that was used in the kitchen or pantry. The top half has doors with perforated metal or wire screen surfaces. This allows for air circulation. The lower half generally has solid doors. This cabinet was used to store pies, cakes and breads.

pie spatula—A triangular piece of metal with an attached handle. It is placed in the bottom of the pie pan. The bottom crust is then placed in the pan. When the pie is ready to be cut, the first cut is made on either side of the spatula. This piece is then lifted out with ease.

pie tins—Containers with sloping sides. Rather shallow. Used for baking pies and tarts. Can be made of metal, glass or ceramic. Available in various depths and diameters. *(See Tins)*

pie weights—*(See Baking Beads)*

piece *(Fr)*—Portion, joint of meat

piece de resistance *(Fr)*—The main dish of a meal.

pielet—A fruit tart

pig—Hog

pigeon—An edible bird of the dove family.

pigeonneau *(Fr)*—Pigeon, squab

pignoli—*(See Pine Nut)*

pignon *(Fr)*—Pine seed (nut)

pignut—A variety of hickory. The flesh is very bitter. Rarely used in cookery.

pigs in a blanket—1) In restaurant jargon, link sausages served rolled in hotcakes or pancakes. 2) Cabbage rolls.

pilaf, pilaff—A Middle Eastern dish of rice, meat and spices. Today, through misuse and generalization, the word pilaff applies to any rice dish with herbs and spices.

pilau, pilaw—*(See Pilaf)*

pilinut—A nut from a tree growing in the Phillippines. Eaten raw or can be ground for other uses. Has a flavor of sweet almonds.

pilon *(Fr)*—Pestle

pilsner—1) A light beer. Has a strong hops flavor. 2) Tall, slender, footed glass. Generally used for beer.

Pilz *(Ger)*—Mushroom

piment *(Fr)*—Pimento, red pepper

piment vert *(Fr)*—Green pepper

pimento—Sweet red peppers that have been thinly-sliced and cooked in jars. Used as a garnish and in salads and cheeses. Also in some luncheon meats.

pimento *(It)*—Allspice

Pimento dram—A rum and allspice flavored liqueur from Jamaica.

pimenton *(Sp)*—Paprika

pimienta *(Sp)*—Pepper

pimienta de Jamaica *(Sp)*—Allspice

pimiento *(Sp)*—Red pepper

pincee *(Fr)*—*(See Pinch)*

pinch—A unit of measure. The amount that you can hold between your thumb and first finger.

pine nut—The seed of the pine. Used in confectionery and as a snack. Tastes a little like almonds.

pine seed—Same as pine nut.

pineapple—A large, juicy, tropical fruit. Widely used in cookery. Can be purchased fresh, canned or candied. Is canned as slices, chunks and crushed. Also made into a juice.

pink bean—A dried bean with a dull pink color. Widely used in Mexican dishes.

pink ice—Ice with a small amount of bitters added. Usually frozen in cubes. Bitters give it a pink tint. Used in mixed drinks that call for bitters.

pinole *(Sp)*—Parched maize that is ground and mixed with sugar and spices.

pinon *(Sp)*—Pine kernel (nut)

pinon nuts—*(See Pine Nuts)*

pint—Unit of measure which equals 16 fluid ounces or two cups.

pinto bean—Brown, speckled, dried bean. A widely used dried bean. Good for refried beans.

pip—A small fruit seed.

pipkin—A small earthenware or metal pot.

piquant—Tart, sharp tasting.

pique-nique *(Fr)*—Picnic

piroghi *(Rus)*—A large pie

pirogi *(Rus)*—Potato filled pastries

pirozhki *(Rus)*—Small pies or tarts.

pisco *(Sp)*—A brandy from the Andes area of South America.

pisello *(It)*—Pea

pissenlit *(Fr)*—Dandelion

pistachio—A highly prized nut used in confections and baked goods. Grown commercially in the southwest United States. The nut is toasted before eating. Makes an excellent snack nut. Often salted.

pistacchio *(It)*—Pistachio

pistache *(Fr)*—Pistachio

pistacho *(Sp)*—Pistachio

Pistazienmandeln *(Ger)*—Pistachio

pit—The seed of various fruits such as cherries, dates, peaches.

pitanga—*(See Surinam Cherry)*

pitcher—A container with a handle and pouring spout. Used for various liquids.

pithy—The center of many root vegetables will become paper-like if allowed to remain in the ground past maturity. This condition is called pithy. This can happen to radishes, beets and other root vegetables.

pizza—The American pizza is an open-faced savory pie. An uncooked crust, thin or thick, is spread with a tomato based sauce. On top of this are spread cheeses, sausages, green peppers, mushrooms, anchovies and herbs. It is baked in a very hot oven, cut into wedges and served hot.

pizza *(It)*—Literally, some kind of pie. There are many different types, depending on the region of the country.

platter—A flat (oblong, square or round) dish that is used for serving food. Many platters have the sides raised so that any juices will not spill out. They can be made of the same materials as plates.

plonk *(Eng)*—Everyday wine.

pluck *(Sc)*—The innards of the sheep.

plum—A fleshy fruit that ranges in color from yellow to red to purple. There are two distinct types: the eating and cooking variety and the prune variety. Damson and Greengage are varieties used for cooking and canning. Santa Rosa, Burbank and Bluefire varieties are best eaten raw. Plums make excellent jams. *(See Prune)*

plum tomato—Similar to cherry tomatoes.

poche *(Fr)*—Ladle

pocket bread—A flat bread that can be slit on the side to form a 'pocket'. The pocket can be filled with meat or vegetable mixtures. A different kind of sandwich.

poele *(Fr)*—A frying pan, pan, stove, cooker.

poelage *(Fr)*—Pot roasting

poeles *(Fr)*—Butter roasting, especially chicken.

poelette *(Fr)*—Small frying pan.

poelon *(Fr)*—Saucepan

pogy—A flounder-like fish.

poire *(Fr)*—Pear

poire *(Fr)*—A fermented beverage made from pears.

poire d'avocat *(Fr)*—Avocado

poireau *(Fr)*—Leek

pois *(Fr)*—Pea

pois-chiche *(Fr)*—Chickpea

poisson *(Fr)*—Fish

poissoniere *(Fr)*—Fish kettle

poissonnier *(Fr)*—The chef in charge of all fish dishes. Also a fishmonger or seller of fish.

poitrine d'agneau *(Fr)*—Breast of lamb.

poivrade *(Fr)*—Pepper sauce

poivre *(Fr)*—Pepper

poivron *(Fr)*—Common name for green peppers.

Pokel *(Ger)*—A cucumber pickle.

polenta *(It)*—Thick porridge made of Indian meal or semolina. Cheese and spices are added and it is formed into a loaf. It is then sliced and fried in oil or butter.

pollame *(It)*—Fowl

pollo *(Sp)*—Chicken

polyunsaturate—Foods rich in carbon atoms. Can combine with other atoms to form new compounds. Affects the cholesterol level of one's blood.

pomace—Ground pulp of a fruit.

pomander—A ball made of fruits and spices. Used as a sachet. At one time was worn to ward off evil spirits and deities.

pome—Fruits with a thin skin covering the flesh and with the seed(s) at the center. Apples and pears are some of the pomes.

pomegranate—A small, round fruit composed of many seeds. Each seed has a thin layer of flesh. Is rather tart. Can be eaten fresh (a tedious task). The rind is stiff and leathery. The juice makes an excellent jelly. It is used to flavor grenadine syrup. The juice does not keep well. When making juice use caution in squeezing. The yellow membrane, if bruised too much, will give off a bitter substance. This will spoil the juice. A wine can be made from the juice.

pommes *(Fr)*—Apple

pommes de terre *(Fr)*—Potatoes

pommes frittes *(Ger)*—Potato chips, fried potatoes

pomodoro *(It)*—Tomato

pompelmo *(It)*—Grapefruit

pone—Oval-shaped cornbread cakes. The shape itself.

poor boy—A sandwich made on a long French roll. Generally cheeses, luncheon and other cooked meats, lettuce, tomatoes, pickles, onions and various sauces are used for filling. Literally, a sandwich of many ingredients. Can be made to serve several people.

popcorn—A variety of corn that when heated will expand into fluffy kernels. Butter and salt are often added. There are special appliances designed for popping corn. A traditional snack at the movies.

popcorn balls—A cooked sugar syrup is poured over the popped corn. It is then formed into various sized balls. It is best to butter the hands before forming the balls. A holiday confection.

popover—Pastry shell made of eggs, flour, milk and seasonings. Baked in a very hot oven using preheated popover pans. During cooking they puff up and have a hollow center. After baking they are filled with whipped cream or custard.

popover pan—Heavy, muffin-like pans used for baking popovers.

porc *(Fr)*—Pork

porcine—Hog, pig, swine

porcini *(It)*—Dried, wild Italian mushrooms.

pork—The meat of the hog. Pork should be cooked well done.

pork, cuts of

BACKBONE—Often boiled or steamed with sauerkraut.

BACON—Cut from the belly of the hog. It is cured by smoking or with salt and sugar. Generally used as a breakfast meat, it is used in other dishes. Bacon is usually bought pre-sliced although it is available in the slab with the rind attached. Bacon has its own distinct flavor.

CANADIAN BACON—The tenderloin is cured and sliced for use as a breakfast meat. Used in other dishes, most notably Eggs Benedict.

CHOPS—Cut from the loin with the bone attached. Several different cuts are made from the loin. Chops can be pan fried, baked, stuffed, grilled or broiled.

COUNTRY SPARERIBS—Cut from the meaty backbones at the shoulder end. Grill, braise or barbeque.

FEET—Usually cooked then pickled.

HAM—This is the rear leg of the hog. Can be used fresh or cured. Is available as whole ham or cut into two pieces called the butt and the shank. Fully cured hams can be eaten as is or baked. The shank portion can be cut into steaks. Also available are hams that have been boned and processed in cans. Label directions should be followed when preparing canned or other packaged hams.

INTESTINE—Thoroughly cleaned, are used as sausage casings or baked until crispy to become chitterlings.

JOWL—Generally used in pates and liverwursts. Has a strong odor and taste. May be pan fried, braised or sauteed. Stewed for pates.

LOIN—Source of loin roasts, with or without the bone, chops and Canadian bacon.

ROASTS—Can be cut from the loin, shoulder or ham. If boned and tied the loin and shoulder cuts make attractive roasts.

SAUSAGE—Can be made from all parts of the hog. Breakfast sausage is generally ground with spice and cooked fresh. Other sausages may be cured by smoking or with salts, sugars and spices. Breakfast sausages are made in patties or links.

SHOULDER—The front leg of the hog. May be roasted whole. Is less lean than the ham. Also called picnic ham. Is often cured by smoking or with salt, sugar and spices. Boston butt is cut from the shoulder.

SKIN—Can be roasted until most of the fat is removed. The skins are now very brittle and are called 'cracklins'. Can be eaten as a snack with salt, or crumbled and added to cornbread batter. The skin is also tanned to produce pigskin leather.

SPARERIBS—The ribs with little meat and fat attached. Can be roasted or grilled, generally with a basting sauce. Cut from the breast of the hog.

STEAKS—These can be cut from the fresh ham, shoulder or the shanks.

SUCKLING PIG—A hog weighing 20-35 pounds. It is sold and cooked whole. Generally oven roasted or may be spitted over a grill or open fire. Very expensive.

TENDERLOIN—Same as loin.

pork, grades of—Two grades of hog are raised. The meat hog which has a low fat content and the lard hog with high fat content.

porridge—Any cooked cereal.

porro (It)—Leek

port—A dark, red-brown wine. Drunk as an aperitif or cocktail.

porte-couteau (Fr)—Knife rest.

posset—A drink of hot milk, spices and liquor.

pot—Any container used to prepare or cook food in. *(See listings for individual pots)*

pot cheese—A soft, natural cheese. Perishable. Must be kept refrigerated.

pot liquor—This is the liquid in which vegetables, fruits and meats have been cooked. If the pot liquor is not used in the dish being prepared, it should be saved for future use.

pot luck—1) A meal where each guest brings a dish. 2) Words used by a hostess when guests arrive at the last minute—eat what we are having—nothing special has been prepared for guests.

pot pie—A meat pie made with pie pastry. Usually contains meat, vegetables, spices and liquid. It is baked. Can be made as a large pie or an individual one.

pot roast—Generally a beef roast that is cooked in a covered pot on top of the stove. Salt, pepper and onions are often added along with a small amount of water. Vegetables are sometimes added near the end of cooking. Gravy can be made with the pot liquor.

potable—Liquid that is suitable for drinking.

potage—A thick soup, almost a stew.

potage *(Fr)*—Soup

potage fausse tortue *(Fr)*—Mock turtle soup

potajes *(Sp)*—Mixed vegetables cooked together. There are many variations of this dish.

potato—An edible root vegetable. It is a starchy tuber. May be boiled with skin on, peeled and stewed, baked, sliced or grated and fried. Used in soups and stews. There are several varieties. Some are best cooked with water and others are better baked with their skin.

potato bakers—Small devices with sharp, metal rods on which potatoes, onions, meat and poultry are speared. The device is placed on a pan, put in the oven for cooking. Foods, especially potatoes, cook faster in this manner. CAUTION: Do not use in a microwave oven.

potato baskets—Grated potatoes cooked in a special device. The golden brown baskets may be filled with cooked peas or other vegetables for serving. Very attractive. *(See Potato Nest Baskets)*

potato cakes—Cold, mashed potatoes mixed with eggs, flour and seasonings. Dropped by spoonfuls or shaped into small patties, and fried in hot fat. An hor d'oeuvre.

potato chips—Potatoes that have been thinly-sliced and deep fried. Salt is sprinkled on after cooking.

potato flour—A thickening agent. Cooks to a transparency. Tasteless. It will thin out if cooked over 176 degrees. Made from potatoes.

potato nails—Long, thin metal rods that are inserted in potatoes to be baked. The rod should protrude slightly from the potato. Potatoes cook faster. CAUTION: Do not use in a microwave oven.

potato nest baskets—Two wire baskets, one smaller than the other, with long handles. Grated potatoes are put in the larger basket and the small basket is fitted inside. Clamped together it is lowered into hot oil and cooked until the potatoes are golden brown.

potato pancakes—Grated, raw potatoes, sometimes mixed with eggs and flour, and dropped by spoonfuls into hot fat. Chopped green onions may be added.

potato ring—*(See Dish Ring)*

potato starch—Potato flour

potherbs (pot-herbs)—The leaves are tender stems of various plants that are cooked and served as a side dish. Mustard, spinach, dock, nasturtium, kale and beet are a few of the plants used as potherbs. Are also called 'greens.'

potholders—Generally padded squares of cloth that are used to protect the hand when lifting hot pans, pots and dishes. *(See Mitten, Cooking)*

potiron *(Fr)*—Pumpkin

potpourri—A mixture. A meat and vegetable stew.

potstickers *(Ch)*—Pan fried filled dumplings.

pouding *(Fr)*—Puddings of various types.

poudre de cacao soluble *(Fr)*—Powdered cocoa which is soluble in liquid.

poulpe *(Fr)*—Octopus

poultry—*(See Fowl)*

poultry carvers—Same as carving knives but the blades are not as flexible.

pound—A unit of weight. Equal to 16 ounces.

pound cake—A rich cake made with more eggs and sugar in proportion to the flour.

pounder—A mallet headed tool used to tenderize and flatten various cuts of meat. May be made of wood or metal.

Pousse-Cafe—A colorful cordial made by floating several different colored liqueurs one on top of the other. Usually in a tall, thin glass.

powdered milk—*(See Dry Milk)*

powdered sugar—*(See Confectioners Sugar)*

praline—Pecan candy popular in the Deep South. The recipe comes from an almond confection originating in France by the cook to Count Duplessis Praslin.

prepared mustard—Seeds of the mustard ground into a paste. Used as a sandwich spread and in various sauces and bastings pastes. Various regions and even cities of the world have their own distinctive mustards. Some quite hot and others mild or even sweet.

presentation plate—*(See Cover Plate)*

preserved eggs—*(See Hundred Year Old Eggs)*

preserves—Generally fruit or a mixture of fruits, sugar and spices cooked together until the mixture is very thick. Used as a condiment and on toast, rolls, crackers and as a filling for tarts and cakes.

preserving pan—Large, heavy pan with a heavy wire handle hinged on each side. Generally has pouring lips. Used for the making of jellies, jams and juices.

pressure cooker—A pot that can be sealed and is fitted with some type of pressure regulator. Used to cook food quickly. Larger types are used in home canning. CAUTION: Always follow directions when using.

presure *(Fr)*—Rennet

pretzels—A rope-shaped cracker that is brittle, glazed and salted. Usually twisted in a bow shape.

prezzemolo *(It)*—Parsley

prickly pear—The edible pear shaped fruit of an American cactus. Often made into jelly. The cactus pads are also edible. Several varieties grow in the southwest United States and in Mexico. Also called nopal.

processed cheese—A soft cheese spread developed in America. Stores without refrigeration. Generally various cheddars are blended with an emulsifier and then pasteurized. It is formed into loaves. Used as a sandwich filling and in some cooked dishes.

produce—The product of a farm. Fruits and vegetables.

prong—The tine of a fork.

prosciutto—A type of cured ham. It is served cold as an hors d'oeuvre, with melons or as a garnish. This ham is generally not cooked before eating. The curing process is lengthy, from three to 12 months. Expensive.

prosciutto *(It)*—Ham

protein—A large class of chemicals that are a necessary food item.

provencale *(Fr)*—Certain dishes from the Provence region in southern France. Cooked liberally with garlic, oil and tomatoes.

provolone—A hard cheese that is wrapped in a net and smoked.

prune—A variety of plum that is dried. May be eaten as is or stewed. Can also be made into a paste for use in cakes and other confections. Of the two main prune varieties—Japanese and European —the sweeter European is used for prunes.

prune *(Fr)*—Plum

pruneau *(Fr)*—Prune

prunelle *(Fr)*—Sloe

pt.—Abbreviation for one pint.

pudding—Thick dessert sauce made of eggs, milk, sugar and flavorings. Sometimes fruit, nuts and coconut is added.

pudin de pasta *(Sp)*—Dumpling

puerro *(Sp)*—Leek

puff paste—A basic pastry of water, flour and butter. The amounts of flour and butter can vary depending on the type of puff paste being made.

pulled sugar—Cooked sugar and water that is worked (pulled) with the hands to make a type of candy called taffy.

pullet—A young hen.

pulque *(Mex)*—Mexican alcoholic drink made from the sap of the maguey plant.

pulse—Dried beans, peas, lentils and other legume seeds.

Pumpernickel *(Ger)*—A rye bread of Westphalian origin. Caraway seed is one important ingredient. The seed gives the bread its distinctive flavor.

pumpkin—An orange colored squash of the gourd family. Most pumpkin flesh is used for pies. The flesh is also added to some cake and bread doughs. The flesh is sweet and bright orange, turning a golden brown when cooked. Pumpkins are also used to make jack-o'lanterns.

punch—A sweet drink that can be made of fruit juices, fruit and carbonated beverages. Liquor or wine is added to some punches. Punch is generally served in a large bowl and dispensed in small cups or glasses. Champagne or sparkling wine is often used.

punch bowl—A large bowl, sometimes with matching cups, for the serving of punches. Can be made of metal, glass or ceramic.

pungent—Tart, sharp taste, acrid

pure—Unmixed. Such as apple juice which has no other ingredient. Plain.

puree—Foods that have been processed so that they become a paste.

puree *(Fr)*—Thick soup of mashed vegetables and seasonings, cooked well and put through a sieve.

puree de pois *(Fr)*—Pea soup

puree d'oignons *(Fr)*—Onion soup

pureer—Tool that separates the pulp of fruits and vegetables from the skins and seeds. Handy tool to have when making your own tomato sauce, apple sauce and purees.

puris *(Ind)*—A flat bread made of whole wheat flour, yogurt and other ingredients. Can be deep or pan fried.

purple broccoli—Same as purple cauliflower.

purple bush bean—A string bean that when mature is purple in color. The bean turns bright green when it is cooked. A built-in timer. Freezes and cans well.

purple cauliflower—A variety of cauliflower whose head is purple in color. During cooking the head will turn bright green. Tastes slightly like broccoli. It is cooked and served the same as white cauliflower.

qt.—Abbreviation for quart.

quail—Game bird that is usually roasted. They are quite small.

quartre epices *(Fr)*—Four spices. Generally thyme, bay, mace and nutmeg tied together and used in cooking certain dishes. Spices are discarded after use. Some chefs have their own combination of spices.

queen—Inside the lobster, near the head, the small bag usually containing gravel or sand. Nonedible.

Queensland nut—Macadamia nut

quenelle *(Fr)*—Forcemeat ball. Generally used as a garnish.

queso *(Sp)*—Cheese

queso anejo *(Sp)*—Aged cheese

queso asadero *(Mex)*—A California made cheese similar to jack cheese. Used in Mexican cookery. Melts well. Should be found in large supermarkets in California. Also in Mexican groceries.

queso fresco *(Sp)*—Fresh cheese

quiche—Basically a custard baked in a pastry shell. Various additional items may be added. Such as bacon, cheese, onions and spices. Can be served as an appetizer, side dish or luncheon and supper entree.

quiche Lorraine *(Fr)*—The old recipe for this quiche contains eggs, cream and a little salt. It is baked and served very hot. The modern version generally has bacon and cheeses added.

quiche pan—Generally a dish made of porcelain with low fluted sides. Various sizes and shapes—round, square, rectangle, oval—are available.

quick bread—Breads made with leavening agents that permit the immediate cooking—pancakes, waffles, biscuits.

quick freezing—A process where meats, fruits and vegetables are frozen very fast. They then may be stored for long periods of time in the freezer.

quince—A yellow apple-like fruit that is mostly used in jams and jellies.

Quitte *(Ger)*—Quince

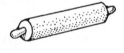

rabano *(Sp)*—Radish

rabbit—A small herbivorous animal used for food. It is raised commercially. Can be pan fried, braised, roasted or made into stew. Is the basis for the German dish Hassenpfeffer.

rable de lievre roti *(Fr)*—Roast baron of hare. Whole roasted rabbit.

radicchio *(It)*—A salad green. Red colored and with a slightly bitter taste.

radis *(Fr)*—Radish

radish—Fleshy root vegetable. Usually eaten raw. Available as red, white or black globes and the long white. The Japanese type (daikon) is very long. Some can be lightly braised in butter or added to other vegetable dishes. The raw radish is served on the relish tray and sliced into green salads. Makes an attractive garnish.

ragout—A thick, highly seasoned stew.

raidir *(Fr)*—To sear quickly in butter or other smoking fat.

raifort *(Fr)*—Horseradish

raised pie mold—Loaf-shaped tins that are quite deep. The sides are removable. Used for meat and game pies. Some have decorative designs embossed in the sides. When the sides are removed the design is visible in the crust.

raisin—Certain grapes that have been dried. Seedless grapes are usually used for raisins. Thompson seedless is a good variety. Two methods are used to dry grapes. Nature's way in the sun or by treating with certain chemicals and exposing to artificial heat. Raisins are used in cakes, cookies, candies, pies and eaten as a snack. Are added to certain sauces and salads.

raisin *(Fr)*—Grape

raisin de Corinthe *(Fr)*—Currant

raisins de table *(Fr)*—Dessert grapes

raisins secs *(Fr)*—Raisins

raki *(Tur)*—Alcoholic beverage made from grapes or plums and flavored with aniseed and mastic.

ramekin—Individual baking and serving dishes.

ramp—An onion-like vegetable with a taste of garlic. Strong. A wild growing plant.

rampions—Same as ramps.

rancid—Generally meat or fat that has become old and has developed an unpleasant taste and smell.

range—Kitchen stove

rapa *(It)*—Turnip

rape—A potherb of the mustard family. It is less pungent than common mustard. Bright green in color.

raper *(Fr)*—A grater

rare—Degree of doneness. Generally used to refer to beef and lamb. The meat will be pink. Only cooked until it is hot thru.

rarebit—Melted cheese with mustard served over toast points. Excellent luncheon or supper entree.

rasher—A portion or serving of food—such as a rasher of bacon.

raspberry—A bramble fruit. May be eaten raw or made into jams and jellies. Added to ice creams and as a filling in pastries and cakes. Freezes well. Available in red, black and in some areas yellow. does not ripen after picking.

raspings—Fine crumbs

ratatouille *(Fr)*—1) Thin slice of meat wrapped around a stuffing then cooked. 2) A type of stew with eggplant, zucchini, tomatoes and various spices.

ravanello *(It)*—Radish

rave—Root vegetable

ravigote—A thick stock using a basic stock, herbs, lemon juice, shallots and white wine.

ravioli *(It)*—Squares of pasta (not dried) filled with meat, cheese and cooked in tomato sauce.

rayu *(Or)*—Sesame oil with chili powder added. Should be available in Oriental groceries.

rechauffe *(Fr)*—To reheat a dish that has been previously cooked.

recipe—Directions for preparing a dish. It will contain a list of ingredients, quantities to use and how to put them together and the method of cooking. A recipe is a guide.

red beans—A dull, red-colored, dried bean. Slightly smaller than a kidney bean. Good for chili and in pork dishes.

red cabbage—A deep red-purple colored cabbage.

red-eye gravy—Gravy made from the drippings of ham that has been fried. A small amount of brewed coffee and water are added. It is not thickened.

red flannel hash—Corned beef hash that has chopped, cooked beets added.

red hots—1) American slang. A hot dog. 2) A candy about the size of a pea. Cinnamon flavored and red in color.

red wines—Wines that are light to very dark red in color.

refried beans *(Mex)*—Dried beans that have been boiled, drained, mashed then put in a pan with a little fat and heated (refried)

refrigerator—A kitchen appliance used to store perishable foods at cool temperatures. Many are equipped with built-in freezers and ice cube makers.

reggamo—A hard cheese. Variety of parmesan.

reglisse *(Fr)*—Licorice

Reis *(Ger)*—Rice

relish tray—A plate with an assortment of fresh vegetables and various pickles. Used as an appetizer.

remolacha *(Sp)*—Beet

remolade, remoulade *(Fr)*—Sauce resembling mayonnaise. Generally a sauce that is served with cold dishes.

rennet—A substance used to curdle milk. Some custards and ice creams are made in this manner. Rennet powder is available in most grocery stores. Also used in making some cheeses.

restes *(Fr)*—Leftovers

Rettich *(Ger)*—Radish

Reuben—A sandwich made of corned beef or pastrami, sauerkraut and cheese. Made on rye bread and lightly grilled in butter.

Rhine—A white wine from the Rhine River area in West Germany.

rhubarb—A perennial plant whose fleshy stalks are edible. Can be made into jams, jellies and pies. The flavor is rather tart. The color of the stalks can be red or green. CAUTION: The leaves of the rhubarb are poisonous.

rhum *(Fr)*—Rum

rice—A cereal grain. Often boiled and served plain as a substitute for potatoes. Also served as a breakfast cereal hot with sugar, cinnamon and cream. It is also ground into a flour. *(See Fried Rice)*

rice noodles *(Or)*—Noodles made with rice flour. They are off-white, brittle, thin and slightly wavy. They puff up when fried.

rice pudding—Cooked rice combined with sugar, eggs, milk and seasonings. Baked and served as a dessert with milk or cream. Raisins and nuts may be added.

rice sticks *(Or)*—*(See Rice Noodles)*

rice vermicelli—*(See Rice Noodles)*

rice vinegar—A vinegar made from rice wine.

ricer—A utensil that cooked foods are put through to prepare them for creaming. Good for potatoes.

rich—A dish that has a very strong but pleasant taste. A mousse with sugar, eggs and whipped cream could be described as being a rich dessert. A stew with lots of fats and spices can also be called rich.

ricotta—A soft, natural cheese. Perishable. Must be refrigerated.

rijsttafel—An Indonesian dish. Midday meal of rice with small portions of meat, vegetables, condiments, etc.

rim—The edge or border.

rind—The outer covering, usually tough, of some meats, fruits, vegetables and cheeses.

Rinderbraten *(Ger)*—Roastbeef

Rindfleisch *(Ger)*—Beef

ripe—1) A fruit or vegetable that is mature and ready to eat. 2) Meat that has reached a degree just short of being spoiled.

ripopee *(Fr)*—Bad wine. Mishmash

ris de veau *(Fr)*—Calf's sweetbread

rise—In bread making, the action of yeast which expands and increases the volume of dough. This action also takes place with other breads and leavening agents when they are baked.

riso *(It)*—Rice

rissole *(Fr)*—A filled pastry in the shape of a turnover and deep fried. A fried pie.

rissoler *(Fr)*—To brown

rissotto *(It)*—A dish consisting of rice, broth, onions, cheese, chicken and seasonings.

riz *(Fr)*—Rice

roast—A dish identified as having been cooked by dry heat, e.g., a beef roast.

roaster—A pan for roasting meats. Generally has a tight-fitting lid.

roasting pans—Large, metal pans used for oven cooking of roasts, fowl, ham and other large quantities of food. Some are deep while others have rather short sides. May have covers or not.

rock candy—Large crystals of sugar.

Rock Cornish game hen—Same as Cornish hen.

rock salt—*(See Cooking Salt)*

rocket—A leafy green. A member of the mustard family. Has a peppery taste.

Rocky Mountain Oysters—*(See Mountain Oysters)*

roe—Fish eggs

Roggen *(Ger)*—Rye grain

rojo *(Sp)*—Ginger

roll—Various types and shapes of small breads. A bun.

rolled oats—Oatmeal

rolling pin—A long cylinder used to flattened and spread out various types of dough. Can be made of wood, marble, glass or metal.

rolling pin, type of

AMERICAN—Straight cylinder with handles at each end. The handles are not attached firmly, but revolve on ball bearings. Some models have a rod running through the length of the pin, with handles at each end.

FRENCH STRAIGHT—Cylinder with tapered ends. Has no handles. Various lengths. Very good for use with puff paste.

SPRINGERLE—Of German origin, the surface of the pin is covered with raised designs. After rolling the dough, the designs are cut out.

TAPERED PIN—A small diameter pin with tapered ends. Good for rolling dough into circles.

INDIAN—A small tapered end pin and a special round board. Used for making the thin chapattis.

roly-poly pudding—Dish made of suet pastry, spread with jam and rolled in the shape of a sausage. Tied in a cheesecloth or muslin bag it is cooked in water. Also called English suet roll pudding.

romaine—A long leaf lettuce. Widely used in salads.

romano—A hard cheese. When very dry it can be grated into a powder.

romano bean—A large, flat string bean. Has a flavor that is distinctively its own. Used extensively in Italian cooking. Also called Italian bean.

romero *(Sp)*—Rosemary

root—That part of a plant which is below ground. Many vegetables form their edible parts there.

root beer—A carbonated beverage. Non-alcoholic.

rooster—The male chicken.

Roquefort *(Fr)*—A semi-hard cheese from the Roquefort region of France. Has blue mold throughout the interior. Used in salad dressings and as a snack cheese. The American cheese of this type is called Blue (Bleu) cheese. Sheep's milk is used to make true Roquefort.

roquille *(Fr)*—Candied orange peel.

rosbif *(Fr)*—Roast beef

rose—A pink wine used at the table and as an aperitif or cocktail.

Rosenkohl *(Ger)*—Brussels sprouts

rosewater—Water that has been flavored with rose petals.

Rosine *(Ger)*—Raisin

rosmarin *(Fr)*—Rosemary

Rosmarin *(Ger)*—Rosemary

rosmarion *(It)*—Rosemary

rosten *(Ger)*—Toast, roast, grill.

rot *(Fr)*—A roast

rotary beater—Tool with one or two whisks that are revolved by turning a handle. The beater is held by one hand and the handle turned by the other. Used for light mixing, beating egg whites and whipping cream.

roti *(Hin)*—Bread

roti *(Fr)*—A roast, roast meat

roti *(Fr)*—A piece of toasted bread; toast.

rotissage *(Fr)*—Roasting

rotisserie—A revolving spit over coals on which food is cooked.

roulade *(Fr)*—Thin slice of meat spread with forcemeat and rolled like a sausage.

roulette *(Fr)*—Pastry wheel

roulle de veau *(Fr)*—Fillet of veal.

round—Cut of beef, generally a steak.

roux *(Fr)*—Flour and fat (usually butter) cooked together to form a paste that is used as a thickening agent. Length of time and amount of heat affect the color and flavor.

royale *(Fr)*—A garnish, of flavored molded custard. Used for clear soups.

royan *(Fr)*—Sprats

R.S.V.P. *(Fr)*—Repondez s'il vous plais. Abbreviation used on invitations meaning 'please reply.' Can also be written rsvp.

Rube *(Ger)*—Turnip

rum—A spirit distilled from the juice of sugarcane or molasses. Light and dark types are made. Used in cooking to flavor various confections and in mixed drinks and cocktails.

rum *(Eng)*—Far in England's past this word meant any strong and pleasant drink.

rum baba—A redundancy: to use these words means you would be saying "rum rum cake."

Runkelrube *(Ger)*—Beet

rusks—Slices of bread, generally round, that are baked again until dry and crisp.

russet—1) Various winter apples with red-brown and yellow-brown skins. 2) Variety of potato that is good for baking in the skin.

Russian dressing—A salad dressing made of oil, catsup, vinegar, onion and seasonings.

rutabaga—A large, yellow turnip. Is prepared in the same manner as white turnips.

rye—A cereal grain. Can be ground into flour for breads.

rye flour—A bread flour made from rye grain.

rye whiskey—A whiskey distilled from rye grain.

S

Saat *(Ger)*—Seed

sabra *(Heb)*—A desert pear.

sabayon *(Fr)*—Zabaglione

saccharin—An artificial sweetener.

Sachertorte *(Ger)*—Chocolate cake filled with jam and iced with chocolate.

saddle cut—That cut of meat that includes the rear haunches and rump.

Safran *(Ger)*—Saffron

safran *(Fr)*—Saffron

sago—A starch is produced from this palm tree. It is native to the East Indies.

saignant *(Fr)*—Underdone, rare

saindoux *(Fr)*—Lard, fat

Saint John's bread—*(See Carob)*

sake *(Ja)*—Rice wine. Served warm in small cups.

saki *(Per)*—Cupbearer

sal culinarius *(L)*—Common salt

sal de mesa *(Sp)*—Table salt

sal gemmae *(L)*—Rock salt

sal soda—A soda used for cleaning. It is not edible.

salad—A mixture of fresh vegetables such as various types of lettuce, spinach, mustard, tomatoes, radishes, onions, cucumbers served with a sauce (dressing). Cooked cold vegetables, meats, fruits, croutons, cheeses and pastas are sometimes added. The ingredients for salads are almost limitless. European style is to serve the salad after the main course.

Various fruits, fresh or canned, nuts and coconut may also be combined to make a salad. Various ingredients can be added to flavored gelatin for an attractive salad.

salad dressing—1) Sauce that is poured over green salads. 2) A manufactured sauce similar to mayonnaise. Salad Dressing is stiffer and the taste is slightly different than mayonnaise. It is cooked and not often made in the home. For sale in grocery stores. Use as you would mayonnaise. 3) Various kinds of liquid dressings are manufactured and bottled. Flavors such as sour cream, cucumber, spice, French (American), and Italian are generally available at the market.

salad dressing mix—A dry packaged mix that when various liquids are added, will produce an acceptable dressing for green salads. Some of these mixes can be added to sour cream for a chip dip.

salade *(Fr)*—Salad

salaisons *(Fr)*—Foods that have been treated with salt to preserve them.

salad knife—These long, narrow-bladed knives are used to cut vegetables for salads. Usually the edges are serrated or scalloped.

salamander—A hand tool used to brown or glaze the tops of prepared dishes away from the stove. It can be either electric or manual (heated over an open flame). Good for browning meringues.

salame *(It)*—Salt meat, salt pork, sausage.

salami—A spiced luncheon meat. Popular for sandwiches and the cold cuts tray.

Salat *(Ger)*—Salad, lettuce.

Salbei *(Ger)*—Sage

sale *(Fr)*—Pickled or salted food-stuffs. Salt pork.

sale fino *(It)*—Table salt

salep, salop—A gelatinous mixture of orchid root powder, wine, sugar and lemon juice or grated lemon rind.

salero *(Sp)*—Saltcellar

saliere *(Fr)*—Saltcellar

Salisbury steak—Ground meat patties with onion, sausage or bacon, and various seasonings. Broiled or pan fried. Often served in an onion gravy.

salit *(col)*—Any of various vegetables whose tops are used as a potherb. In some areas, salit refers to wild greens.

Sally Lunn—A baking powder bread that originated in England. It has eggs added and is baked in a muffin tin.

salmagundi—A mixture of anchovies, boiled eggs, chopped meat and onions served as a salad. (Also generalized to mean a potpourri.)

salmis *(Fr)*—Ragout of pre-cooked game.

salmon—Pink fleshed fish. Can be baked or grilled. Can be purchased fresh or canned.

salometer—Device used to measure the salt content of liquids.

salpicon *(Fr)*—A mixture of one or more ingredients diced and bound with a sauce. Can be used as stuffing for tartlets, canapes or made into croquettes. Can be hot or cold.

salsa *(Mex)*—Uncooked sauce made with tomatoes, onions, celery, green peppers, green chilies and spices.

salsa *(It)*—Sauce

salsa *(Sp)*—Sauce. In Spanish cooking, sauces tend to be an integral part of the dish, instead of being served separately or poured over the prepared dish.

salsa verde *(Sp)*—Green sauce

salsify—A root vegetable with slender above ground stalks. Can be boiled then stir fried. Makes an excellent soup when combined with leeks. Also called 'oyster plant' because the root has a faint oyster flavor when cooked.

salt cellar—Usually a small table dish, with spoon, for the serving of salt.

salt, cooking—Unrefined common salt. It is used when making ice cream in a home freezer and as a bed for baking oysters. This type is used when making a salt crust. It comes in varying degrees or coarseness. Some cooks prefer it for cooking.

salt crust—A crust of flour, coarse salt and water. Used to incase various cuts of meat and poultry for baking. The crust acts much like a clay pot, continuing the moisture. When seasonings are placed inside with the meat, their flavor is more distinctive and tasted throughout the meat. The crust becomes very hard and must be broken off. It is not eatable. An eye catching way of serving a baked hen or duck.

salt grinder—Small grinder used to grind rock salt to a powder.

salt mill—*(See Salt Grinder)*

salt shaker—Small cylinder with a lid which is pierced with holes. Used for dispensing salt.

salt, table—A fine white crystalline substance (sodium chloride) used to season foods. Also used in preserving. It is preferable to use iodized table salt in seasoning because it contains iodine, a necessary element in our diet. When using salt in preserving foods, plain salt should be used. Iodized salt tends to turn pickled foods dark. Also when soaking fruits and vegetables, plain salt should be used. A salt water bath will help cut fruits and vegetables from turning dark. Table salt is treated to prevent caking.

saltpeter (saltpetre)—A salt used in curing meats.

salumeria *(It)*—Delicatessen. Pork butcher shop.

salver—A small tray

salvia *(It, Sp)*—Sage

samovar *(Rus)*—Metal urn used to boil water for tea.

samp—Hominy grits

sandwich—Two or more slices of bread between which various meats, vegetables, cheeses, spreads and condiments are placed. Generally taken up and eaten in hand. The bread can be toasted. Can also be made with the bread laid on the plate and the various fillings placed on top. It is then eaten with a knife and fork. This is called an 'open faced' sandwich.

sandy pot—Clay pot made with sand. Can be used on top of the stove or in the oven. The pot is enclosed in a wire mesh for reinforcement. The pots are fragile.

sanglier *(Fr)*—Boar, wild boar

sangri *(Fr)*—Maderia wine mixed with water, sugar and a little nutmeg. A refreshing beverage when served chilled.

sangria *(Sp)*—Wine punch with fruit.

sanjaki cucumber—Chinese cucumber three or more feet long.

sansho *(Ja)*—Japanese fragrant pepper. Look for in Oriental markets.

sapodilla—*(See Sapote)*

sapote—Fruit from a West Indian tree. Eaten raw or in fruit drinks and sherbets.

sarcrauti *(It)*—Sauerkraut

sarsaparilla—A soft drink. One of the first, if not the first, soft drink made and served. Flavoring comes from the sarsaparilla plant. A tropical plant. The dried roots are used, with other flavorings, in the making of rootbeers and other soft drinks.

sassparillee—Dialectic for sarsaparilla flavored soft drink. In some areas can mean any soft drink.

sate *(Ma)*—Marinated meat that is cooked on skewers.

sauce—A liquid mixture of various ingredients that is used in and on a variety of dishes. Sauces can be of varying thicknesses. Gravy, salad dressing and mayonnaise can be called sauces.

sauce a la menthe *(Fr)*—Mint sauce

sauce au beurre *(Fr)*—Butter sauce

sauce aux capre *(Fr)*—Caper sauce

sauce blanche *(Fr)*—White sauce

sauce Bernaise *(Fr)*—Hot mayonnaise and mustard sauce.

sauce financiere *(Fr)*—Madeira wine sauce with truffles.

sauce hollandise *(Fr)*—Hot sauce made of butter, egg yolk and lemon juice.

sauce meuniere *(Fr)*—Sauce made of browned butter, parsley and lemon juice.

sauce piquante *(Fr)*—Any sharp, pungent sauce.

saucer—A flat container (plate) in which a cup is designed to set.

sauce releve *(Fr)*—A rich, highly seasoned sauce.

sauce verte *(Fr)*—A green sauce.

saucisse *(Fr)*—sausage

saucisson *(Fr)*—Salami

Sauerbraten *(Ger)*—Beef roast that has been marinated in vinegar and spices. It is cooked in the marinade with onions added. Near end of cooking, carrots and potatoes can be added. The cooking liquid is thickened with ginger snaps.

sauerkraut—Cabbage that has been thinly-sliced or finely-chopped and cured in salt. Can be served hot or cold.

sauge *(Fr)*—Sage

saumon *(Fr)*—Salmon

sausage—Meat that is ground and combined with spices and put into tubular casings. Pork sausage is often made into patties and fried.

sausage pricker—Paring knife with small pins protruding from the handle. Used to cut apart sausage links and to prick holes in the sausages before cooking. A cork should be stuck on the pins when not in use.

saute pan—A heavy pan, with handle, used for sauteing. A heavy sauce pan.

sautoir *(Fr)*—Saute pan

savarin *(Fr)*—1) A yeast cake that is soaked in rum, kirsch or flavored syrup after baking. 2) A round pan with the center portion slightly raised. When the gelatin or cake is turned out it has a raised ring on the top. This pan can be used for molding aspics, gelatins and baking of cakes.

scales—Device used for weighing. Some types sit on the counter while others are suspended.

scallion—Onion without the enlarged bulb.

scallop—1) A marine mollusk with a large edible muscle. Very delicate taste. 2) Thin slices of veal cut from the leg. They are pounded flat before cooking. *(See Scallopine)*

scalloped edge knife—Various sized knives whose cutting edge is scalloped or wavy. Used to cut soft foods, such as cucumbers, tomatoes, grapefruit.

scallopine—Very thin slices of veal cut from the leg. To obtain the most delicate cuts, the leg should be boned, the membranes and sinews removed then sliced. It is pounded until the slices are quite thin. Usually breaded and fried quickly in hot fat.

scalogno *(It)*—Scallion

scaloppina *(It)*—Veal cutlet

scampi *(It)*—Large shrimp, prawns

scarlet runner bean—A popular string bean in England. can be used as a snap bean or the seed dried.

Schalotte *(Ger)*—Shallot

Schiedam *(Du)*—Holland gin

Schinken *(Ger)*—Ham

Schlagobers *(Ger)*—Whipped cream

schmalts or shmaltz *(Yid)*—Literally, cooking fat.

schnapps—A strong gin. Holland gin. Some are flavored with peppermint.

Schneck *(Ger)*—Snail

Schnecken *(Ger)*—Coffee cake

Schnee *(Ger)*—Snow

Schnittlauch *(Ger)*—Chives

Schnitzel *(Ger)*—A cutlet

Schokolade *(Ger)*—Chocolate

Schweinefett *(Ger)*—Lard; fat

Schweinefleisch *(Ger)*—Pork

scissors—Various types of scissors are available for use in the kitchen. All purpose, paper, kitchen cutters, fish, poultry and grape are some types. Scissors should be kept sharp.

scone—A small biscuit made of cornmeal, oatmeal and bran. It is baked on a griddle.

scoop—Small open-sided device used for dipping various dry foodstuffs such as flour, sugar and meal. Some types can be used as measures.

Scotch whiskey—A distinctively flavored whiskey that is distilled in Scotland. Not often used in cookery. Used in highballs and other mixed drinks. An apertif is made by combining scotch with shaved ice in a champagne glass.

scrapple—Scraps of pork and cornmeal combined and cooked in a loaf pan.

scratch—To make a dish, such as a cake, by combining all of the ingredients yourself. This is opposed to using prepared mixes.

scrod—Young cod or haddock. A small fish prepared for planking.

scullery—Area near the kitchen where the pots and pans are stored and cleaned. Found in larger houses and restaurants.

scum—The solids that form on the top of a boiling liquid. Such as when boiling meat, certain fats and blood from the meat will solidify and rise to the top. Should be skimmed off and discarded.

sea biscuit—Hardtack

sea salt—Salt obtained by evaporating sea water.

seafood—Fish or mollusks taken from the ocean and used as food.

sebile *(Fr)*—Wooden bowl

sec *(Fr)*—Dry. Used to describe an extra dry wine or champagne.

sedano *(It)*—Celery

segala *(It)*—Rye grain

seigle *(Fr)*—Rye grain

sel blanc *(Fr)*—Table salt

sel de mer *(Fr)*—Sea salt

selle *(Fr)*—(See Saddle Cut)

selle de mouton *(Fr)*—Saddle of mutton.

Sellerie *(Ger)*—Celery

seltz *(Fr)*—Seltzer water

seltzer water—Soda water that is naturally sparkling or is effervesced with carbonic gas under pressure.

seme *(It)*—Seed

semilla *(Sp)*—Seed

semi-sweet chocolate—Cocoa with a small amount of sweetener added. Usually formed into solid bars or cakes.

semola *(Sp)*—Semolina

semolina—Cereals, mostly wheat, that are coarsely-ground and used in pastas, soups, puddings, groats and other dishes.

semolino *(It)*—Semolina

semoule *(Fr)*—Semolina

Senf *(Ger)*—Mustard

seppia *(It)*—Squid

server—A small tray or salver.

service plate—*(See Cover Plate)*

Sesam *(Ger)*—Sesame

sesame *(Fr)*—Sesame

sesamo *(It)*—Sesame

sesamo *(Sp)*—Sesame

Seville orange—A bitter orange used in certain liqueurs, beverages and in confections. The blooms are used to make orange blossom water.

shad roe—Eggs of the shad (fish) baked or poached.

shake *(sl)*—A milk shake.

shallot—Vegetable from the onion family. Has a slight garlic taste.

sharab *(Hin)*—Wine

shark—A carnivorous fish whose flesh is tough. Chinese cooks esteem the fin for making soup.

sharpening steel—A rather thin steel rod that is used to sharpen cutting knives. The surface is criss-crossed with very small grooves. Some steels are made of a ceramic material. Cutting knives should be treated to the steel every time they are used.

shears—Similar to garden pruning shears. Used for cutting small bones.

sheep—A food and wool animal. rather small in size. *(See Lamb and mutton)*

shepherd's purse—*(See Corn Salad)*

sherbet—A frozen confection of fruit juices, sugar, milk and water, and flavorings. Often served at the end of a heavy or spicy meal. Very refreshing. Commercial sherbet (that you buy at the market) must contain one-two percent milk fat and two-five percent solids. Sherbet usually contains more sugar than ice cream.

sherry—A fortified wine with a nutty flavor. Can be sweet or dry. Served as an apertif, digestif or in certain dishes. Caution should be taken not to use an overly amount in cooked dishes. The wine can easily overpower the dish's flavors.

shiitake *(Ja)*—A type of mushroom

shirred—Eggs baked with cream until the whites are just set. Can have a crumb topping.

shoat—A young hog.

shoestring potatoes—White potatoes that have been sliced in thin strips and deep fried. Available at the market in cans.

shoofly pie—One crust pie made with brown sugar, spices, molasses and other ingredients.

short (pastry)—*(See Short Flake)*

shortcake—A dessert made with rich pastry, biscuits or sponge cake. Fresh fruit is ladled over and topped with whipped cream.

shortening—Solid vegetable or animal fat used in cooking. Can also mean butter, margarine or oil. Vegetable shortening or oil should be used for deep frying.

short flake—A crust where the fat is allowed to blend with the flour. A tender and firm crust. This type of crust can be cut with a fork. It will not flake or cumble.

shrimp—A small sea crustacean that is related to the lobster. Widely used in cooking. Can be steamed, boiled, sauteed or fried. Any of various sauces are served with shrimp. Can be used in certain casseroles and sauces.

shuck—Husk of corn.

Sicilian fennel—The young stems of this vegetable are prepared like celery and asparagus. Grown mostly in southern Italy.

sideboard—*(See Buffet #2)*

side dish—A dish of some kind that is served along with a meat or vegetable dish.

side of—One-half of a beef, veal or hog. A side includes the front leg, mid section and rear leg. In one piece. When butchered the animal is cut in two pieces, sides.

sieve—A utensil with a screen that is used to separate large particles from small ones. Necessary tool for the kitchen. Can be bowl, drum or conical in shape. Degree of fineness of screens are available.

silence cloth—Same as table silencer.

silent butler—A small dustpan shaped device used at the table to remove crumbs from the tablecloth. A small brush is used to sweep the crumbs into the device.

silver—Any article used at the table that is made of silver. This can include cutlery, dishes, platters and serving dishes. Can also refer to any cutlery used at the table or in the kitchen regardless of material.

silverside *(Eng)*—*(See Round)*

silver thread bread *(Ch)*—A special shaped yeast bread that is cooked by steaming. Usually in a covered wok.

single cream *(Eng)*—Light cream

sink—The basin in the kitchen where foods are cleaned and prepared. Also used for the cleaning of dishes, pots and pans.

siphon—A heavy bottle for dispensing carbonated water. They are equipped with a tight-fitting cover with a spout and handle to release water. Some types are designed to accept a gas capsule to provide the effervescence. In this type, plain water is used in the botttle.

sirloin—A cut of beef. Can be a roast or steak.

sirup—Syrup

sizzlers—New England dessert similar to fried fruit pies.

skewer—Slim metal rod on which food is threaded then grilled.

skillet—A frying pan. Made of many different materials. Used mostly on top of the stove. Those without wood or plastic handles can be used in the oven. Many have lids. Electric skillets with temperature controls are available.

skim milk—Milk that has had the cream removed. It is sold fresh in grocery stores. Can be purchased in the dry form and reconstituted with water.

skimmer—Long handled tool used to remove batter coated foods from the cooking pot. Can also be used to remove the scum from soups, stews and the like. The 'bowl' is flatish and is pierced or meshed.

skirret—A root vegetable. The roots can be stewed, braised, baked, creamed, batter fried or mashed and added to mashed potatoes. The raw root can be added to green salads. The flavor is sweet and mild.

slab—Thick slice of any food, especially roast beef or cheese. Also a large piece of bacon with rind attached.

slaw—Cole slaw

sliver—A thin slice.

sloe—Fruit of the sloe tree. Very sour and sharp tasting. Used to make a jam and in flavoring certain alcoholic drinks and some wines.

sloe gin—Gin that is flavored with sloe berries.

sloppy joe—An American sandwich served on a hamburger bun. The filling is made of ground beef cooked with tomato sauce and various seasonings. Can be open faced or closed. The prepared sauce and seasonings may be purchased at the market. This sauce is added to the browned ground beef.

slow cooker—(See Crock Pot)

slumgullion—A meat stew cooked in a skillet on top of the stove. Some cooks make it with ground beef, onions, celery, peppers and their vegetable leftovers. Tomatoes or tomato sauce and spices can be added. Mushrooms, olives, water chestnuts, cheeses and pastas can also be added. A fast main dish.

slump—A dessert of cooked fruit topped with biscuit dough or dumplings. From Maine.

slush—A confection made of shaved or finely-crushed ice with flavored syrup poured over. Generally sold in a paper cup.

smelt—Small food fishes found in coastal or inland waters.

smoked—Various meats are preserved by exposing the meats to wood smoke for a length of time. Bacon, ham and turkey are an example. Some cheeses and fish are smoked.

smokers—Enclosed devices used for smoking meats. It is used out of doors.

smorgasbord *(Sw)*—A buffet type of meal service. Generally there are many selections of meats, vegetables, breads and desserts both hot and cold.

snack—Generally light food eaten between meals.

snail—A small edible mollusk. Considered a delicacy.

snail dish—Pans with indentations to hold each snail. Snails are cooked and served in this pan. Available in sizes to hold 6 or 12 snails.

snail fork—Small tined fork designed for removing snails from their shells. Used in conjunction with special tongs that hold the shell steady. Usually made of stainless steel.

snail, sweet—A coffee cake. Generally the dough is rolled and filled then cut and baked. Many variations.

snail tongs—Small tongs used to hold the snail steady while removing the meat.

snake-eyed gravy—*(See Red-Eye Gravy)*

snap—A cookie

snow—Crystals of ice formed from water vapor in the air. In cookery, shaved or grated ice is called snow.

snow cone—A confection of shaved or finely-crushed ice with flavored syrup poured over. Served in a paper cone.

snow ice cream—A confection made of new fallen snow, cream, sugar and flavorings. It is eaten immediately. It should be made outside in the cold. The ingredients are stirred together until just mixed.

snow pea—The pod of this pea is eaten when the seeds are immature and the pods tender. Good stir fry vegetable. Used extensively in Oriental cookery. When cooking, the pods should be briefly boiled or steamed. Can be used as a crudite.

soaker—A baking powder biscuit is placed in a cup or small bowl and covered with hot coffee. Eaten with a spoon. Generally the biscuit is cold. Some people add sugar and cream.

soba *(Jp)*—Buckwheat noodles.

soda, baking—A leavening agent. Used with sour milk and buttermilk. Over use will cause breads to turn dark and have a disagreeable odor and taste. Can be used as a cleansing and freshening agent.

soda cracker—Thin square cracker made of white flour, soda, water and salt. Baked lightly. Eaten with soups, stews and as a base for some canapes.

soda pop—Flavored beverage charged with carbon dioxide. can be purchased in bottles or cans.

sodas—*(See Soda Pop)*

soda water—*(See Seltzer Water).* Also American colloquial for soda pop.

sodium chloride—Salt

sofrito *(Pr)*—A thick, liquid seasoning. Used extensively in the cookery of the Caribbean and especially Puerto Rico. Should be available in markets that handle foods of this area.

soft boiled—Degree of doneness of an egg when boiled in the shell. Generally this will be about two minutes. The white will be set and yolk still a liquid.

soft cheese—Cheese whose consistency permits it to be spread with a knife.

soft drink—Non-alcoholic beverage. One generally thinks of a carbonated beverage. Soda pop.

soft ice cream—*(See Frozen Custard)*

soft water—Water that has a low amount of salts, minerals and impurities present. Best water for cooking and drinking.

soft wheat flour—Flour milled from a soft wheat which has a low gluten content. Use for pastries, crackers, cookies, cakes and pretzels.

sop—A morsel of food soaked in liquid. A soaker.

sopa *(Sp)*—Soup

sopaipillas *(Mex)*—Small squares or triangles of a sweet rolled dough that are deep fried. Served with sugar and honey. They puff up while frying. Best served warm.

soppin' gravy—*(See Red-Eye Gravy)*

sorbet *(Fr)*—Sherbet

sorbetto *(It)*—Ice cream; sherbet

sorghum, sweet—The sap from this plant is cooked to produce a thick syrup called molasses. Molasses is also called sorghum or sorghum molasses. The plant (cane) is round and very tall. The sap is pressed out by passing the canes through steel rollers. This syrup is very dark colored with a strong taste.

sorrel (rumex)—The fresh leaves of this herb have a citrus like flavor. Can be cooked as spinach. Also can be pulverized and made into a green sauce for serving with cold meat, fish and fowl. Can be added to certain soups, notably the French 'soupe aux herbes'. Sorrel is related to the 'docks.' The root can be made into an astringent and is useful as a diuretic.

S O S *(mil, sl)*—Chipped beef in a cream sauce or gravy. Served on toast or biscuits. Sometimes ground beef and onions are used instead of the chipped beef. (Ask a military person what the letters SOS mean.)

sotol *(Mex)*—A yucca-like plant from which an alcoholic beverage is distilled

souffle—A slight and fluffy dish made of egg whites beaten stiffly and a cream sauce with cheese, vegetables or liqueurs added. Served directly from the oven. Some sweet souffles are not baked.

souffle dish—Round, straight-sided dishes used for baking and serving souffles. Made of porcelain, stoneware or glass. They are quite deep. Can also be used for molding cold (uncooked) souffles and puddings.

soup—Flavored liquid in which meats and/or vegetables have been cooked. Various herbs and spices are often added. Can be served with solids present or can be strained for a broth. Some soups are made thick by pureeing the solids. Often milk or cream is added to this type of soup.

soup ladle—A long handled spoon with a deep bowl, used for serving soup. Comes in many sizes.

soupe aux herbes *(Fr)*—A creamed vegetable soup that among other ingredients contains fresh sorrel.

soupe grasse *(Fr)*—Meat soup

soupe maigre *(Fr)*—Thin soup made without meat.

sour—A tart and acid taste.

sour cream—A commercial product made by adding a culture to fresh cream or milk. This produces a smooth creamy slightly acid product. Much used in the kitchen as a base for dips, sauces and in breads, cakes and other confections.

sour dock (rumex)—A wild green. Found along roadsides and fence rows. One of the first spring potherbs. Generally not cultivated. Use only the smallest and tenderest leaves. The larger leaves are bitter and unpalatable. Also called curly dock, wild spinach and yellow dock.

sour salt—Citric acid in a crystalline form. It is used by some as a substitute for salt. Use like lemon juice.

sourdough starter—A mixture of water, yeast, sugar and flour that is mixed and allowed to become bubbly and spongy. A part of this starter is used in making yeast breads and some other breads. When starter is used a like amount of flour, water and sugar is added to the starter bowl. This keeps it alive. Store in the refrigerator.

soursop—A fruit of an American tropical tree. It is eaten raw and in fruit salads.

souse—Pickled meat. Food steeped in vinegar.

sous-nappe *(Fr)*—*(See Table Silencer)*

soy bean—A legume whose seed is eaten whole, ground into a flour or made into a milk. An oil is derived from pressing the seed. Excellent boiled and added to cold vegetable salads.

soy flour—Flour made from the dried soy bean.

soy milk—A liquid made by steeping the dried bean in water.

soy sauce *(Or)*—The liquid from soy beans that have been fermented. Used as a condiment and a seasoner. Widely used in Oriental cooking. Salty taste.

spaghetti—Solid, round, long, thin pasta.

Spanish cream—A pudding made of eggs, sugar, butter, sherry and flavorings. Usually topped with fruit or fruit puree.

Spanish peanut—A variety of peanut that is almost round and is small in size. The skin covering the nut is generally red in color. Toasted and used as a snack.

spareribs—Ribs of the hog which are often baked, steamed or grilled with a sauce.

Spargel *(Ger)*—Asparagus

Spargelkohl *(Ger)*—Broccoli

sparkling burgundy—An effervescent dark red wine.

spatchcocking *(OE)*—The splitting and flattening of chickens and game birds for grilling.

spatula—Flexible knife-like tool used for scooping, spreading or mixing soft foods. Length of blade can range from four inches to over nine inches. Some have a serrated edge for slicing or cutting soft foods.

spear—A long piece of cucumber pickle. Usually a large pickle is cut into several spears. A stalk of asparagus.

Speisekarte *(Ger)*—Menu

spice—Various aromatic plants and plant products used to season and flavor foods.

spice mill—Small mill used for grinding various spices and herbs. The hand held types are similar to salt and pepper mills. Mills that clamp to the work surface are handy for grinding large quantities, such as poppy seed. These mills should be used only for spices and herbs.

spinach—A pungent potherb. Should be cooked briefly. Steaming is best. Should never be boiled. Excellent as a fresh salad green.

spinach noodles—Egg noodles with cooked spinach added to the dough before rolling and drying. Dull green in color.

spinacio *(It)*—Spinach

Spinat *(Ger)*—Spinach

spirits—Whiskies, gins, vodkas or any alcoholic beverages that have a high alcoholic content. Spirits does not apply to wines, beers or liqueurs.

split pea—Dried peas that are green or yellow in color.

split pea soup—A thick soup made from dried peas.

sponge—A yeast batter. Sourdough starter.

sponge cake—A cake that is made without shortening.

spoon—A hand tool with a slim handle and an open bowl on one end. Many types—teaspon, soupspoon, cooking spoon (solid or pierced bowl), measuring spoons, dessert spoons, etc.

spoon bread—Cornmeal bread cooked in a casserole, served warm from the baking dish. Whole kernel corn, chopped onions or green peppers are added.

sprats—Smoked sardines that are marinated in oil, vinegar, shallots and chopped parsley. Served at room temperature. Smoked herring may be substituted.

spread—1) A table set with food. A feast. 2) A sauce designed for putting on bread.

sprig—The end part of a stalk or branch, usually with several of the leaves attached.

spring form pan—A baking pan whose sides are removable. Generally two or more inches deep.

spring lamb—The first lambs available in the spring. Generally smaller than the summer lambs.

spritz—A crisp cookie.

sprouts—Seeds of various grains, beans and peas that are moistened and permitted to start growing (sprout). They are eaten raw or very lightly cooked. Used on sandwhiches, in salads and in various Oriental dishes.

spud *(sl)*—Potato

spumante *(It)*—Sparkling wine; champagne

spun sugar—Sugar syrup that has been cooked to the hard stage and then drawn into thin threads. It is used for decorating confections and for making nests for cakes and such.

squash—1) Any of several varieties of edible gourds. Most of them may be stewed or baked. Some make good pies, similar to pumpkin, which is a squash. Butternut can be stewed, baked or made into pies. Scallop or summer squash can be stewed or sliced and fried. Yellow neck is best stewed. When stewing or steaming, care should be taken not to overcook as they will become mushy. 2) A cool drink of which part is fruit and fruit juice. Such as a lemon squash will have the juice of the lemon and some of the pulp.

squid—A shell-less sea mollusk.

spumoni *(It)*—Layered ice cream or sherbet of different flavors, colors and textures. Candied fruits and nuts can be added.

stalk—Main axis of a plant, generally long and slender. Such as a stalk of celery.

staples—Basic foodstuffs such as flour, milk, sugar, shortening.

starch—A carbohydrate found in many foods such as corn, flour, etc. Very important in the diet.

star fruit—*(See Carambola)*

steak—Any of a variety of cuts of beef such as T-bone, rib eye, filet mignon and sirloin. Cooked by grilling, pan frying, broiling or braising. It should be noted that there can be diferent names in different parts of the country for the same cut.

steamer—Various devices for holding foods above simmering water so that they are cooked in steam.

steer—Bovine raised for its flesh. *(See Beef)*

steig *(Sc)*—Steak

stew—Dish of meat and vegetables cooked together in a liquid.

stifle—A New England meat or fish stew.

Stilton scoop—A Victorian tool used to scoop Stilton cheese from the top of the round.

stockpots—Large, two-handled metal containers. Used for making soups, stews and for large quantities. Used on top of the stove.

stocks—The flavored liquid from which many sauces and gravies are made. Stocks are also used in the cooking of meats, vegetables and fruits.

Stollen *(Ger)*—A rich fruit cake.

stone—The seed of various fruits—cherry, peach, plums, apricots, etc.

stopper—An object which is used to close the opening of a bottle. Can be made of glass, cork, wood or plastic.

stoved hens *(Sc)*—Chicken casserole

strainer—Kitchen utensil with a fine sieve used to strain foods. Small sized ones are used for straining tea and coffee.

straw case—The wrapping of straw in which bottles are transported.

straw potatoes *(Eng)*—White potatoes that are prepared the same as shoestring potatoes but are cut slightly thicker.

strawberry—Berry from a small bushy plant. Used in making shortcakes, jams, preserves and eaten fresh with sugar and cream. Also made into pies and tarts. Berries should be fully red when using. The berry does not ripen after picking. They may be dried and made into fruit leather.

strawberry huller—Small tool used to remove the stem from strawberries and other berries.

Streussel *(Ger)*—A topping made of sugar, flour, butter and flavorings. It is spread over the bread, cake or pie before baking. Also a yeast roll with this type of topping.

Stritzel *(Ger)*—A braided sweet bread. In some parts of Europe a traditional Christmas bread.

string bean—The long pods of various beans can be stewed, steamed or boiled. Widely used in cookery. Can be cooked with bacon, pork fat and diced onions. Also mushrooms, waterchestnuts, pearl onions, new potatoes and toasted almonds can be added. Cold cooked string beans can be combined with cooked dried beans for a colorful salad. There are green and yellow varieties.

strudel—A light rich yeast pastry that is stretched very thin with the hands. It is then filled with various fruits, preserves or meats. Rolled and baked whole.

strutto *(It)*—Lard (fat)

stuffing—*(See Forcemeats)*

submarine—Same as a Poor Boy sandwich.

subrics *(Fr)*—Small preparations that can be used as hors d'oeuvres or garnishes. An example—diced, cooked beef, eggs, flour and cheese combined then dropped by spoonfuls into hot fat, cooked on both sides. Meats and vegetables are precooked before being made into subrics.

succotash—Lima beans and whole kernel corn cooked together with seasonings.

sucre *(Fr)*—Sugar

sucre en morceaux *(Fr)*—Sugar cubes

sucrose—Cane or beet sugar.

suet—The fatty tissue from the loins of the beef, oxen and some other animals. Not the swine. A hard fat.

sugar—A sweetener made from sugar cane and sugar beets. It is soluble. In its refined state it is white in color. Used in cakes, cookies, candies, punches, beverages and wherever a sweet taste is desired. See separate listing of types of sugar.

sugar boiler—Saucepan used for melting sugars. Has a large lip for pouring. Copper is the best material.

sugar iron—*(See Salamander)*

sugar pea—Snow pea. Garden pea.

sukiyaki *(Ja)*—Strips of beef that are quickly fried. Usually the cooking is done at the table, where the diner is served immediately. Vegetables can be cooked in this manner. Cooking is done on a small grill and little fat is used. Various condiments usually accompany this dish.

sultana—Raisins made from the sultana grape. Also called white raisins.

sunchokes—Jerusalem artichokes

sundae—A confection made up of scoops of ice cream with various flavored syrups and preserved fruit spooned over the top. Sometimes whipped cream and chopped nuts are added. Generally served in a tall sherbet glass. May also be called a parfait.

sunflower—The mature seeds of this flower can be toasted and eaten as a snack. Can be used as a garnish on various dishes. A desirable cooking oil is made from the seed.

summer lamb—The lambs that are available in the summer months.

sunny side up—Method of frying eggs. The eggs are broken into a skillet with fat and cooked until the whites are set. They are not turned over.

sun tea—Method of brewing tea. Tea is placed in a glass container with water and set in the sun for a few hours. The heat of the sun will warm the water enough to brew the tea. Brewed in this manner, the tea has a softer taste than that brewed with hot water.

supper—The last meal of the day. In some areas the evening meal (dinner) is called supper.

supreme *(Fr)*—1) Literally, the best. 2) The breast of chicken or other choice cut of meat. 3) Chicken in a cream sauce.

surinam cherry—Fruit of a South American tree that is also grown in California and Florida. It is eaten raw and used in salads. Can also be used in fruit cakes.

sushi *(Ja)*—Raw fish that is cut into fancy shapes and eaten with various condiments.

susina *(It)*—Plum

sweet and sour—A dish that is both sweet and sour tasting. Such as sweet and sour ribs.

sweet breads—The pancreas or thymus of beef, lamb and hog used for food.

sweet butter—Same as unsalted butter.

sweet chocolate—Cocoa with ample sweeteners added so that it can be eaten as is. Usually formed into bars or cakes.

sweet pepper—Same as bell or green pepper. Any pepper that is not hot tasting.

sweet potato—An edible tuberous root vegetable that is sweet tasting. Can be yellow or orange colored. It is generally stewed and served with butter or placed in a casserole, topped with marshmallows and browned. Can be sliced and fried in butter and sugar. Orange juice is sometimes added to the stewing liquid. Small potatoes can be baked whole with the skins on.

sweetmeats—*(See Sweets)*

sweets—Sweet foods such as candy, cookies, cakes, pies, tarts and the like.

sweet sherry—*(See Cream Sherry)*

Swiss cheese—A hard cheese, pale yellow to dull white in color. Rather sweetish. Has large holes throughout. A sandwich and cooking chees.

Swiss meringue—The most popular and widely used of the meringues. Superfine sugar is beaten with the egg whites. It is used on pies, cakes, alaskas and other desserts. Used for making meringue baskets and decorative garnishes. Poaches well.

swizzle—An alcoholic drink made of rum or other spirit, sugar and bitters. Served over crushed ice.

swizzle stick—A glass, plastic or wood rod used to stir an alcoholic drink.

syllabub—Beverage made of champagne, wine or sparkling wine, fruit juice, sugar, spices and whipped cream. Should be light and frothy.

syrup—A thick sugar solution. Can be flavored with fruits or other flavorings.

T

t—Abbreviation for teaspoon.

T—Abbreviation for tablespoon.

Tabasco—Trademark name for a sharp-tasting sauce used on meats, fish, etc.

table d'hote *(Fr)*—The host's table. Common table in a hotel. A meal at a fixed price and hour. A fixed menu as opposed to an ala carte menu.

table service—Generally refers to the utensils and dishes used at a meal. Can also mean that food and drink will be served at the table in a restaurant.

table silencer—Heavy cloth or pad used under the tablecloth to protect the surface of the table and to silence the movement of dishes.

table wine—Wine that is served at the table with meals.

taco *(Mex)*—A Mexican corn tortilla fried then folded over and stuffed with cooked meat, lettuce, tomatoes, onions, cheese and hot sauce. It is eaten as a finger food. Can be likened to a sandwich.

Tafelsalz *(Ger)*—Table salt

taffy—A type of pulled candy. After the ingredients are cooked, according to the particular recipe, the candy is worked (pulled) with the hands until it is milky in color. It is stretched in ropes and cut in the desired lengths. It is a rather hard candy. There are many varieties, such as salt water, white and chocolate.

tagine—An earthenware pot used in the Moroccan kitchen for cooking stews.

tagliatelle *(It)*—Long, narrow noodles.

tahini—A paste made from ground seasame seeds.

tallow—Hard animal fat (beef or sheep) rendered and used in making soap and candles. Sometimes added to solid shortening and lard. Will smoke when heated. Generally not used in cooking.

talmouse *(Fr)*—A type of cheesecake

tamale or tamal—Dish made of chopped meat, cornmeal mush and seasonings. Can be made in a casserole or individual ones wrapped in corn husks and steamed. Various chopped or grated cooked meats can be used. Sometimes cheese is used to top the casserole type tamale.

tamale pie—Tamales baked in a casserole.

tamarin *(Fr)*—Tamarind

Tamarinde *(Ger)*—Tamarind

tamarindo *(It, Sp)*—Tamarind

tamis *(Fr)*—Sieve

tanaka *(Tur)*—Pot used for making Turkish coffee. It is narrow necked with a long handle. It is spouted and is available in many sizes.

tang—Flavor, small taste.

tangelo—A citrus fruit that is a cross between a tangerine and grapefruit. It is eaten raw and can be used in fruit salads,

tangerine—A citrus fruit with a bright orange or red peel that separates very easily from the flesh. It is eaten raw or added to fruit salads. It is also available canned.

tankard—Container used to drink beer from. Made of ceramic, metal or glass. Generally has a hinged lid and handle.

tapas *(Sp, col)*—Generally, snacks served with drinks before a meal. Snacks, hot or cold.

tapioca—Thickening agent made from the cassava root. Used especially in puddings.

tart—1) Agreeable sharp to the taste, as the apple was tart. 2) Pastry shell filled with pudding, fruits or other filling.

tarta de fruta *(SP)*—Fruit pie

tartar—The acid potassium tartrate used in baking powder.

tartare—A mayonnaise sauce with chopped onion, green olives, sweet pickle, capers, parsley and vinegar added. Served with fish.

tarte *(Fr)*—Pie

tartine *(Fr)*—Bread spread with butter or jam.

tartlets—Small tarts

tartlet tins—Small fluted or decorative tins used for baking tartlet cases.

tartufo *(It)*—Truffle

taste buds—Sensors on the tongue that permit us to perceive the flavors of food and drink.

te *(It)*—The beverage tea

te *(Sp)*—The beverage tea

tea—1) A beverage that can be brewed from many different plants. The tea shrub is the source of black and green teas. The leaves are dried and then combined with hot water to produce the beverage tea. Can be served hot or with ice. Sugar, lemon and milk are often added. Orange pekoe is the most common tea used in America. Many other varieties are available—Oolongs, Darjeiling, Assam, Gunpowder, India and Formosa Black. 2) Light snacks usually served between meals. 3) An afternoon social function where tea, cakes, cookies and small sandwiches are served. Usually to honor someone or an event.

tea bag—A small amount of dried tea enclosed in a porous bag. Enough to brew one cup.

tea cozy—Padded cloth cover placed over the teapot to keep the tea hot.

tea infusers—Small containers in which leaf tea is placed for brewing.

tea kettle—Stove top container in which water is heated.

teapot—Utensil for brewing tea. Made of porcelain, glass, pottery or metal.

Tee *(Ger)*—The beverage tea.

tempura *(Or)*—Fresh vegetables, fruit, meat or seafood dipped in batter and fried in hot oil. Served hot.

tenderizer—*(See Pounder and Meat Tenderizer)*

tequilla *(Mex)*—Alcoholic beverage distilled from the maguey or other mescal yielding plants. Not often used in cooking.

ternera *(Sp)*—Veal

terrapin—An edible fresh water turtle.

terrine—1) An unglazed earthenware casserole with lid. Usually oblong shaped. Soak in water before using. 2) The dish cooked in such a pot. 3) Potted meat.

terrine a pate *(Fr)*—Same as a terrine. Can be called a clay pot.

terrine de foie gras *(Fr)*—Goose liver cooked in earthenware.

tete de veau *(Fr)*—Calf's head

the *(Fr)*—The beverage tea.

thermometer—Instrument used to measure temperature. A meat thermometer is inserted in the cut of meat before the start of cooking. Liquid thermometers are suspended in the liquid during cooking.

Thermos—Brand name for a container enclosed in a vacuum that permits food and drinks to be kept cold or hot for long periods of time. Through common usage the word Thermos has come to mean any type of vacuum bottle or container. Handy for trips.

thermostat—A device that regulates the temperature of an appliance. Ovens, crockpots and waffle irons are usually equipped with them.

thimbleberry—An old name for raspberry

thon *(Fr)*—Tuna

thousand island dressing—A salad dressing made with mayonnaise, pickle relish, spices and herbs.

thousand year eggs—*(See Hundred Year Old Eggs)*

Thunfisch *(Ger)*—Tuna, tunny

thym *(Fr)*—Thyme

ti leaves—Leaves from the ti plant are used for wrapping food. Decorative only. The leaf is not edible. Shiny and oblong. Should be available through florists.

Tia Maria—A Jamaican liqueur flavored with coffee.

timbale—1) Mold shaped like a drum with straight sides. 2) The dish prepared in a timbale.

timballo *(It)*—Meat pie

timer—Devices used to measure cooking time. Can be hand wound or electric. Some ranges are equipped with timers.

timo *(It)*—Thyme

tines—The slender, pointed parts of a fork.

tins—Metal containers used primarily for baking cakes, pies, breads and pastry cases. Pie and bread pans should be allowed to darken with use. Dark pans brown better. Cake and cookie tins usually are kept shiny and bright.

tipple—A small portion of liquor.

toast—1) Slices of bread that have been browned by dry heat on both sides. Generally in an electric toaster. 2) To pay honor to someone or something by saying words of praise followed by the drinking of wine or other beverage.

toaster—An electrical device used to toast bread. Can toast 2 or 4 slices at a time. Equipped with an automatic timer. A non-electric model sits over the flame of a stove burner.

toasting fork—Long handled fork with large tines. The tines are wide spaced. Used to toast or warm bread, rolls, wieners and marshmallows over an open fire or charcoals.

toast points—Bread that has been toasted and then cut into triangular shapes. One slice of toast will make four toast points.

toddy—An alcoholic drink of rum or whiskey, spices, sugar and hot water.

toffee—A brittle candy. Can be coffee or chocolate flavored.

tofu *(Or)*—Molded bean curd. Rather bland in taste. Used in stir-fry dishes.

tofu cheese—Tofu that has had the water pressed out.

Tom and Jerry—*(See Eggnog)* This drink is served hot.

tomatillo—Small (about the size of a walnut) green berries that are used in Mexican cookery. Should be deep green in color and the husk a tan color. Husk is not eaten. Used in making salsa verde and can be added fresh to green salads. Usually available in Mexican groceries.

tomate *(Fr, Sp)*—Tomato

Tomate *(Ger)*—Tomato

tomato—A fleshy fruit from a bush of the nightshade family. Colors range from bright red to pink to yellow to white. A widely used fruit. Native of the Americas. Can be served fresh, made into sauces, catsups, added to stews, soups and casseroles. Should not be stored in the refrigerator as this will cause a chemical action and the fruit can become bitter tasting. Although it is a fruit, it is thought of as a vegetable and used as such. Size can range from the very small to ones five inches in diameter.

tomato paste—Same as tomato sauce but is cooked until most of the water is removed. Must be combined with water for use. Used the same as tomato sauce. Very thick. Available at the market.

tomato sauce—A sauce made of tomatoes, sugar and seasonings. Cooked until quite thick. Used in soups, stews, casseroles and as a base for some spahetti sauces. Is available at the market.

tomillo *(Sp)*—Thyme

tongs—A tool for lifting and holding. Similar in shape to scissors.

tono *(It)*—Tuna

tools—Various devices used in preparing and serving foods and drinks. See individual listings.

toothpick—A short, round, slim piece of wood that is used to dislodge food particles from between the teeth. Should be used with discretion or in private.

topinambour *(Fr)*—Jerusalem artichoke

toque *(Fr)*—A tall hat worn by cooks.

toronja *(Sp)*—Grapefruit

torsk *(Dan)*—Fresh cod

torta *(It, Sp)*—Cake; pie

Tortchen *(Ger)*—Pie

Torte *(Ger)*—A rich cake

tortellini *(It)*—On small rounds of pasta a bit of filling is placed. It is folded over, sealed and formed into a créscent. Cooked in a liquid. Can be served with a meat sauce.

tortilla *(Mex)*—A flat, thin cake, unleavened, baked on a heated stone or iron. Can be made of cornmeal or flour. Use as a wrapping for meat, beans or other ingredients. It is also eaten like bread.

tortilla *(Sp)*—An egg dish similar to an omelette. It is not folded or filled. Various ingredients are mixed and cooked with the eggs. It is cooked on both sides.

tortilla press—Small hand tool used to form tortillas.

tortue *Fr)*—Turtle

tortue clair *(Fr)*—Clear turtle soup.

tostaditas *(Mex)*—Fried corn tortilla chips. Used as a snack and for dipping.

tostada *(Mex)*—A corn tortilla is fried then ground cooked meat, lettuce, tomatoes, onions, cheese and a hot sauce are layered on it. Usually the cheese is added last. It is best eaten with a fork. Literally, an open faced sandwich.

tournedos *(Fr)*—Choice cut of beef fillet.

tourte *(Fr)*—Tart, pie

toute epice *(Fr)*—Allspice

tracklements *(Eng)*—Condiments

trail—The intestines of wild fowl.

transparent noodles *(Or)*—*(See Mung bean noodles)*

Traube *(Ger)*—Grape

treacle—The drippings from sugar vats. Molasses.

treacle *(Engl)*—Molasses

tree ear fungus— *(Ch)*—*(See Cloud Ear Fungus)*

tremper *(Fr)*—Soak

trencher—A wooden platter for serving food.

trifle—A desset concoction of fresh or canned fruits combined with beaten egg whites and frozen. Can also be a combination of fruits, pudding and sponge cake. Many variations of this dish.

trigo *(Sp)*—Wheat, maiz, corn

tripe—Stomach tissue of a ruminant used as food.

Triple Sec—An orange flavored liqueur.

trivet—A small metal or ceramic stand used to rest hot dishes on. A necessity for the dining table.

trota *(It)*—Trout

trout—A freshwater food fish. Related to the salmon.

trucha *(Sp)*—Trout

truck farm—An agriculture operation that grows a variety of fruits and vegetables for the produce market. Generally the acreage is small. It is well worth the effort to find one in your area.

trufa *(Sp)*—Truffle

truffe *(Fr)*—Truffle

Truffel *(Ger)*—Truffle

truffle—An underground fungus whose dark wrinkled fruit is esteemed in cookery. Found in Europe. It is gathered by using trained pigs and dogs to locate them.

truite *(Fr)*—Trout

truite au bleu *(Fr)*—Brook trout

truite de lac *(Fr)*—Lake trout

truite saumonee *(Fr)*—Salmon trout

trussing needle—A long needle with a large eye to accommodate heavy twine. Used for trussing fowl.

tube pan—Round cake pan with a hollow tube in the center. In some types the tube is removable. Angel food cakes are almost always cooked in this type of pan. Some pans have decorative sides and bottoms. Can be shallow or deep.

tucker *(col)*—Food

tumbler—A round drinking glass

tun—Large wine cask

tuna—A popular sea fish. Member of the tunny family. Purchased in cans it is used in salads, sandwiches, casseroles and as croquettes. Is sometime availabe fresh in fish markets.

Tunke *(Ger)*—Sauce

tunny—Fish of the mackerel family.

tureen—Large, covered bowl used at the table for serving soups and stews. Usually has a matching ladle.

turkey—A large fowl. Can be purchased at the market ready to cook. The whole birds can weigh from six pounds to over 20 pounds. Are also available as parts, leg, thigh and the breast. Are available fresh, smoked or frozen. The whole bird is generally roasted while the parts can be grilled or roasted. Turkey is a traditional Christmas and Thanksgiving Day meat. Leftover meat can be served cold in sandwiches, in a cream sauce or in casseroles. The carcass, after all meat is removed, can be made into an excellent broth.

Turkish delight—A candy that is usually jelly-like cubes covered with powdered sugar.

turners—Handled tool with a flattened end. Used for turning pancakes, eggs, removing cookies from the baking sheet and anywhere the cook needs help in turning something.

turning knife—Short bladed knife, 2-3 inches. Used to shape vegetables into decorative forms. Sharp pointed.

turnip—An edible root vegetable. Usually white in color with a purple skin. Generally stewed but can be added to soups and stews. Usually the smaller roots are the most tender. Peel before cooking. Excellent stuffed with sausage and bread crumbs.

turnover—A round of pastry dough. Filling is placed on the dough, it is folded over and baked. Can be a sweet or savory.

turntable, cake—Round, revolving device on which a cake is placed while it is being iced and decorated.

tutti-frutti—Mixed fruits, as in a salad. Flavor of ice cream with various candied fruits in it. A condiment of candied fruits in a heavy syrup.

TV Dinners—Trademark name for frozen meals that are complete in themselves. Each meal is on its own plate. They are placed in the oven to be heated.

twist of—A strip of peel, from a citrus for instance, is twisted over a drink or dish. This sprays the aromatic oils in the peel onto the surface of the food or dink.

two-minute egg—*(See Soft Boiled Egg)*

Tymian *(Ger)*—Thyme

When turned out the fruits and sugars form the icing for the cake.

utensil—Any tool, pot, pan, dish used in cooking.

utensile *(It)*—Utensil

utensilio *(Sp)*—Utensil

uva *(Sp)*—Grape

uval *(Fr)*—Grape

uva passa *(It)*—Raisin

uva seca *(Sp)*—Raisin

uzhin *(Rus)*—Supper

U

ukha *(Rus)*—Fish soup

umkokolo fruit—The small, yellow fruit of this tall shrub is cooked. The taste is similar to cranberries. Also known as 'kei apple.' Can be grown in California and Florida.

unbleached flour—A mixture of hard and soft wheat flours. Good bread flour. It is bleached by aging. Don't let the name fool you. Off white in color.

unsalted butter—Butter that has had no salt added during churning. Ideal for pastries and other confections.

until set—To let a dish, like custard or gelatin, sit until it is firm.

uovo *(It)*—Egg

USDA—United States Department of Agriculture. Inspects meats and agriculture products. Assures set standards are maintained.

upside down cake—A cake where the topping is put in the pan before the batter, then baked.

V

vaca *(Sp)*—Cow

vache *(Fr)*—Cow

vache a lait *(Fr)*—Milk cow

vacherin *(Fr)*—A dessert made of several 'crowns' or rings of baked meringue. The rings are stacked one on the other with whipped cream, fruit or chantilly cream between the layers.

vacherin *(Swiss)*—A soft cheese from Switzerland.

vainilla *(Sp)*—Vanilla

Vandermint—A Dutch liqueur flavored with chocolate and mint.

vaniglia *(It)*—Vanilla

vanilla sugar—Granulated or confectioner's sugar that has been flavored with the essence of the vanilla bean. *(See Chapter III)*

vanille *(Fr, Ger)*—Vanilla

vatrushki *(Rus)*—Open tarts filled with cream cheese and other ingredients.

veal—A very young calf. The flavor is different from beef. Flesh is light in color. Cuts are basically the same as beef. The cuts are naturally smaller.

veal scallopine—Prepared scallopines are usually breaded and quickly fried in fat. Various herbs and spices and seasonings can also be used. *(See Scallopine)*

veau *(Fr)*—Veal

vegetable—The edible part of a plant, usually served with the entree of a meal. *(See individual listings)*

vegetable pear—Name given to the chayote in Florida.

vegetal *(Sp)*—Vegetable

vegetale *(It)*—Vegetable

vegetarian—1) A person who eats no meats or meat fats. 2) Method of cooking using no meats or meat fats.

veloute *(Fr)*—Soft and smooth to the palate.

venaison *(Fr)*—Venison

venison—The flesh of the deer.

verjuice—The juice of unripened grapes.

verjus *(Fr)*—Verjuice

vermicelli—Pasta in long strands. It is smaller in diameter than spaghetti.

veronique *(Fr)*—Meat or fish dishes that contain seedless white grapes.

Vesperbrot *(Ger)*—Light afternoon meal, a tea.

viande *(Fr)*—Meat, flesh

viands—Provisions, food

Vichy-Celestins—A mineral water from France's Vichy region.

vichyssoise *(Fr)*—Type of potato soup with leeks and cream. Served cold.

Vienna sausage—Small, spiced frankfurters. Used as hors d'oeuvres.

vin *(Fr)*—Wine

vinagre *(Fr, Sp)*—Vinegar

vinaigrette dressing—Sauce made with vinegar and spices and herbs. Generally served on cold vegetables, especially asparagus.

vin chaud *(Fr)*—Hot spiced wine.

vin coupe *(Fr)*—Mixed wine

vin de paille *(Fr)*—Wine from grapes that are dried on straw and exposed to the sun.

vin d'honneur *(Fr)*—Literally, the wine drunk in honor of an honored guest.

vin du pays *(Fr)*—Wine of the neighborhood or country.

vinegar—A sour acidic liquid used in cooking and pickling. Obtained by fermenting cider, wine, malt, etc. Some salad vinegars have had certain herbs or spices added to them. Wine vinegar is popular as a green salad dressing. An excellent household cleaner.

vinning okra—A vegetable gourd that resembles okra. While young it is tender and can be eaten like zucchini and cucumbers. Used in Chinese cookery. Also known as Chinese okra, gee gwa and sing qua. Should be available in Chinese markets.

vino *(It, Sp)*—Wine

vino de casa *(It)*—Literally, common wines to quench the thirst. Housewine.

vin ordinaire *(Fr)*—The house wine in a restaurant or any non-vintage wine. Any inexpensive (cheap) wine.

vin pur *(Fr)*—Wine without water.

Virginia peanut—Variety of peanut eaten as a snack and ground for peanut butter. The nut is long, slim and light colored. The skin covering the kernel is removed before using.

vitamins—Various organic substances essential to man. Generally obtained when we eat plants and meats. May be added to the diet by the consummation of certain tablets.

vitello *(It)*—Veal

vodka—A neutral grain spirit that is odorless and tasteless (ideally). Not often used in cooking.

vodka *(Rus)*—Literally, little water. A strong alcoholic drink that is almost tasteless.

volaille *(Fr)*—Poultry, fowl.

vol-au-vent *(Fr)*—A kind of puff paste case.

wafer—Thin crisp cake or cracker

Waffel *(Ger)*—Waffle

waffle—Soft but crisp cake generally made from a pancake type batter and cooked in a special baking utensil. Usually served at breakfast with butter and syrup. Can also be used as a base for various creamed dishes or desserts.

waffle iron—An electrical appliance used for the baking of waffles. Usually have an automatic baking control.

Waldorf salad—Salad made with apples, celery and walnuts. Served with a mayonnaise based dressing.

walk-in box—In restaurants and markets, a refrigerator that can be walked into. It is generally room sized.

walnuts—Any of several varieties of a popular walnut. English and Black are the ones mostly used in American cookery. Walnuts are used in pies, cakes, cookies and other confections. Can be used as garnish for various fruit, vegetable and meat dishes as well as a part of these dishes. A flavorful cooking oil is made from the nut meats. Also known as Persian Walnut.

warming tray—A small tray with electrical heaters in the surface that keep the top warm. Excellent for use at the buffet or patio table.

wash—Brushing the surface of a pastry before or after baking. A wash can be of egg, milk, water, fat or whatever the recipe calls for.

wassail—A sweet spiced alcoholic drink that is generally served during a holiday season. Usually from a punch bowl.

Wasser *(Ger)*—Water

water—The liquid which composes rivers, lakes and oceans. That which falls from the sky as rain. The liquid the body must have to survive. Snow, hail and sleet are frozen water. Water is not a beverage.

water bath—1) In canning the process of covering the filled cans with boiling water and processing (boiling) the prescribed time. Used for acid fruits and vegetables only 2) The pan itself.

water chestnut—The edible fruit from an herbaceous water plant. Can be boiled or roasted. The flesh is similar to the chestnut. Flavor is bland. They are crisp and crunchy. Widely used in Oriental cookery.

watercress—Leafy green vegetable used in salads, soups and sandwiches.

weep—The separation of egg whites after they have been beaten. This indicates that the whites were not beaten long enough.

Wein *(Ger)*——Wine

Weizen *(Ger)*—Wheat

well done—Degree of doneness of food, such as steak. The flesh has lost all of its pinkness in cooking. The flesh should still be moist.

Welsh onion—A non-bulbous, bunching onion. It is mild. Similar to the leek in that it is cultivated to produce a long white stem. Widely used in the Orient.

Welsh rabbit—*(See Rarebit)*

western omelet—*(See Denver Omelet)*

wheat—A cereal grain used as a breakfast cereal and ground into flour. There are three types of wheat grown in America. Hard, Soft and Durum. See listings for each type.

wheat flour—Any of various types of flour milled from wheat grain. Only the inner part of the grain is used for white flours.

wheat germ—The wheat embryo that is separated during milling. Rich in vitamins.

whey—The watery part of milk that separates when the milk sours. Also the liquid that remains after the cream is churned. Cheeses and buttermilk are made from this whey.

whipped topping—A creamy white substance with the taste and consistency of whipped dairy cream. It is sold frozen in small containers and in aerosol cans. Caution—

After thawing or dispensing the 'cream' will not hold its form very long. Add it when ready to serve. There is also a dry powder that when mixed with a liquid and beaten will produce a topping. This type can be used for frosting cakes and other confections.

whisk—Kitchen tool used to beat and whip eggs, sauces and other liquids. One type is made of stiff steel wires bent in a pear shape. Another type is made with coiled wires. Handy for making smooth sauces and gravies. The design of whisks are such that large amounts of air can be incorporated.

whiskey or whisky—Any of several alcoholic spirits distilled from various grains. *(See Bourbon, Scotch, Rye, Irish Whiskey, Canadian Whiskey and Alcohol)*

whisky de seigle *(Fr)*—Rye whiskey

whisky irlandais *(Fr)*—Irish whiskey

white beans—Same as navy beans.

white flour—Any flour milled from the inner part of the wheat grain. Usually bleached by chemicals.

white fudge—Similar to chocolate fudge in texture. It is made without chocolate or corn syrup.

white sauce—Basic sauce made with milk, flour and fat.

white walnut—Another name for the butternut

white wine—Wines that are clear to amber in color.

whole wheat flour—Graham flour

Wienerschnitzel *(Ger)*—Breaded veal cutlet. The meat is flattened, breaded and fried in oil or butter until crisp.

wild rice—Not a rice but a wild grass seed. It is used in various dishes and stuffings. Has an interesting flavor and texture. Dark colored. Expensive.

wilted lettuce—A method of preparing fresh leaf lettuce or other tender greens. Hot bacon fat or butter is poured over the prepared greens just prior to serving. Sometimes crisp fried bacon or chopped hard boiled eggs are added. The blade of green onions can also be used. A little salt and fresh ground pepper are usually sprinkled over the salad.

wine—A fermented beverage made from the juice of grapes, berries, fruits and other plants. Wine is used as an accompaniment at meals as well as an aperitif, digestif and cocktail. A rule of thumb to follow in serving wine with meals is that red wine with red meats and lamb, and white wine with light meats, seafood and fowl. Champagne can be served with any course. The alcohol content of wines can range from approximately 12 to 20 percent. White wines should be served chilled. Red or dark wines should be served at room temperature. Wine should be served in wide mouthed glasses, with the exception of heavy wines served as aperitifs and digestifs. Smaller glasses should be used for these. Almost all wines are used in cooking. Use a non-vintage wine for cooking. Sparkling wines should be allowed to 'die' before cooking. Alcohol will cook out. *(See Cooking Wines)*

wine basket—A shallow wicker or metal container in which a bottle of wine can be laid.

wine cellar—Place where wine is stored. A cellar used to store wine. Temperature is usually constant.

wine cooler—1) A ceramic tube in which a bottle of wine is set. The holder is immersed in water before use. The natural evaporation will keep the wine chilled. 2) An alcoholic drink made of wine and some type of effervescent. Fruits or juices can be added. Served in a tall glass with ice.

wine glassful—A measure used in old recipes. It is equal to about four ounces.

wine press—A machine for extracting the juice from grapes.

wine rack—Stands designed to hold wine bottles in the horizontal position. Some are small for the table top, while others can be of cabinet size.

winery—Place where wines are made.

winter cress—Watercress

wishbone—The forked bone located in the front of a fowl's breastbone. Often cut as a separate piece. After eating this piece, sometimes two people each grasp a side of the bone and upon making a silent wish, will pull the bone apart. Usually the one getting the larger part will have their wish come true. A tradition of unknown origin.

wok—A saucer-shaped Oriental cooking pan. Used for stir frying and steaming.

wood sorrel—A species of sorrel that is small in size.

woodcock—A game bird.

wooden pick—A small sliver of wood that is inserted in a cake to test its doneness. A wooden toothpick or clean broom straw can also be used. Pick is inserted in the middle of the cake and withdrawn. If pick is clean the cake is done.

woody—The flesh of many vegetables, if permitted to overripen, will become stringy and tough. This is particularly true of asparagus.

Worcestershire sauce—A highly seasoned sauce used mainly on steaks and other cuts of beef. Generally used at the table.

Wurst *(Ger)*—Sausage

Wurze *(Ger)*—Spice, condiment, seasoning.

xeres *(Fr, It)*—Sherry

XXXX sugar—Confectioner's sugar

yam—Edible tuber of a vining tropical plant. Starchy and widely used in the tropical regions of the world. Sometimes the American sweet potato is called a yam.

yaourt *(Fr)*—Yogurt

yard long bean—A variety of cowpea which can reach a length of up to three feet.

yard long cucumber—Chinese cucumber

yeast—A leavening agent used in making most loaf breads and dinner rolls. Coffee cakes, too. Breads made in this manner are allowed to rise before baking. Baking yeast can be purchased dry (granules) or moist (cakes). Use before the expiration date on each package.

yearling lamb—A lamb over one year and under two years of age.

yema *(Sp)*—Egg yolk

yerba *(Sp)*—Herb

yoghurt—Yogurt

yogurt—A fermented semifluid milk food. Thick and tart. Made of milk solids and skimmed cows milk. Flavorings and fruit are often added.

Yorkshire pudding—Not a pudding in the general sense. A mixture of flour, eggs, milk and salt is poured into a pan with drippings from the roasting beef roast. It is baked. During cooking it becomes brown and slightly brittle. Always served warm with the roast. Can be placed under the roast and the drippings allowed to fall upon the pudding. This is the original method of cooking this dish.

yum-yum *(sl)*—Sugar

zabaglione *(It)*—Basically a light custard made without milk. Some variations call for whipped cream or beaten egg whites. Generally Marsala wine is used. Any light fruit wine can be substituted.

zabaglione pan—Domed bottom pan used for whisking eggs when making Zabaglione. The pan is held over the fire (heat) with one hand while whisking with the other. Made of tin lined copper.

zabaione *(It)*—Same as zabaglione

zafferano *(It)*—Saffron

zakuski *(Rus)*—Hors d'oeuvre usually eaten after drinking vodka.

zanahoria *(Sp)*—Carrot

zaque *(Sp)*—Wine skin

zarzaparilla *(Sp)*—Sarsaparilla

zenzero *(It)*—Ginger

zest—The colored part of the peel of the orange, lemon and lime. Used in various confections. Removed with a special tool.

zester—Small hand tool used to cut very small strips of zest.

Zimt *(Ger)*—Cinnamon

Zitrone *(Ger)*—Lemon

zucca *(It)*—Pumpkin

zucchero *(It)*—Sugar

zucchini—A variety of edible gourd. They are long and green or almost black in color. Can be lightly stewed, steamed or breaded and lightly fried. Can be used raw in green salads. Used in some cakes and breads. Can be pickled.

zucchini blossoms—The bloom can be dipped in batter and fried. Not seen in markets very often.

Zucker *(Ger)*—Sugar

Zuckerwerk *(Ger)*—Candy

zwieback—Rusks that have been baked twice. A sweet bread.

Zwiebel *(Ger)*—Onion

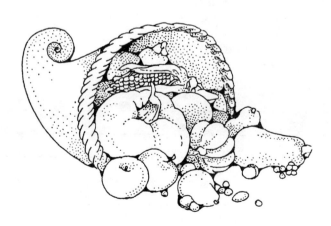

Notes

CHAPTER II

Spices, Herbs
and
Edible Flowers and Wild Plants

acacia—The blooms of this plant can be dipped in a batter and fried as fritters. Use as a snack or garnish. The flowers can also be made into a wine.

allspice—This spice is the dried ripe fruit from an evergreen tree. The flavor resembles a blend of nutmeg, cloves and cinnamon. Whole allspice may be used in soups, stews, pot roasts, sauces, pickles and fish dishes. Ground allspice is added to cakes, cookies, fruit pies and other confections. Adds flavor to meatloaf, barbeque sauces, French and other salad dressings. It is also known as pimento, Jamaica pepper and Jamaica pimento.

angelica—When candied, the stems of this tall growing herb are used in various confections. Stems can also be used fresh and prepared like asparagus. The liqueurs Chartreuse and absinthe, gin and vermouths use angelica in their flavoring. Bitters is made from the leaves. Man has used this herb for many centuries.

anise—This spice is the seed of a plant belonging to the parsley family. It has a strong licorice flavor. May be used whole or crushed in cookies, cakes, breads and candies. May also be used to enhance the flavor of applesauce, beef stew, fruit pies, pickles, fish and shellfish dishes. Available as whole seeds or as an extract. Use sparingly.

aniseed—Same as anise.

anise pepper—This dried red berry is used in Chinese cookery. It is hot and aromatic. Is one of the five ingredients in Chinese Five Spices. Should be available in Chinese groceries.

annatto—The seeds of this spice are orange in color and have a light sweet earthy taste. They are ground before using. Used in Caribbean and Latin American cookery. The pulp surrounding the seed is used as a flavorless coloring agent.

apple blossoms—The blossoms may be fried then dusted with sugar and served as a dessert or used as a garnish.

banana buds—The bud of the banana is husked and the inner portion used like a vegetable. Can be added to stir-fry dishes and in paellas. In some areas of the world the buds are pickled. The bud is located at the end of the banana stalk.

basil—One of the most widely used herbs. May be used in meat dishes as well as cooked vegetables and green salads. Has an aromatic clove-like aroma. If possible use the fresh leaf. Available as a dried leaf which is crushed before using. Is also called the 'tomato herb' because it is used in so many tomato dishes.

bayberry—1) Waxy grey berries from a seacoast growing shrub. Used in making candles. 2) In Jamaica a tree whose leaves produce an oil that is used in the making of bay rum.

bay—The dried leaves of this herb are from an evergreen tree or bush. Has a strong and pungent flavor. The flavor increases during cooking. Whole leaves are removed before serving. Used in fish, chicken and beef dishes. Also in salad dressings and various marinades. Available as whole leaves or powdered.

beebalm—*See Oswego tea*

black currant buds—The buds of the currant may be used to flavor liqueurs, such as Cassis. Cooked in sugar syrup they can be added to ices and creams.

black mustard—Seeds of this wild plant are used in pickling. Can also be used as a condiment.

blend—A balanced mixture of compatible spices, herbs and seeds either ground or whole.

borage—The three to five-inch leaves of this herb are used fresh in green salads. Can be grown in a pot. The flowers may be dipped in egg whites then in sugar and used as a garnish.

bouquet garni—A variety of herbs and spices tied together in a cheesecloth bag and used in the cooking of a variety of dishes.

burnet—*See salad burnet*

calendula—A variety of marigold.

camomile—The dried leaves of this herb can be used to make a tea, beer or to flavor sugar syrup. Some dry sherries (especially those from Spain) are flavored with the flowers of this plant.

caraway—The small brown seeds of this herb have a sweetish flavor. Should be used sparingly. Used to flavor rye breads, cooked sauerkraut, cabbage, noodles and other meat and vegetable dishes. Available in whole seed form. The young fresh leaves are good in salads and soups. The mature roots can be cooked like carrots and parsnips.

cardamon—The aromatic seeds of this spice have a pungent sweet taste. It is a member of the ginger family. Used in pastries, sweet breads, in pickling, puddings and barbeque sauces. Can also be added to hot spiced wine. Available whole or ground.

carnation—From the dianthus family, carnations and pinks are both used in cookery. The petals of the blossoms may be used dried or fresh. Can also be made into vinegars and scented waters. The petals can be used to flavor jellies and sugar candy.

carob—A tree whose fleshy pods are ground into flour that is sweet and tastes like chocolate. Used in breads, cakes, beverages. In some recipes it may be used as a chocolate substitute. It is caffeine free.

cassia—A spice that tastes like strong cinnamon.

catnip—The plant that cats love. The leaves can be made into a tea. A cup after a large meal acts as a carminative (to expel gas). Some people drink the tea with honey as an old-fashioned cough remedy.

cayenne pepper—Finely ground red chili pepper.

celery seed—From the Mediterranean and Southeast Asia areas this celery-like plant produces a seed with a celery flavor. Whole or ground it is used in stews, soups or wherever a light celery flavor is desired. Use sparingly.

chervil—This herb is used fresh in green salads. It has a flavor more delicate than parsley.

chicory—The roots of one variety of this plant are dried, ground and used as an addition to coffee. The root should be used sparingly as they are quite pungent. Another variety is raised as a salad green. The leaves are blanched before adding to the salad. Caution should be used when adding to salads.

chilies—Several varieties of peppers that are pungent. The intensity of pungency (hotness) varies greatly in the different varieties. Their color can range from bright red to yellow to deep purple. There are a great number of sizes, from the very small to ones a foot long. They are dried and ground to produce chili powder. Caution should be used when handling any type of chilies.

chili powder—A slightly sweet earthy flavored spice. Some types are very hot. Widely used in Mexican cookery.

China tea—The beverage tea made from the tea shrub as opposed to those teas brewed from herbs, spices, flowers, roots and barks.

Chinese five spices—A ground spice mixture used in Chinese cookery. Generally equal parts of anise, pepper, star anise, cassia, cloves and fennel are used. Chinese grocery stores should have this mixture.

Chinese tea—*See China tea*

chives—The small green blades of this onion-related herb are used for light seasoning and as a garnish. Chives have a delicate flavor. The blades are clipped from the growing plant. Blades are chopped before using. The bulb is generally not eaten. Good in salads, cooked vegetables or mixed with sour cream for baked potato topping. Can also be found in the frozen section at the market. Available dried.

chrysanthemum—This fall flower is used in Chinese cookery. The petals of the blossoms are used in salads and when preserved, in a salt solution, added to hot tea. A wine is also made from the blooms.

cinnamon—A mild, sweet spice. Comes from the inner bark of an evergreen tree of the laurel family. Widely used in confections, pastries, breads and some meat, fruit and vegetable dishes. The essence is used to flavor applebutter. The whole sticks are used in pickling and as swizzle sticks for cider, wine and other beverages. Available ground, whole sticks and as an essence.

citronella—A grayish-green grass that is used fresh or dried. Used in Southeast Asian cookery. Is also used to make an insect repellent. Has the flavor of lemon peel.

clover—Both the red and white clover blossoms can be used to make wine and vinegar. The dried flowers can be made into a tea. Dried seeds and flowers are ground into flour for bread.

clove—A strong, sweet, pungent spice from the unopened bud of an evergreen tree. Available ground or whole. Whole, the clove is used to stud hams, pork roasts, fruits and beef. May also be added to stews, soups and teas. Pomade balls may be made by studding an apple with the whole cloves. Ground clove can be used in any number of pastries, cakes, pies, salads and sauces.

cola nuts—Used in the flavoring of various soft drinks.

comfrey—Considered an animal food or weed, this herb has many culinary uses. The young leaves may be treated as a pot-herb, raw in green salads or added to other cooked vegetables. The roots can be chopped and added to soups and stews. May be available in health food and organic food stores. The leaves can be dried. Very rich in minerals and a source of vitamin B-12. Also known as 'boneknit' for its healing powers.

condiments—Aromatics added to food after they are cooked, generally at the table. They include salt, pepper, mustards, sauces, nuts, relishes, chutneys, spices and herbs. Pickled vegetables (cucumbers included) may also be considered condiments. Spiced preserved fruits, jams and jellies are also in this category.

coriander—This versatile herb is the seed of a plant related to the parsley. The flavor is mildly lemon. Whole seeds are used in sweet pickles, after dinner coffee, punches and wassil bowls. Crushed, it is used in candies, cookies, gingerbreads and Danish pastries. Excellent in fish and chicken dishes. Also used in vegetable and beef soups, apple pie, rice pudding, applesauce, fruit sauces, beef, pork and lamb dishes. Available whole or crushed. When the immature umbels are used for flavoring, they are called 'cilantro.'

costmary—The leaves of this herb are used in soups, wild game, poultry and other dishes. It grows wild in the midwestern states. In England, where it is called alecost, it is used to flavor a home brew.

cowslip *(Am)—See Marsh Marigold*

cowslip *(Eng)*—An European primrose with yellow flowers. Both the flowers and buds are used to make syrups, wines and conserves. The buds can also be pickled.

creme de noyau—An essence made by macerating the kernels of various fruits, such as peach, cherry, apricot and bitter almond. This produces an almond-like flavored liquid. It is sweet and is believed by some cooks to be superior to almond extract.

cumin—A seed from a plant of the parsley family. This herb has a strong earthy flavor. Use sparingly. Is used in cheese and rice dishes, with vegetables and in various sauces. Can be used with all types of meat.

curry—A blend of several spices and herbs in powder form. The kinds of spices and herbs varies according to manufacturer. It has an exotic aroma. Indian curry powder is very hot. It is used in soups, sauces, salad dressings, breads and curries.

dandelion—Considered by many to be a bothersome weed this plant is one of the most nourishing in nature. The young leaves may be eaten as a salad green, lightly stewed or steamed. Can be cooked alone or with other greens. The buds (hearts) may be added to omelets. The buds can also be batter fried or added to fritters. New varieties have been developed that are not as strong tasting as the wild plants. It is now being grown commercially.

daylily—The young leaves, buds and tubers of this flower are edible. They can be stir-fried or added to salads. Can also be added to other vegetable dishes.

dill—A spice plant of the parsley family. It has a pleasant fresh flavor. The dried seed is used in pickling, added to sauerkraut, green beans, soups, sauces and dressings. The immature umbels and stalks are used in pickling and as a flavorful garnish.

elephant garlic—A clove of this garlic variety is about the size of a small egg. Has a mild and delicate flavor. Use the same as the smaller sized garlic. Can be stewed and served in a cream sauce.

fennel, common—This variety of fennel is considered an herb. The seeds are used for flavoring. They are yellow-brown in color and have a mild licorice flavor. Used in fish and egg dishes, stews, breads, spaghetti and other sauces, cakes and cookies. *See Fennel in the dictionary section.*

galingale—A rhizome that is dried then powdered. Used in Southeast Asian cookery. Should be available in Oriental and gourmet-type food stores. Can be used as a substitute for ginger root although it is not as pungent.

garlic—A bulbous root herb. The bulb is composed of several cloves which are peeled before using. The cloves are used whole, sliced, minced or pulverized. May also be squeezed in a garlic press to produce juice. Garlic may also be purchased as dried flakes, flavored salt or as juice. Large cloves can be stewed and served in a cream sauce. Generally, the longer garlic is cooked the milder it becomes.

geranium—The dried flower petals can be used to flavor a dusting sugar. It is used to dust various pastries. The fresh petals can be added to punches and used as garnish for puddings. The rose geranium is very flavorful.

gilliflower—*See Carnation*

ginger—The root of the ginger plant is a sweet and hot spice. Fresh roots when grated or sliced are used in pickling, sauces, teas and beers. The ground root is used in baking and many Oriental dishes. When crystalized in sugar it is used as a confection. The branched roots are called 'hands.'

goldenrod—A tea or wine can be made from the flowers.

Good King Henry—Considered by many a weed, this plant's stalks and leaves are edible. The tender stalks may be cooked as asparagus and the young leaves as a pot-herb. The larger leaves are bitter. Not known to be grown commercially.

heather—An ale can be made from the flowrs of this plant. Bees placed near the heather will make a dark brown honey from the nectar of the blossoms.

herb seasoning—A commercially prepared mixture of various spices and herbs used to flavor various dishes.

herbs—The aromatic leaves, stems and sometimes the flowers of various plants growing in a temperate climate. Also some bulb plants are considered herbs. They can be used fresh or dried for flavoring.

hollyhock—Chinese cooks use hollyhock in their cooking. The fresh buds and petals are served, with a dressing, as a salad. The tender stalks can be prepared in the same manner as salsify.

horehound—A plant which is dried and used to flavor a hard sugar candy. May also be combined with honey to produce a syrup that some people use as a cough suppressant. It is a native of England but has been transplanted to other parts of the world.

horseradish—A pungent root. It is ground fresh and used as a condiment. Generally served with roast beef, ham and corned beef. It is very hot.

hyssop—A tea can be made from the fresh green tops of this herb. An oil made from the green parts of the plant is used in the manufacture of perfumes.

jasmine—The flowers of the jasmine are used to make an essence. The essence can be used to flavor candies, sugar syrups and liqueurs.

juniper berries—Fruit of a bush that grows wild. The berries are used to flavor marinades, certain foods and the alcoholic beverage gin. Berries can also be made into a tea.

laos—A southeast Asian seasoning. Small amounts are used to flavor poultry, meat and vegetables. Use sparingly. It is related to the ginger.

lamb's quarters—The leaves of this weed may be eaten fresh in salads or cooked as a pot-herb. The dried seeds can be ground and used as a flour. Some gardeners cultivate this plant. Also known as pigweed and wild spinach.

lemon blossoms—The blossoms are used to flavor ice cream, puddings, butters and jams. They can also be prepared as a fritter to use as garnish or snacks. Lemon sugar and lemon water can be made from the blooms.

lemon verbena—The dried leaves of this plant may be used as a substitute for lemon or mint in poultry, fish and stuffing recipes.

lemongrass—*See citronella*

licorice—A flavoring made from the dried root of a perennial leguminous plant. It is used in confections, liqueurs and as a medicinal flavoring. A popular candy is made in long thin ropes.

lime blossoms—Lime blossoms from the lime tree may be used in the same manner as lemon blossoms.

mace—A spice that has a taste similar to nutmeg, but more delicate. Mace is the shell of a tree-borne fruit. It covers the seed (nutmeg). When dried, the shell and seed are separated. Generally available ground. When mace is sold whole it is called 'blades of mace.' Used in baked goods, vegetable dishes, fruit salads, dressings and in candies.

maidenhair fern—This fern when boiled with sugar and water produces a thick liquid. This is called capillaire syrup.

marigold—The blooms of this flower can be eaten fresh, candied, added to puddings, made into a conserve and to flavor wine.

marjoram—This herb is a member of the mint family. It is aromatic and pleasing to the palate but should be used sparingly as it has a bitter undertone. Used in meat, poultry, game, fish and tomato dishes. Also in various sauces, vegetable dishes and stuffings. Available as whole dried leaf or ground.

marmite—A yeast extract often used in vegetarian cooking. Various herbs and spices are added to provide additional flavor.

marsh marigold—The leaves of this flower can be used as a pot herb and the blossoms made into wine. The unopened flowers (buds) can be picked for use in salads and as garnish.

mastic—A resinous substance from trees of the genus 'pistacia.' One variety is used to flavor bread, pastries and the Greek liqueur 'mastiha.'

may apple—A two-leafed plant with one bloom. The fruit when ripe can be eaten as an apple. CAUTION: When the fruit is green it is poisonous.

mignonette pepper—A coarsely-ground black pepper used in some French dishes. It is slightly sweeter than regular black pepper. Also called 'shot pepper.'

mimosa blossoms—These fluffy blooms are treated with gum arabic and a sugar syrup to form tasty treats.

mint—An herb whose use dates to ancient times. The fresh and dried leaf are used in cooking. An oil is extracted from the plant. Mint has a cool, clean and slightly sweet taste. Can be used in many dishes. Mint tea made from the dried leaves is a refreshing beverage. There are many varieties of mint with spearmint and peppermint the most widely used. Some other varieties are apple, curly, orange, water and Corsican. Available in the dried leaf and as an extract.

mormon tea—Used by the Aztecs, this plant found its way north to America. Believed to be used by the early Mormons as a substitute for coffee and tea. The dried stems are used to brew the beverage. The plant has no leaves. Should be available in health food stores.

mustard—The seeds of this herb have a pungent flavor. There are many varieties. It is available ground or whole. The whole seeds are used in pickling and such dishes as boiled beef, sauerkraut and coleslaw. Ground, it is used in egg and cheese dishes, dressings and sauces. Finely-ground seed are the main flavoring in various prepared mustard spreads.

narcissus—The bulbs of this flower are edible and are cooked the same as Jerusalem artichokes.

nasturtium—A versatile flower. The young leaves can be added to salads, butters and used as a sandwich filling. The flowers can be stuffed with tuna salad for a colorful dish. The buds and berries (seeds) can be pickled and used in place of capers. The blooms can be fried in butter and then added to chicken stock for a unique soup. The tender stems can be chopped and added to various soups.

nettle—The young tender leaves of the stinging nettle, a weed, can be used as a pot-herb or as a salad green.

noyau—*See creme de noyau*

nutmeg—One of the two spices from a fruit-bearing tree. the nutmeg is the seed (kernel) of the fruit. The covering of the seed is mace. Nutmeg has a sweet spicy flavor. It is used in breads, pies, tarts, cakes and puddings. Also used to enhance the flavor of meats, vegetables and fruits. Available whole or ground. Fresh grated nutmeg is most desirable.

orange flower—These fragrant blossoms can be used to flavor water, jellies, chopped and added to butters and sauces or candied.

orchid—The petals may be eaten fresh. The roots can be dried, then ground and made into a salep.

oregano—The dried leaf of this herb has a very distinct flavor. A basic seasoning in Italian dishes and other tomato dishes. Can be used, sparingly, in sauces, soups, salads, stews, gravies, beef and lamb dishes. Available as whole dried leaf or crushed leaf. The fresh leaves may also be used. In various areas of the world oregano is known as sweet, wild or winter marjoram.

oswego tea—Also called beebalm, the dried or fresh parts of this plant can be made into a refreshing beverage.

pansy—The blooms of this flower can be made into a wine, candied or used to flavor a sugar syrup.

paprika—This spice is the powder of a dried sweet red pepper. Rather sweet in taste and used mainly to add color to bland dishes such as potato salad, macaroni salad and coleslaw. Often used in salad dressings and in Chicken Paprika.

parsley—This bright green, curly-leafed herb is very high in nutritional value. Has a mild fresh odor and a refreshing taste. Used mainly as a garnish. It can be added to salads, soups and stews. May be used fresh or dried.

peach blossoms—The peach bloom can be used to flavor sugar syrup, vinegar or a liqueur. A beverage can be brewed from the blooms. Sip while hot.

peony—These flowers can be used to flavor sugar syrup or water. Can also be added to a vinegar-spice sauce.

pepper, black and white—This spice is the dried berry of a climbing vine. Is used whole or ground. Can be added to many dishes as a flavor enhancer. Can be hot. Black pepper is obtained by picking the berries when they are green and then drying until they are hard and black. White pepper is obtained when the berries are permitted to ripen. Then they are treated to remove the skin and flesh. The remaining seed is the source of white pepper. About the only difference in black and white pepper is the color.

peppercorns—Whole pepper berries. *See pepper, black and white*

pickling spice—A commercially prepared savory blend of whole and broken spices, herbs and seeds. Is used mainly in the pickling of cucumbers. A small amount can be tied in a cheesecloth bag and added to roasts, vegetables and fruits while cooking. This will add a definite spiciness to the dish.

pine, eastern white—The inner bark of this tree can be used and prepared as a spaghetti-like food.

pinks—*See Carnations*

poke weed—A wild growing plant. The young leaves can be used as a vegetable.

poplar—Tree whose sap layer produces a noodle-like substance that can be used in soups and stews.

poppy seed—The Egyptians cultivated the poppy over 3,000 years ago. They used both the seeds and the oil from the seeds. It is not narcotic. Generally it is lightly toasted before it is sprinkled over salads, fruit compotes or whenever a nutty flavor is desired. Can be sprinkled on various breads before baking. May be added to cookies and made into candies. The oil from the seeds is a very fine cooking fat. The blooms can be used to make a brandy.

poultry seasoning—A commercially prepared blend of herbs used in the seasoning of poultry stuffings. Can be used in other meat dishes.

pumpkin pie spice—A commercially prepared blend of cinnamon, ginger, allspice, nutmeg and cloves. The mixture is ground. Used primarily in pumpkin pies. May also be used in cakes, cookies and other desserts where a strong spice taste is desired.

purslane—Considered by many a weed, the purslane is an excellent salad green. A native of Africa and India, it was brought to the New World by early settlers, and introduced to Europe in the 15th century.

red pepper—Dried, ground, red peppers. A hot and pungent powder. Used in Mexican and Italian dishes. Adds zest to sausages and some pickles. Also called cayenne.

rose—This elegant flower has many uses in the kitchen. An oil pressed from the flower petals is used to flavor wines, icings, candy and other confections. The petals can be candied and used as garnish.

rose hips—The seed pod of the rose. Can be made into jelly. Also used in other confections and dishes.

rosemary—A sweet fragrant herb from a small perennial evergreen. Used fresh or dried in lamb dishes, with fish, soups, stews, sauces and vegetables. When cooking meat over hot coals, sprinkle with rosemary for an interesting taste.

rue—This herb is not often used in cooking. It has a very strong taste, so use sparingly. A few fresh leaves can be chopped and added to a green salad.

safflower—A desirable cooking oil is derived from the seeds. The dried blossoms can be used as a substitute for saffron. A red dye can be made from the flower.

saffron—An herb native to the Mediterranean area. The stigmas of the blooming flower are collected and dried then powdered. It takes approximately 60,000 stigmas to equal a pound and is very expensive. Used to color various foods. Little or no taste.

sage—An aromatic and slightly bitter herb. Grey green in color. Used mainly in poultry stuffings. Is used sparingly in other dishes. Available as dried leaves or ground.

salad burnet—When bruised, the leaves have a smell and taste of fresh cucumbers. Can be used fresh in green salads, butters, cream cheeses, vinegars and as a garnish.

salam leaf—Far Eastern variety of bay leaf.

sarsaparilla—The dried root of a tropical plant. Used to flavor various soft drinks.

sassafras—Although an herb, this plant resembles a tree, often reaching a height of 100 feet. The dried bark and root are used to brew a tea. It is a native American plant. Was one of the first commercial exports to Europe by the New World.

savory—The dried brown-green leaves of this herb have an aromatic piquant flavor. Generally used with other herbs in meat, poultry, fish and egg dishes. Available as a powder or in the leaf form.

sesame seed—The dried seed of a tropical herb. It has a rich nut-like flavor when toasted. Use as a topping for cookies, pies, tarts before cooking. Toasted seeds may be sprinkled over any dish where a nut-like flavor is desired. Mixed with honey and dried fruits to make a delightful sweetmeat. An excellent oil is pressed from the seeds.

seed—The aromatic dried whole fruits or seeds from plants cultivated in a more temperate region.

shot pepper—Mignonette pepper

spice—The aromatic seeds, flower parts, bark and roots of plants usually grown in tropical regions. Used to flavor various foods and beverages.

squash blossoms—Blossoms from various squash plants may be stir-fried, added to scrambled eggs or treated as fritters.

star anise—This star-shaped fruit is picked before it ripens. It is dried then powdered. The flavor is similar to anise but more pungent and slightly bitter. Used mainly in Chinese cookery.

sunflower—The mature seeds may be toasted and eaten as a snack. A desirable cooking oil is made from the seed.

sweet cicely—Leaves of this herb have a sugary licorice flavor and the seeds are spicy. The roots can be eaten raw or boiled. Leaves are used in green salads, soups and stews. When green, the seeds are used in salads and when ripe added to herb mixtures.

sweet woodruff—This herb is used when dried. Used to flavor sodas and wine. Makes a pleasant room deodorizer.

tamarind—The pods of this tree are macerated in hot water to produce a brown juice. Used as a flavoring agent in Indian curries, chutneys, candies and various beverages. Rind of the pods is dried and made into a paste. The juice, rind and paste should be found in food specialty shops.

tansy—Dried leaves of this herb are used in salad dressings and in omelets. It is very strong. Tansy is also used in the making of the liqueur Chartreuse.

tarragon—The dark green leaves of this herb are very aromatic. Use sparingly in meat, fish, poultry and egg dishes. May be added to green salads. Place a few leaves of tarragon in a bottle of vinegar for an interesting taste.

thyme—The grayish-green leaves of this herb are one of the herbs in a bouquet garni. Is also used to season meat, fish and poultry dishes. Good in tomato and cheese based dishes. Available in powder or leaf form.

tomato herb—*See basil*

turmeric—The root of this herb is dried, then ground. It adds color to some dishes. A major ingredient in prepared mustards and curry powders. Can be used in egg dishes, cream sauces, salad dressings and to season chicken.

vanilla—Vanilla is the fruit (bean) of a climbing orchid. It is made into a liquid extract that is used widely in confections. The whole bean can be used to flavor various liquids, then dried and used again. A whole bean placed in a container of sugar will flavor the sugar so no extra extract will be needed when using the sugar. Extract is available in a dark color or as a clear liquid. The clear is used when discoloration of white foods is not desired. An imitation vanilla is also available, but does not have the depth of aroma and taste of the extract.

violets—Flowers can be crushed and used to flavor ices, mousses and other confections. They can be used to make a jelly and a flavored syrup. The flowers are very pretty when candied and used as garnish.

wild strawberry—Fruit of this wild plant can be used same as the domestic variety. The fruit is generally smaller.

wintergreen—Leaves and berries are used to flavor various candies and chewing gum. The leaves were used by the Maine Indians to brew a tea. The bright red berries are sweet, tender and flavorful. They may be candied. Rarely found in markets.

wormwood—An herb related to tarragon. Has a bitter taste. Used mainly in the flavoring of various liqueurs and vermouths. It is slightly narcotic.

yarrow—Although not widely used in the kitchen, the dried yarrow can be used as a substitute for nutmeg and cinnamon. Is used in home medicinal remedies.

yucca—The flower petals of this desert plant can be made into a soup or added to green salads. Only the white petals should be used as the centers are quite bitter.

THYME

Notes

CHAPTER III

Weights & Measurements
Equivalents, Temperatures, Substitutions

ABBREVIATIONS

c, C	.... cup	l, L	.... liter	t	.... teaspoon
cc	............cubic centimeter	lb	.... pound	tsp	.... teaspoon
		ml	.... milliliter	oz	............ounce
fl	...............fluid	T	........Tablespoon	pt	.... pint
gal	...........gallon	Tbsp	.....Tablespoon	qt	..............quart

EGGS

The quality of fresh eggs is indicated by a letter code - AAA, AA, A, B. AAA is the highest quality.

The size of eggs, JUMBO, EXTRA LARGE, LARGE, MEDIUM, SMALL, is determined by their weight per dozen, heaviest being JUMBO.

8 to 10 egg white .... 1 cup
10 to 14 egg yolks .... 1 cup
4 to 6 whole eggs .... 1 cup

Various Weights, Measures & Equivalents

U.S. DRY MEASURES

1 Tablespoon		....	3 teaspoons
1/5 pint	2/5 cup	....	6½ tablespoons (approx.)
1/4 pint	1/2 cup	....	8 tablespoons
1/3 pint	2/3 cup	....	12 2/3 tablespoons
1/2 pint	1 cup	....	16 tablespoons
1 pint	2 cups	....	32 tablespoons
2 pints	4 cups	....	64 tablespoons
2 pints		....	1 quart
1 quart	4 cups	....	64 tablespoons
8 quarts		....	1 peck
4 pecks		....	1 bushel
1 lug		....	20 to 24 pounds

U.S. LIQUID MEASURES

60 drops .... 1 teaspoon	16 ounces .... 1 pint
3 teaspoons .... 1 tablespoon	2 cups .... 1 pint
2 tablespoons .....1 liquid ounce	2 pints .... 1 quart
4 tablespoons .... 1/4 cup	4 quarts .... 1 gallon

British & American Comparison

LIQUID MEASURE

BRITISH	AMERICAN	AMERICAN	METRIC
1 teaspoon	1 1/4 teaspoon	—	6 cc
1 tablespoon	1 1/4 tablespoon	—	17 cc
1 fluid ounce	1 fluid ounce	—	30 cc
2 fluid ounce	2 fluid ounce	1/4 cup	60 cc
2 2/3 fluid ounce	5 1/3 tablespoon	1/3 cup	—
4 fluid ounce	8 tablespoon	1/2 cup	120 cc
5 1/3 fluid ounce	10 2/3 tablespoon	2/3 cup	—
8 fluid ounce	8 fluid ounce	1 cup	240 cc
10 fluid ounce or 1/2 Imperial pint	10 fluid ounce	1 1/4 cup	—
16 fluid ounce	16 fluid ounce	2 cup	.480 liter
20 fluid ounce	20 fluid ounce	2 1/2 cup	.568 liter
1 Imperial pint	1 1/4 pint	—	—
1 3/5 Imperial pint	2 pints	4 cups	—
1 3/4 Imperial pint	—	—	1 liter
2 Imperial pts or 1 Imperial qt	2 1/2 pint	5 cups	—
6 2/5 Imperial pints	1 gallon	16 cups	3.785 liters
8 Imperial pts or 1 Imperial gal	10 pints	20 cups	4.546 liters

British & American Comparison (cont'd)

VOLUME

KNOWN	MULTIPLY BY	TO FIND
teaspoons	5	milliliters
tablespoons	15	milliliters
fluid ounce	30	milliliters
cups	0.24	liters
pints	0.47	liters
quarts	0.95	liters
gallons	3.8	liters

WEIGHT

ounces	28	grams
pounds	.46	kilograms

LENGTH

inches	2.5	centimeters
feet	30.0	centimeters

British standard measuring cup is 10 fluid ounces.

American standard measuring cup is 8 fluid ounces.

American and British dry measures are equivalent.

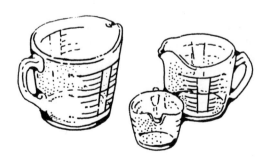

Temperatures

In America, we use Fahrenheit as the unit of heat measurement. In Europe the Celsius scale is used. Centigrade is another name for Celsius.

Converting from Fahrenheit to Celsius: From the Fahrenheit temperature, subtract 32 and multiply by 5/9.

Example: From 100 degree F subtract 32, then multiply by 5 and divide by 9, which will equal 37 degrees C.

$$\text{or } (100-32) \times 5 \div 9 = 37$$
$$\text{or } 100 - 32 = 68 \times 5 = 340 \div 9 = 37$$

Converting from Celsius to Fahrenheit: Multiply Celsius temperature by 9/5 and add 32.

Example: Multiply 37 degrees C by 9, then divide by 5 and add 32, which will equal approximately 100 degrees F.

$$\text{or } 37 \times 9 = 333 \div 5 = 66.8 + 32 = 98.6$$
$$\text{or } (37 \times 9) \div 5 + 32 = 98.6.$$

Note: the results may not be exact.

ABBREVIATIONS

F = Fahrenheit   C = Celsius or Centigrade   deg = Degree

Various Cooking Temperatures

SYRUPS, SUGAR

Thread stage	230-234 F
Soft ball stage	234-238 F
Med. ball stage	238-245 F
Firm ball stage	245-250 F
Hard ball stage	250-265 F
Soft crack stage	265-272 F
Med. crack stage	272-290 F
Hard crack stage	290-310 F
Caramel stage	320-345 F

WATER

Simmers at	180 F
Boils at (sea level)	212 F

JAMS & JELLIES

Jells at	220 F

BAKING OVEN (American)

Warm	200 F
Very slow	250 F
Slow	300 F
Moderate slow	325 F
Moderate	350 F
Moderate hot	375 F
Hot	400 F
Very hot	450 F
Broil	500 F

BAKING OVEN (European, gas)

¼	225 F	107 C
2	300 F	150 C
4	350 F	178 C
6	400 F	205 C
8	450 F	233 C

Roasting Temperatures for Meats

(using a meat thermometer)

BEEF

130 F	Rare
160 F	Medium
180 F	Well done

PORK

160 F to 185 F ....Done

LAMB

140 F	Rare (pink)
145 F	Medium rare
165 F	Well done

VEAL

165 F to 170 F ....Done

NOTE: End of thermometer is placed near the bone but not touching it.

Equivalents

ALMONDS, unshelled, 1¾ pounds .... 2¼ cups nutmeats

APPLES, one bushel ....44 pounds

APRICOTS, one lug ....22 pounds

BUTTER, one pound .... 2 cups

CONFECTIONERS' SUGAR, one pound .... 2½ cups

CORNSTARCH, 1 tablespoon ....½ ounce

CORN SYRUP, one pound .... 1½ cups

FILBERTS, unshelled, 1⅛ pounds .... 1¾ cups nutmeats

FLOUR, one pound .... 4 cups

        1 tablespoon ....¼ ounce

GRANULATED SUGAR, one pound .... 2¼ cups

HONEY, strained, one pound .... 1½ cups

OLEOMARGARINE, one pound .... 2 cups

PEACHES, one bushel ....48 pounds

        one lug ....20 pounds

PEANUTS, unshelled, ¾ pounds .... 1½ cups nutmeats

PEARS, one bushel ....48 pounds

PECANS, unshelled, 1¼ pounds .... 1½ cups nutmeats

PLUMS, one bushel ....50 pounds

POTATOES, one peck ....15 pounds

WALNUTS, BLACK, unshelled, 2¾ pounds .... 1½ cups nutmetas

        ENGLISH, unshelled, 1¼ pounds ....2 cups nutmeats

Yields for Dried Beans

TYPE OF BEAN (1 cup)	YIELD (cups cooked)	TYPE OF BEAN (1 cup)	YIELD (cups cooked)
Black	4	Lima, Baby	3½
Black-eyed peas	3½	Navy	4
Garbanzo/Chickpeas	4	Pink	4
Great Northern	4	Pinto	4
Kidney	4	Red	4
Lentils	4½	Small white	4
Lima	2½	Split pea	4½

Dried beans, with the exception of lentils, should be soaked in water before cooking. When cooking, make sure the beans are always covered with liquid. Start cooking the beans in the soak water.

Cooking times will range from ½-hour to over 3 hours.

CAN SIZES

Can No.	Net Weight	Cupfuls
10	6 lbs., 10 oz.	13
3	2 lbs., 1 oz.	4
2½	1 lb., 12 oz.	3½
2	1 lb., 4 oz.	2½
1 (tall)	1 lb.	2
8 oz.	8 oz.	1
303	1 lb.	2

Net weight and contents can vary slightly with different manufacturers. Types of foods can also cause a variation.

CANNING SYRUP

For	Use
Thin syrup	1 C sugar and 3 C water*
Medium syrup	1 C sugar and 2 C water*
Heavy syrup	1 C sugar and 1 C water*

*Fruit juice can be substituted for one-half of the water

Substitutions

NEED	USE
1 t baking powder	1/3 t baking soda and 1/2 t cream of tartar
1 bouillon cube	1 t beef extract
1 C bread crumbs	3/4 C cracker crumbs
1 C brown sugar	1 C sugar and 5 t molasses
1 C buttermilk or sour milk	1 C sweet milk & 1 t of vinegar
1 square chocolate	3 T cocoa & 1 T shortening
1 C coconut, flaked	1 C coconut, grated
1½ C corn syrup	1 C sugar & ½ C water
1 C heavy cream	¾ C milk and 1/3 C butter
1 fresh egg	¼ C dried egg mix & ¼ C water
1 whole egg	2 egg yolks
1¾ C flour	2 C cake flour
1 T flour, as thickener	½ T cornstarch or arrowroot or 2 t quick tapioca
2/3 C honey	1 C sugar & 1/3 C water
1 T fresh horseradish	2 T bottled horseradish
1 C milk	½ C evaporated milk & ½ C water
1 C milk	1 C reconstituted dry milk & 2½ t butter
1 C molasses	1 C honey
1 C sour cream	1 C yogurt
1 C sugar, baking	⅞ C honey & a pinch of baking soda
1½ T quick tapioca	¼ C pearl tapioca
1 T dry yeast	1 package dry yeast or 1 cake of compressed yeast
1 C yogurt	1 C buttermilk

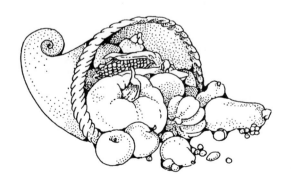

Notes

CHAPTER IV
Helpful Hints

AIR—Freshen the air by simmering together vinegar and spices such as whole cloves and stick cinnamon. Orange or lemon peel can be used in the same manner without the vinegar.

ANNATTO SEEDS—Use an extra pepper mill for grinding these seeds. Faster than using a mortar and pestle.

APPLES—Place apples in a brown paper bag to ripen. Punch several holes in bag to permit gasses to escape.

AVOCADOS—Ripen at room temperature or place in a brown paper bag for several days. Store in refrigerator after ripening. Coat cut surface with lemon juice or water to prevent darkening.

BAKING—For easy pouring, use a pitcher for batters like crepes, cupcakes, pancakes and waffles.

BAKING SODA—It is not used alone as a leavening agent. Some other leaveners must be present for the proper chemical action to take place. Soda is used when any acid ingredient is in the recipe—sour milk, buttermilk, molasses, apple sauce, etc. Baking soda can be used as a cleansing agent and freshener.

BAKING STONES—Unglazed terracotta tiles may be used as a base for baking breads and pizzas.

BANANA—Ripe bananas can be stored in the refrigerator. Though the skins will turn very dark, the flesh should remain in excellent condition.

BEANS, DRIED—Place dried beans that have been soaked, several hours or overnight, in plastic bags and freeze. No need to thaw before cooking. Bring dried beans to a boil in the soak water. Drain water off and cover with fresh cold water and continue to cook until done. Should help prevent stomach gases from forming. If baking soda is added it will kill the vitamin B-1 in the beans.

BEEF, ROAST—Leftover sliced roast beef should be heated by the gravy or sauce. Additional cooking will toughen the meat.

BEETS—Add a little vinegar to beets when cooking. Helps prevent color drainage.

BREAD—Fresh bread and rolls may be stored in the freezer. Wrap tightly or place in freezer bags. To thaw, place unwrapped in a hot oven, then turn oven off. Should be thawed in about 10 minutes.

BREAD, WARMING—Baked bread should be removed from the pan to prevent sweating. To reheat, place bread in the baking pan or a brown paper bag, or wrap in aluminum foil and heat in a hot oven.

BROWN SUGAR—To soften brown sugar that has hardened, place a cut apple in the closed container with the sugar. To make your own brown sugar add two (2) tablespoons of unsulphured molasses to one-half cup of sugar.

BUTTER—Butter balls, plain or herbed, can be made and placed in plastic bags and stored in the freezer for later use.

CANDIED FRUITS—To finely-chop these sticky morsels, use your food processor. Or dredge with flour, cornstarch or powdered sugar and mince on the cutting board.

CANNING LIDS & RINGS—Rings should be free of rust. Rings can be used more than once. Lids are used one time only.

CANNING SYRUP—Light corn syrup can be substituted for one-half of the sugar. One-third of the sugar can be replaced with honey. Add to the hot sugar syrup. Boiling or simmering will cause a change in the honey's taste.

CARROTS—Carrot tops should be cut off before storing.

CELERY—Dry unused leaves. Store in a closed container.

CHEESE—Place cheese in the freezer for a few minutes for easy grating. Hard and semi-hard cheeses may be grated and then stored in the freezer.

CHOPPING—Rub the knife blade with vegetable oil before chopping garlic, dried fruits and raisins. Helps keep them from sticking to the blade.

CITRUS JUICE—Freeze lemon, lime or other citrus juice in ice cube trays. When frozen, transfer cubes to a plastic bag and store in the freezer. For a fresher taste, aerate canned and frozen juices before serving. Do this by hand or in the blender.

CITRUS PEEL, CANDIED—When candying your own peel, be sure to remove all the white membrane before adding to the sugar syrup.

CLARIFYING—To clarify stocks and soups, add an egg white and several egg shells. Simmer a few minutes then strain.

COCONUT—Freshen dried out coconut by steaming briefly.

COOKIES—Use a small ice cream scoop for forming drop cookies.

CORER—Use a melon baller to remove the cores from apples and pears.

CORN—Use a dampened towel to rub the silk from ear of corn.

CORN FLAKES—Place corn flakes in a bowl and crush with a round sided cup.

CREAM, FRESH—Add a pinch of baking soda to the cream when pouring over fresh fruit. Keeps cream from curdling.

CREAM, WHIPPED—Bowl, beaters and cream should be well chilled. Don't overwhip; you could end up with butter. Add any sweeteners and flavorings at the last. Add a scant tablespoon of light corn syrup to a pint of cream. Should whip higher.

CRUMBS, BREAD—Dry slices of bread in a slow oven. Cool and place a few in a muslin sack and roll with a rolling pin to the desired fineness. Can also be crushed between two sheets of paper or in a heavy plastic bag. Crackers and cookies can be crushed in the same manner.

CUTLERY CARRIER—Use empty foil, waxed paper and plastic wrap boxes for holding utensils and other small items when going on a picnic.

DRIED FRUITS—Store dried fruits in sealed containers on the shelf, in the refrigerator or in the freezer. Freeze newly-dried fruits for several weeks. Destroys any insects or insect eggs.

DRYING—Exposing some fruits to sulfur fumes before drying will help retain their color.

EGG—A stale egg will float in a container of water. Two tablespoons of mayonnaise can be substituted for one egg in a recipe.

EGG STRAINER—Use your hand to separate eggs. Break an egg in a clean hand and let the whites slip through the fingers.

EGGS, TOPPING—Sprinkle toasted sunflower or sesame seeds over fried or poached eggs for a tasty treat.

EGG WHITES—Must be at room temperature for beating. Use stainless steel, glass or copper bowl. Bowls and beaters must be free of grease. If the whites start to separate during beating, add one tablespoon of powdered sugar per each 10 egg whites. DO NOT use a plastic bowl or beater.

EGG YOLKS—Cover egg yolks with water when storing in the refrigerator. Pour off water before using.

FISH—Place frozen fish in milk to thaw.

FISH, FREEZING—Place fish in a container, like an empty milk carton, fill with water and freeze.

FLOUR—Should always be sifted before measuring (unless recipe says not to) and when combining with other dry ingredients. When using as a thickener, cook well so that it will lose its floury taste. Keep flour in a muffineer for light dusting.

FRUITS, CUT—When cutting fruits, immediately immerse the cut pieces in lightly salted water. Helps prevent darkening of the fruit.

FRUITS, DRIED—Instead of sugar, use various fruit juices to cook the dried fruit in.

GARLIC, PEELING—For easy peeling of cloves, drop them into boiling water for about a minute.

GREASING PANS—Slip a small plastic bag over the hand, dip into grease and apply to pans. Bag can be discarded.

HANDS, CLEANING—Lemon juice rubbed over the hands will remove strong smells such as fish, garlic and onion. Rinse off.

ICE CREAM—Scoop individual portions of ice cream ahead of time and place in freezer.

JARS—When canning, check for cracks and chips on the top. Don't use if any are present.

KIRSCH—Substitute grenadine or maraschino cherry juice.

KITCHEN TOOLS—Sharp pointed tools may be stuck into a dry sponge, styrofoam or cork.

LEMON EXTRACT—Make your own extract by adding two teaspoons of lemon zest to a pint of vodka. Let set four weeks. For a less pronounced flavor, remove zest after two weeks.

LEMONS—Have lemons at room temperature or warmer before squeezing. This will produce more juice.

MEASURING—A small medicine dropper can be used to measure a small amount of flavoring and colorings.

MEAT LOAF—Form meat loaf into individual loaves. Makes for an attractive dish.

MEAT LOAF & MEAT ROLLS—Place bread slices under the loaves or rolls before baking. Prevents sticking to pan. Used bread slices can be given to the cat or dog.

MILK—When drinking, sip it. Milk curdles when it reaches the stomach.

NAPKIN RINGS, EDIBLE—Make rings out of small pieces of bread dough and bake.

NUTS—Store nutmeats in sealed bags in the freezer or in the refrigerator.

OATS—Lightly toast 'old fashioned' oats. Adds a nutty flavor.

OIL DISPENSER—Use a pump type syrup dispenser for cooking oil. Handy and no drip. Plastic squeeze bottles are also excellent.

ONION—Use the onion skins when making soups and stews. Adds a nice color. Easily removed before serving.

PANS, BAKING—Give baking pans a light coat of oil before storing. Helps prevent rust. Wash off before using again.

PARAFFIN, CANNING—Lay a piece of string across top of jars of jams and jellies, then pour on paraffin. Permits the paraffin to be easily removed.

PASTA—Have water boiling before adding pasta. Stir with fork to keep separated. When done, rinse in running water to remove any flours.

PASTRY SLICER—For delicate filo and strudel pastries, cut with a sharp pizza cutter.

PEPPERS, STUFFED—Set stuffed peppers in muffin tin to cook.

PIE, CREAM—The cream filling should be cold when it is poured into the cold baked crust.

PLUMPING—Dried fruits, raisins, currants can be plumped by steaming over boiling water for a few minutes.

POTATOES, BAKED—Use only baking potatoes. Prick skins of each potato with a fork. Rub each with bacon drippings or other fat. Bake in a hot oven.

POTATO CHIPS—Freeze them in sealed plastic bags to stay crisp.

RAISINS—Coat with flour before adding to cake batter. Will help prevent them from sinking to the bottom.

RAISINS, STORING—Store raisins in a closed container with a small amount of Kirsch, brandy or other liqueur added. Adds an extra flavor to cakes and cookies.

RIPENING FRUIT—Fruits placed in a plastic or paper bag will ripen faster. Punch a few holes in bag to permit some of the gasses to escape.

ROLLS, SERVING—Place a piece of aluminum foil in the bottom of the serving basket. Place napkin over the foil.

RUST, PREVENTION—Coat pans and iron utensils with oil after washing. Helps prevent rust. When using again, wipe or wash.

SAUSAGE, BULK—Add a little to meat loaf for an added flavor.

SLICING—For ease of slicing uncooked pork, beef or fowl, place in the freezer until very firm.

SOUP STOCK—Soup stock can be frozen in ice cube trays. The cubes are then stored in plastic bags. Each cube wil be equal to about one tablespoon.

STRAINERS—For disposable strainers, use dampened paper coffee filters.

STRING, SLICING—String can be used to split layer cakes, coffee cakes and the such.

SUGAR—To make superfine sugar, grind sugar in a blender or food processor. Can be ground quite fine. CAUTION: Excess grinding can cause the sugar to heat up and melt.

SUGAR, CONFECTIONERS—Sift before measuring and using. Add liquids a little at a time.

SUGAR, FLAVORED—Granulated and confectioners sugar can be flavored by placing citrus zest in a closed container with the sugar. Whole spices can be used but the flavor will not be as intense.

TOMATO SAUCE & PASTE—Leftover sauce and paste can be frozen in ice cube trays and stored in plastic bags for future use.

TOMATOES, STUFFED—Set stuffed tomatoes in muffin tins for baking.

TWEEZERS—Handy for removing small bones from fish.

VANILLA SUGAR—In a closed container, place two to four cups of sugar and a vanilla bean that has been split. Bury the bean in the sugar. Good for granulated or powdered sugars. Let set at least two weeks before using. The vanilla bean is reusable.

VEGETABLES, SURPLUS—Store surplus vegetables, cooked and raw, in the freezer for later use in soups and stews.

YEASTS—Use before expiration date on packages.

YEAST BREADS—Always allow breads to rise at room temperature. Either the flour or liquid should be an exact measure.

ZEST—Zest can be made ahead of time and frozen. Can be left in strips or chopped.

COOK BOOKS

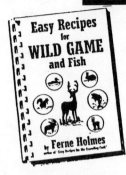

Great recipes, yet easy-to-fix, by hunter-traveler cook Ferne Holmes. Large game animals, small game, wild fowl, fish, side dishes, too! More than 200 recipes, fully indexed. *Easy Recipes for Wild Game* (160 pages)...$6.50

An ideal cook book for those who do not want to fuss over meals while traveling. More than 200 recipes to make in your RV, camper or houseboat. Suggests utensils, supplies, food and daily menus. Special section on campfire cooking. *Easy Recipes for the Traveling Cook* by Ferne Holmes. (128 pages)...$5.00

Tempting recipes for luscious pies, dazzling desserts, sunshine salads, novelty meat and seafood dishes! Plus tangy thirst-quenchers with oranges, grapefruit, lemons, limes, tangerines, etc. *Citrus Recipes from the Citrus Belt* by Al and Mildred Fischer (128 pages)...$3.50

Enjoy the versatility of dates in these tempting recipes for breads, puddings, cakes, candies, fruitcakes, waffles, pies and a myriad of other fantastic taste treats. It's all in the *Sphinx Ranch Date Recipes* by Rick Heetland (128 pages)...$5.00

There's more to pecans than pecan pie! Indulge your pecan passion with recipes for pralines, macaroons, ice cream, bread pudding, torte, rolls, muffins, cakes and cookies, casseroles, nippy appetizers, hearty main dishes and, of course, a variety of tantalizing pecan pies! *Pecan Lovers' Cook Book* by Mark Blazek (128 pages)...$5.00

COOK BOOKS

More than 200 recipes for Mexican festival desserts, custards, fruits, puddings, gelatines, cakes, pies, cookies, ice creams, sherbets and beverages. The only book of its kind! *Mexican Desserts* by Socorro Munoz Kimble and Irma Serrano Noriega (144 pages)...$6.50

More than 250 easy-to-follow home-style favorite family recipes for tacos, tamales, menudo, enchiladas, burros, salsas, frijoles, chile relleno, carne seca, guacamole and sweet treats! *Mexican Family Favorites Cook Book* by Maria Teresa Bermudez. (144 pages)...$5.00

Treat yourself to the California lifestyle with this cornucopia of 400 recipes for avocados, citrus, dates, figs, nuts, raisins, Spanish and Mexican dishes, wines, salads and seafoods. *California Favorites Cook Book* by Al and Mildred Fischer (144 pages)...$3.50

Chili cookoff prize-winning recipes and regional favorites! The best of chili cookery, from mild to fiery, with and without beans. Plus a variety of taste-tempting foods made with chile peppers. *Chili-Lovers' Cook Book* by Al and Mildred Fischer (128 pages)...$3.50. *More than 90,000 copies in print!*

A taste of the Old Southwest, from sizzling Indian fry bread to prickly pear marmalade, from sourdough biscuits to refried beans, from beef jerky to cactus candy. *Arizona Cook Book* by Al and Mildred Fischer (144 pages)...$3.50. *170,000 copies in print!*

ORDER BLANK

Golden West Publishers
4113 N. Longview Ave.   Phoenix, AZ 85014

Please ship the following books:

Number of Copies		Per Copy	AMOUNT
	Arizona Cook Book	3.50	
	California Favorites Cook Book	3.50	
	Chili-Lovers' Cook Book	3.50	
	Citrus Recipes	3.50	
	Cook's Book, The	5.00	
	Easy Recipes for the Traveling Cook	5.00	
	Easy Recipes for Wild Game & Fish	6.50	
	Mexican Desserts	6.50	
	Mexican Family Favorites Cook Book	5.00	
	Pecan-Lovers' Cook Book	5.00	
	Sphinx Ranch Date Recipes	5.00	
Add $1.00 to total order for shipping & handling			$1.00

Check (or money order) enclosed...$_____

Name _____

Address _____

City _____ State _____ Zip _____

Notes

Meet the author!

John C. Lawrence was born near Bakersfield, California, and attended school there.

In the eighth grade, he enrolled in the "boys" cooking class. He had already been cooking at home and had learned much from several aunts—farm women who were excellent cooks.

Over the years he has worked in various types of eating establishments, from fast foods to dinner houses. He has been a waiter, maitre d'hotel, cook and bartender. He especially enjoyed preparing and serving palatable and delectable food.

Lawrence also held positions as personal chef and caterer, during which time he avidly studied cook books and food magazines, furthering his education in this field.

During his years of experience in food preparation, he was often frustrated by not finding information he needed in his work. He set about to compile a book that cooks of all kinds would find useful. The result is his first book: *The Cook's Book of Useful Information.*

Lawrence's personal preference is for cooking from "scratch," grinding his own flour for breads and pastas. Among his novelty cooking ideas are fruit juice in place of water when cooking rice and biscuit dough for various tarts and turnovers.

He grows herbs, spices, vegetables, fruits and nuts in a small home garden, practicing organic methods.